SHARP®

CAROUSEL CONVECTION MICROWAVE COOK BOOK

Design & Production: Cy DeCosse Incorporated

CONTENTS

Microwaves and other ultra-high frequency radio waves operate a variety of familiar systems, such as mobile telephones, remote control toys, air traffic control radar and remote television tuners.

What are Microwaves?

Microwaves are high frequency, non-ionizing, electromagnetic waves. Other familiar forms of non-ionizing energy are infrared heat waves from a toaster or electric range, and visible light waves from the sun or a light bulb.

Microwaves are similar to radio waves or the signal from a remote control television tuner. In fact, they are very short radio waves which can be confined within the metal walls of an oven to form a miniature broadcasting system. The magnetron broadcasts a microwave signal which is converted to heat in food. The microwave energy field alternates between positive and negative directions. Like a magnet, the positive direction attracts minus particles in food molecules, while the negative direction attracts plus particles.

How Microwaves Work

Magnetic game illustrates that "positive" ball is attracted by the blue negative energy field, but bounces away from the red positive field. When microwave energy activates the particles in food molecules, they "bounce" about 2½ billion times a second; friction between them produces heat in the food.

Test for Yourself

Pour 1 cup of water into a 2-cup measure. Microwave at HIGH (100%) until water boils, 2 to 3 minutes. Remove cup from oven. The water is boiling hot, and has heated the glass around it, so the cup feels hot. Handle feels slightly warm, but the air in the oven is still cool.

PRECAUTIONS TO AVOID POSSIBLE EXPOSURE TO EXCESSIVE MICROWAVE ENERGY

a) Do not attempt to operate this oven with the door open since open-door operation can result in harmful exposure to microwave energy. It is important not to defeat or tamper with the safety interlocks.

b) Do not place any object between the oven front face and the door or allow soil or cleaner residue to accumulate on sealing surfaces.

c) Do not operate the oven if it is damaged. It is particularly important that the oven door close properly and that there is no damage to the: (1) door (bent), (2) hinges and latches (broken or loosened), (3) door seals and sealing surfaces.

d) The oven should not be adjusted or repaired by anyone except properly qualified service personnel.

Advantages of the Carousel

The energy in a microwave oven is not distributed equally throughout the cavity. Some areas are warmer than others, with the consequence that food in those areas becomes hotter.

Stirring helps equalize heat in the food, but there are many foods which cannot be stirred. These foods must be rearranged or rotated if they are to cook evenly. The more often they are moved, the better the results.

The Sharp Carousel™ is a dishwasher-safe turntable which rotates constantly while the food cooks, so no part of it remains in a warm area for any length of time. The carousel simplifies cooking, especially of foods which require frequent rotating, because it moves the food automatically.

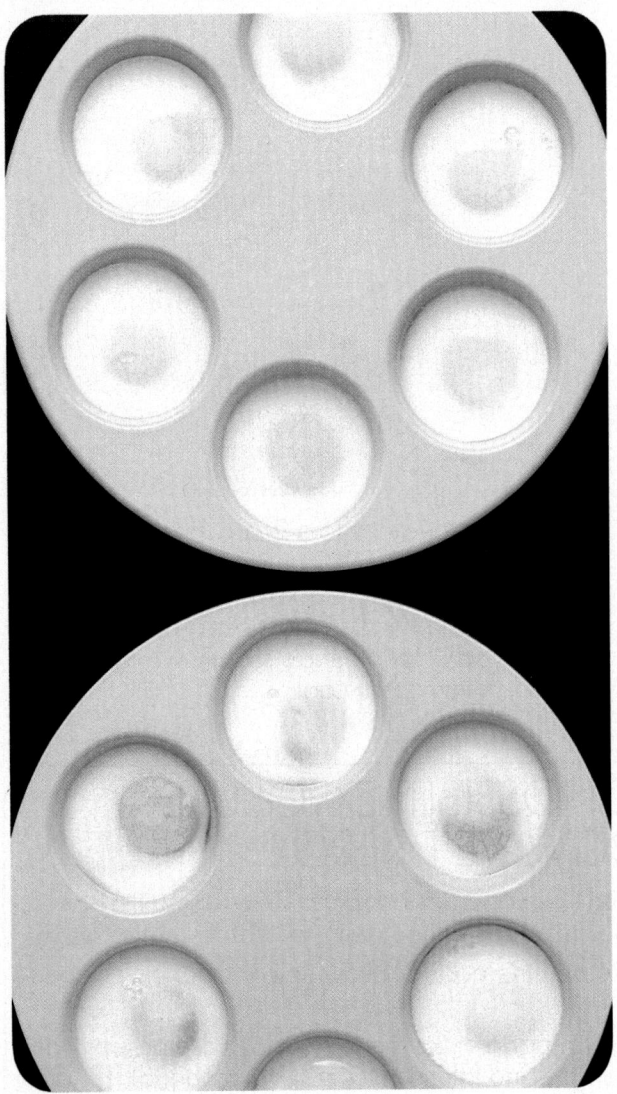

Compare eggs microwaved on the constantly rotating carousel (above) with unevenly cooked eggs microwaved in another oven (below).

Microwave Myths

Not everything you may have heard about microwave cooking is true. A number of myths persist because many people don't really understand how the microwave oven works. As you use your oven, you'll discover that some of them are half-truths, while others are entirely false.

MYTH 1. Microwaves cook from the inside out. They certainly do not. Microwaves penetrate foods from the outside to a depth of about 1 inch. Small foods, under 2 inches in diameter, are penetrated to the center from all sides. With larger foods, energy creates heat in the outer layer; then the heat moves to the center by conduction, as it does conventionally. A few foods may appear to cook more on the inside. One example is an egg. Energy penetrates to the center, where the fatty yolk becomes hotter than the white and cooks first.

MYTH 2. You can't use metal in a microwave oven. False. Metal reflects microwaves; the oven itself is made of metal so microwave energy can't escape. Inside the oven, metal slows cooking because it keeps energy from reaching parts of the food. You can use the reflective properties of metal to protect foods which might overcook in some areas. The magnetrons in most microwave ovens are designed so that they cannot be damaged by the use of metal in the oven.

MYTH 3. Dishes don't get hot in a microwave oven. Keep your pot holders handy. A microwave-safe utensil will not be heated by microwave energy, but it will become hot from contact with hot food. Heat tends to equalize. A warm object heats the air around it, like a radiator in a cool room. When food becomes hot, some of this heat is transferred to the dish.

MYTH 4. Microwaved foods don't stay hot. Not so. They cool at the same rate as conventionally heated foods, and for the same reason. No matter how you heat foods, they cool faster if you serve them in a cool dish. One advantage of microwaving is that you can cook and serve in the same dish, so food stays hot longer.

MYTH 5. Foods don't brown in a microwave oven. True and false. Browning depends on fat content and the amount of cooking time in relation to food volume. Some foods *do* brown: bacon, roast, a turkey. Many small, moist foods cook so rapidly they do not have time to brown.

Do's and Don't's

The purpose of this book is to show you what the microwave oven can do. The recipes were developed for 600 to 700 watt ovens. You'll find many delicious, attractive foods you may not have known you could prepare by microwaving. Each section provides explanations of what you should do, and why, so you cook with confidence.

Read the Operation Manual for information on operating and cleaning. Do not remove the carousel turntable while oven is in use.

You may find that some foods cause the microwave oven to "sweat"; others do not. Humidity and moisture in the food will influence the amount of condensation in your oven. Covered foods cause less condensation than uncovered foods. Condensation is normal in microwave cooking. Be sure the vent of your oven is not blocked.

The door seal on your oven is designed to prevent the leakage of microwave energy during cooking. Occasionally moisture may appear around the oven door. You may also see some small areas of light or feel warm air around the door. None of these situations are abnormal or necessarily indicate that your oven is leaking microwave energy.

Do not cook eggs in the shell. Steam builds up inside the shell and it may explode from pressure. Shelled hard-cooked eggs should be sliced or cut up before reheating in the microwave oven. You may hard-poach eggs for salads and casseroles. Follow directions on page 129 and microwave until yolk and white are as firm as desired.

Pop popcorn only in special microwave poppers, following manufacturer's directions. Do not use oil unless specified by the manufacturer, or heat longer than recommended. Never pop popcorn in paper bags or glass utensils.

Do not heat oil or fat for deep-frying. The temperature of the oil cannot be controlled and it may overheat. Do not attempt to can in the microwave oven as it requires prolonged high temperatures.

Microwave Utensils

The ideal material for a microwave utensil is transparent to microwaves; it allows energy to pass through the container and heat the food. Many ordinary household items, such as paper, plastic or wooden bowls may be used to warm foods to serving temperature.

When a utensil is used for cooking, it must also be able to withstand contact with very hot food or boiling liquid. Manufacturers are now marketing dual-purpose, heat-resistant paper and plastic utensils which can be used in both microwave and conventional ovens; in addition, many traditional cooking containers are suitable for microwaving.

Read this section, then check your cupboards. You may already have microwave oven-safe utensils. If you are not sure, use this test: place the empty dish in the oven; microwave at HIGH (100%) 30 seconds. A dish which becomes very hot should not be used.

Useful for meat cooking are a 12 × 8-inch utility dish or a 10-inch casserole and a rack or trivet to fit. Special microwave thermometers are available for meats and candies. Oven glass cups and bat- ter bowls can be used for both measuring and cooking. Ring shapes are ideal. Make your own by placing a glass in a 2½- to 3-quart casserole. Cook some foods directly on the carousel.

Paper plates and hot drink cups may be used for heating. Paper baking cups absorb excess moisture from cupcakes or muffins and save clean-up. Heat breads or cook bacon on paper towels. Cook frozen vegetables in their cartons. Cover foods with waxed paper to prevent spatters.

Ovenable paper containers come in a variety of shapes and sizes. They are freezer-proof and safe for both microwaving and conventional ovens up to 400°.

Oven glass utensils are inexpensive and widely available. Use them for measuring, mixing and microwaving. Choose clear glass for pies, cakes and breads, so you can check for doneness through the bottom of the dish.

Glass ceramic (Pyroceram®) utensils can be used for microwaving and serving, as well as on range tops or in conventional ovens.

Utensils (continued)

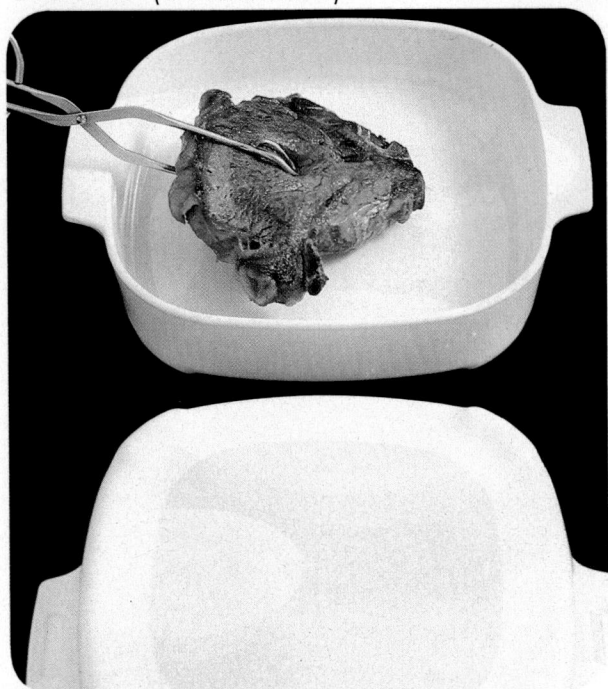

Browning utensils are made of glass-ceramic and are coated on the bottom with a material which absorbs microwave energy. After the empty dish is preheated in the microwave oven, it sears, browns and crisps the surface of foods. The dish cannot be used for conventional cooking.

Pottery, stoneware and porcelain serving bowls, platters, casseroles, plates, and cups make attractive microwave cook-and-serve ware. Many are labeled, "Microwave safe." If you are not sure, use the dish test on page 8.

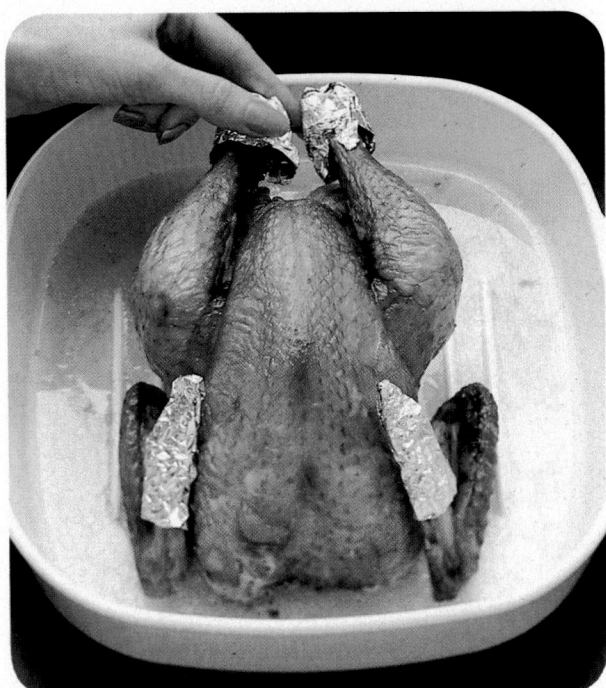

Usable metal includes aluminum foil for shielding, small skewers, and shallow foil convenience food trays. The amount of metal used must be in proportion to the volume of food; foil trays should be two-thirds to three-fourths full.

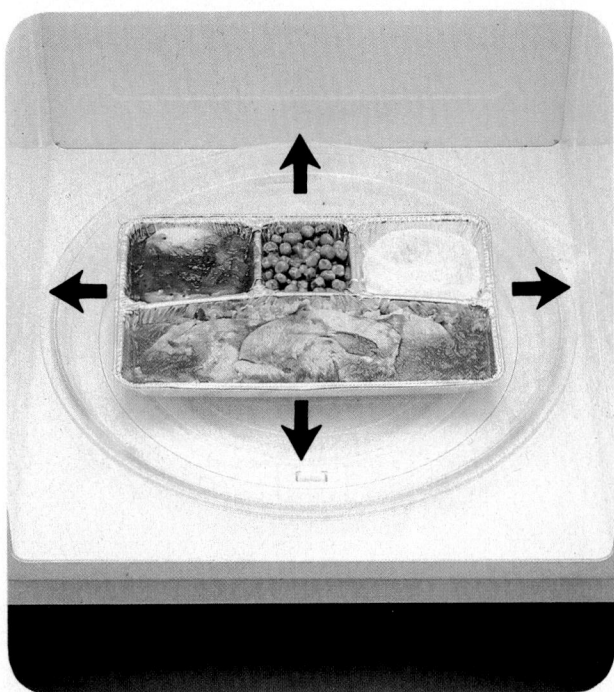

Keep metal at least 1 inch away from oven walls. Deep trays and metal pans are unsuitable because they reflect too much energy away from food. Foil-lined cartons shield food completely, so it does not heat at all.

Plastic film cooking bags and boilable pouches are ideal for microwaving. Do not use metal closures, as plastic may melt from reflected heat. Food storage bags should not be used for cooking. Non-stretch plastic film makes a convenient cover for baking dishes; vent it so steam escapes.

Plastic cookware of polysulfone and thermoset-filled polyesters withstand high food temperatures. Follow manufacturers' recommendations for use with specific foods.

Styrofoam® and "dishwasher safe" plastic storage containers and tableware may be used for heating foods to serving temperature. Do not use them for cooking raw foods, or for heating foods high in fat or sugar content, since they distort at fairly low temperatures.

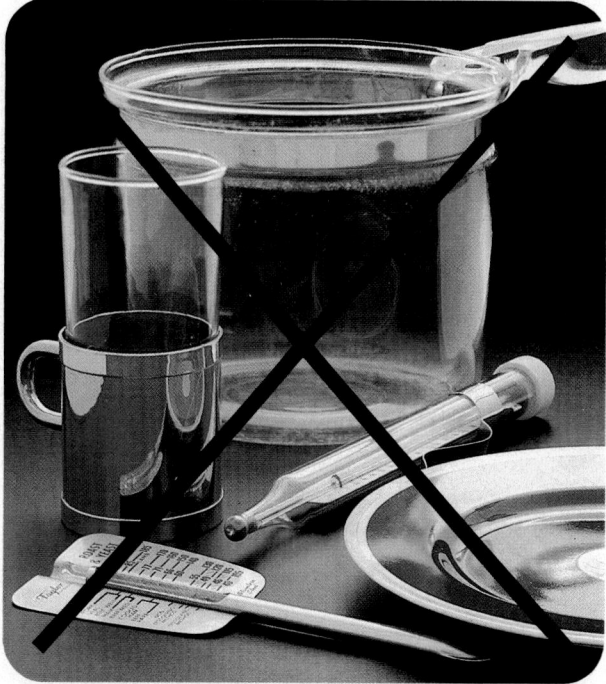

Do not use dishes with metallic trim; utensils with metal screws, bands or handles; Melamine® or Centura® tableware; delicate glassware or plastics which may be sensitive to hot foods; cups or mugs with handles repaired with glue; conventional meat or candy thermometers.

Microwave Cooking Principles

The speed and evenness of microwave cooking is affected by the foods themselves. Microwaves penetrate foods to a depth of ¾ to 1½ inches on all surfaces: top, bottom, and sides. The interior of foods greater than 2 inches in diameter heats by conduction, as it does in conventional cooking. Foods with high water, fat or sugar content respond quickly to microwave energy. Understanding the way food characteristics influence cooking will help you enjoy the benefits of microwaving.

Quantity. Microwave cooking times are directly related to the amount of food in the oven. Because energy is absorbed by the food itself, one potato or a single piece of chicken cooks rapidly. When the energy is divided among several items, cooking takes more time.

Size. Small pieces cook faster than large ones. To speed cooking, cut pieces smaller than 2 inches, so microwaves can penetrate to the center from all sides. For even cooking, make all the pieces the same size.

Shape. Foods which are irregular in shape, like fish fillets, chicken breasts or drumsticks, take longer to cook in the thicker parts. To help them cook evenly, place the thickest parts to the outside of the dish, where they will receive more energy.

Starting Temperature. Frozen or refrigerated food takes longer to heat than food at room temperature. Cooking times in this book are based on normal storage temperatures. Since rooms, refrigerators, and freezers differ in temperature, check for doneness at the minimum time.

Moisture Content. Microwaves are attracted by moisture. Naturally moist foods microwave better than dry ones. Add a minimum of liquid to moist foods, as excess water slows cooking. Prick foods with skins like those on potatoes or squash, so internal steam can escape.

Fat and Bone. Marbling within meat, or a thin, even layer of fat on a roast, speeds cooking. Large fatty areas or excess drippings in dish attract energy away from meat to slow cooking. Center bones do not affect cooking, but bone on the side of meat conducts heat to the areas next to it.

Density. The depth to which microwaves penetrate foods varies depending on their density. Porous foods, like ground beef or mashed potatoes, microwave faster than dense ones like steak or whole potatoes.

Microwave Cooking Techniques

Many of the techniques of microwaving are similar to those used in conventional cooking. They help equalize energy in the food so that it cooks evenly. Some techniques also shorten cooking time, so you get the full benefit of microwave speed.

Depth of food in dish affects both speed and evenness of cooking. Food in a shallow casserole will cook faster than food in a deep dish of the same capacity. Choose casseroles with straight sides; in a dish with sloping sides, the outside top edges receive more energy and overcook.

Ring shapes are ideal for microwaving because energy penetrates food from top, bottom, sides and center. Round shapes cook more evenly than squares or rectangles, which absorb most energy in the corners.

Arrange individual items, like custard cups or baked potatoes, in a ring around the outside of the carousel. Leave space between foods so energy can penetrate them from all sides.

Arrange foods with thin or delicate ends, like drumsticks or asparagus spears, with the thick or tougher portions to the outside of the dish. The parts which need more cooking will receive more energy, so food will microwave evenly.

Shield areas which attract the most energy, like the wing tips or breast bone of a turkey or corners of a square cake. Use small pieces of foil, which reflect microwaves. Covering meats with a sauce also acts as a shield to prevent drying.

Covering the dish holds in heat and steam to speed cooking. Use a casserole lid or plastic wrap. Vent plastic by turning back one edge at the side of dish to form a narrow slot where excess steam can escape. To hold in heat and prevent spatters without steaming, use waxed paper.

Paper toweling placed under breads, crackers, or crumb-coated chicken pieces absorbs moisture from steam which builds up between food and carousel, keeping surfaces crisp and dry. Cover foods with paper toweling to prevent spatters.

Microwave Cooking Techniques (continued)

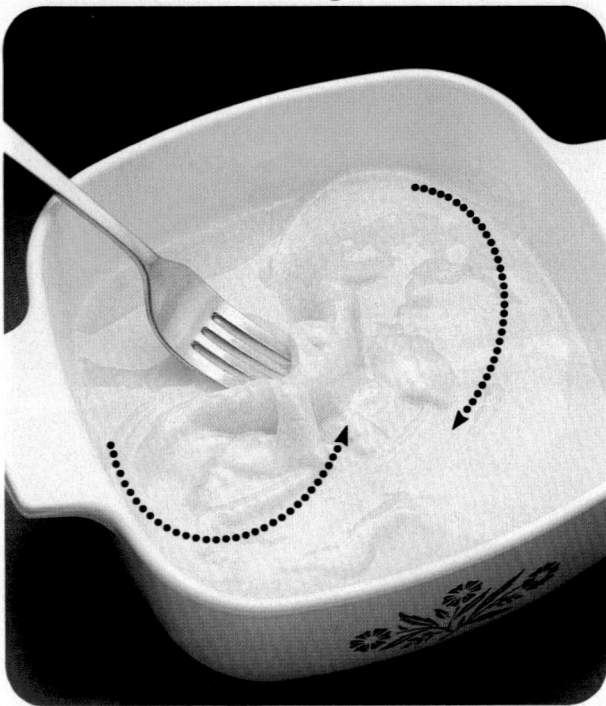

Stir foods from outside to center of dish once or twice during cooking to equalize heat and speed microwaving. Foods will not scorch or stick, so there's no need to stir constantly as you do in conventional cooking.

Turn foods over once during microwaving to speed cooking of medium-sized pieces, like chicken and hamburgers. Large items like turkeys and roasts must be turned over because areas near the top of the oven receive most energy.

Rearrange overlapping areas, like tails of long fish fillets, from top to bottom, and closely packed pieces, like meat balls, from the outside to the center of the dish. Rotating or repositioning dish in the energy pattern is not needed with the Sharp Carousel oven.

Lower power levels cycle energy on and off to equalize heat in foods. When energy is off, heat spreads by conduction from warm to cool areas. Sensitive foods don't overheat, and less tender meats have time to tenderize.

Standing time is one of the most important micro-waving techniques. Heat is in the food, not the oven, and many foods build up enough internal heat so they continue to cook by themselves after they are removed from the oven. Letting roasts, large whole vegetables and cakes stand to finish cooking allows the centers to cook completely without overcooking, drying or toughening the outsides. It also saves energy and money.

Browning develops on roasts and turkeys or chops, steaks and hamburgers microwaved in a browning utensil. Other foods will look cooked but not brown. Browning agents do not affect the quality of microwaved foods, but can add color and flavor. For meats and poultry, use bouquet sauce diluted with water or melted butter; soy, Worcestershire, barbecue or steak sauce; a sprinkling of paprika or dry gravy mix; jelly glaze or crumb coating. Frostings and toppings finish cakes and breads. Top casseroles at the end of microwaving with grated cheese or crumbs.

17

LEARN WHILE YOU COOK

Sixteen simple foods to teach you
the principles of microwave cooking

Cook with Confidence

The best way to learn about microwave cooking is to cook. In this section you'll find 16 easy to prepare foods, from a cup of instant coffee to a pot roast. Try them first. The directions not only tell you what to do, but why you do it, so you can cook with confidence. For example, once you've scrambled eggs, it's easy to understand why you stir from the outside to the center of the dish because you can see for yourself that cooking occurs first on the outside.

The foods in this section were chosen because they illustrate a principle of microwave cooking, demonstrate a useful technique, or point out an advantage of microwaving. Most of them are foods you use every day.

When you've learned to microwave these foods, you'll also be able to microwave several meals with confidence. You can apply the techniques you've mastered to all the recipes in this book.

Coffee

Boiling water for instant coffee demonstrates the way microwaving time is affected by starting temperature and quantity. Using hot tap water shortens the time. Notice that 4 cups take longer than 1, but not 4 times as long. Brewed coffee may be reheated in the same way, but will take a little longer if coffee is at room temperature. The coffee and water are mixed together before heating to enhance flavor. You can add the coffee later, but if the water is close to boiling, it may boil over.

1 cup	½ - 1¼ min.
2 cups	1 - 1¾ min.
3 cups	1¼ - 2¼ min.
4 cups	1¾ - 2½ min.

Spoon instant coffee into 1 to 4 cups or mugs. Add hot tap water. Place in oven. When heating more than 2 cups, space them around the edge of the carousel, leaving the center empty. Microwave at HIGH (100%) until very hot but not boiling.

Cream Soup

A single serving of soup can be mixed, microwaved and served in the same container, making clean-up easy. Cream soup illustrates the heating properties of milk products. Milk boils higher in the microwave oven than it does conventionally, so you should either watch it carefully or select a deep bowl. Milk may be heated at HIGH (100%), but must be stirred after half the time. At MEDIUM-HIGH (70%), the soup can be heated without attention. Reduce the power to MEDIUM (50%) if the soup is diluted with cream.

1 can (7½ ounces) semi-condensed soup
½ can milk

Combine soup and milk in a microwave oven-safe serving dish or mug. Microwave at MEDIUM-HIGH (70%) until soup bubbles but does not boil, 2 to 4 minutes. If soup starts to boil over, open the oven door. Heating will stop immediately.

Bacon-Wrapped Pineapple

The carousel serves as a baking dish when you microwave small items, like these bacon-wrapped appetizers. Several layers of paper toweling absorb fat, so bacon crisps and clean-up is easy. Leave space between the pieces so energy can penetrate from all sides. Because the carousel rotates the food automatically, no further attention is needed until you check doneness.

1 can (8 ounces) pineapple chunks (juice pack), drained (reserve 3 tablespoons juice)
2 tablespoons soy sauce
¼ teaspoon ground ginger
Dash garlic powder
6 slices bacon, each cut into thirds

Makes 18 appetizers

1. Combine pineapple juice, soy sauce, ginger and garlic powder in small bowl. Add pineapple; let stand 1 to 2 hours. Drain. Wrap a piece of bacon around each pineapple chunk; secure with wooden pick. Line carousel with several layers of paper toweling.

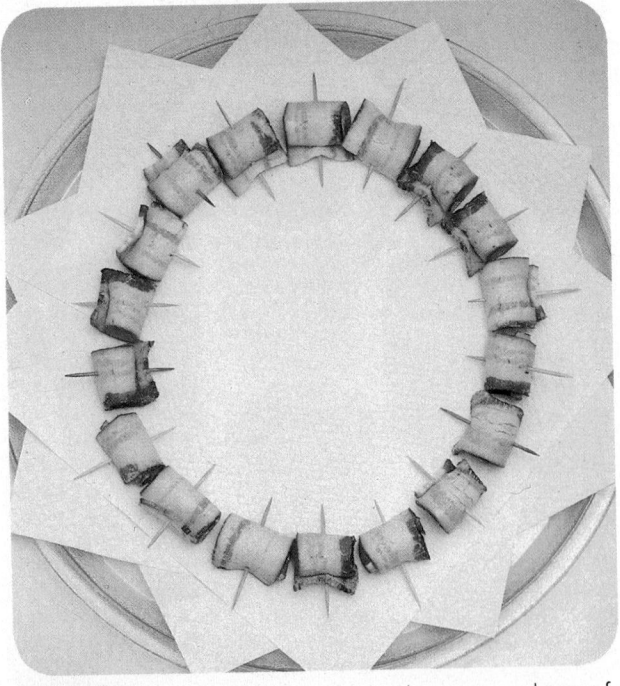

2. Arrange appetizers around outer edge of carousel with space between. Microwave at HIGH (100%) until bacon is lightly browned, 5 to 9 minutes. If using oven other than Sharp Carousel, place appetizers in paper towel-lined baking dish; rotate and rearrange several times.

Nachos

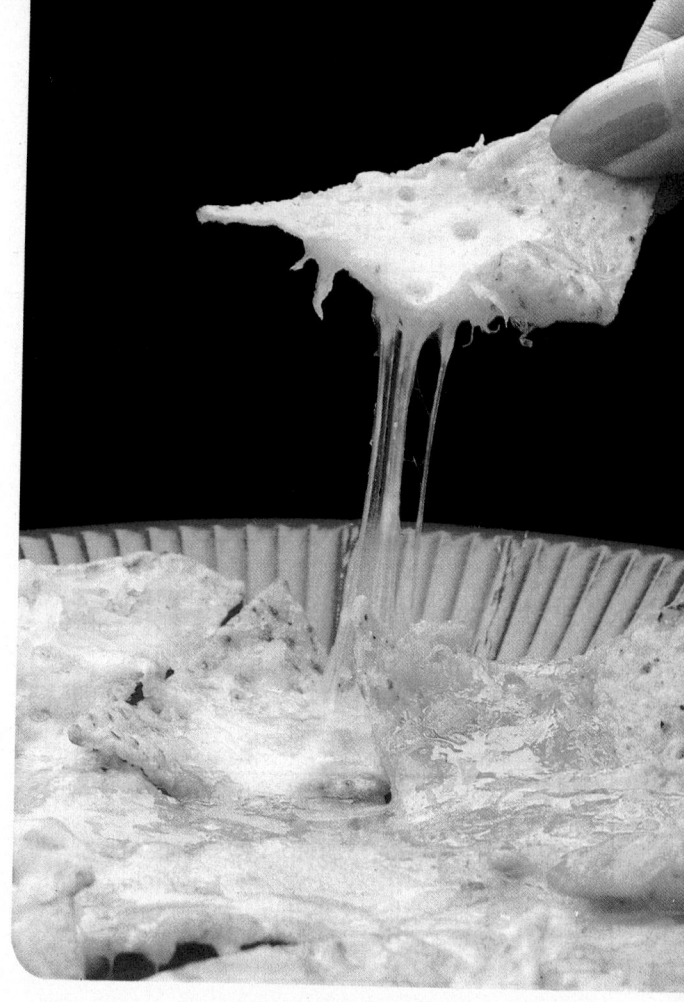

Cheese melts rapidly in the microwave oven because of its high fat content. A lower power setting helps prevent overheating, which can make cheese tough and stringy.

For easy clean-up, prepare and serve Nachos on a plastic or wax-coated paper plate. Don't use an uncoated plate because cheese will stick to it. If you prefer a glass or pottery plate, line it with a 12-inch square of waxed paper to prevent sticking and absorb steam.

16 large tortilla chips
¾ cup shredded Monterey Jack cheese
    (about 3 ounces)
¼ cup shredded Cheddar cheese
    (about 1 ounce)

Makes 16 appetizers

1. Spread tortilla chips on 10-inch plastic or wax-coated paper plate. Sprinkle with cheese. Microwave at MEDIUM (50%) 1½ to 2½ minutes.

2. Microwave just until cheese softens. It will finish melting by internal heat. If using oven other than Sharp Carousel, rotate twice during heating.

21

Scrambled Eggs

When you microwave scrambled eggs, you'll see for yourself how food cooks first near the edge of the dish, and finishes cooking as it stands outside the oven. Cook and serve the eggs in the same dish, which will be much easier to clean than a crusty frying pan. Butter is not needed to prevent sticking; it is used for flavor and can be omitted.

Eggs	Butter	Milk	Time
1	1 tbsp.	1 tbsp.	½ - ¾ min.
2	1 tbsp.	2 tbsp.	1¼ - 1¾ min.
4	1 tbsp.	2 tbsp.	2 - 3 min.
6	2 tbsp.	¼ cup	3¼ - 4¼ min.

1. Place butter in casserole or serving dish. Microwave at HIGH (100%) until butter melts, about 30 seconds. Add eggs and milk and scramble with a fork. Following the chart, microwave at HIGH (100%) for half the time.

2. Eggs will start to set around edge of dish. Break up cooked portions with fork; stir them to center of dish. Microwave remaining time, stirring once or twice more from outside to center.

3. Stop cooking while eggs still look moist, soft and slightly underdone. If cooked until they are as firm as you like, they will be overcooked and tough when served. Let stand 1 to 4 minutes; stir again. If not firm enough, microwave a few seconds more.

Bacon

1. Layer 3 to 5 paper towels, depending upon the amount of bacon to be cooked. Arrange 1 to 6 slices of bacon on the towels. Cover with another paper towel to absorb spatters and pat gently.

Because of its high fat content, bacon browns and crisps in the microwave oven, even though it has a short cooking time. There is less shrinkage and curling, and bacon can be cooked on paper toweling for easy clean-up. If you wish to save the fat, place bacon slices on a roasting rack set in a baking dish.

Cooking time depends on amount of salt and sugar used in curing, as well as thickness of the slices. Check for doneness after minimum cooking time; bacon continues to cook as it stands.

1 to 6 slices	¾-1¼ min./slice

2. Microwave at HIGH (100%) for minimum time and check for doneness. The fat should still be slightly translucent and bubbly. Don't cook bacon until it looks done, or it will be overcooked.

3. Let bacon stand 5 minutes. During standing it will cook evenly and turn brown and crisp. If bacon has a high sugar content, paper toweling may stick slightly and be discolored.

Chicken

Chicken is one of the easiest and most delicious microwaved meats. In minutes, you can cook a single piece or the entire chicken. Plain micro-waved chicken looks poached or steamed. When you're cooking it to use later in a casserole or salad, browning techniques are unnecessary. To serve it as a main dish, use a browning mixture, a crumb coating or a sauce. If you don't intend to eat the skin, remove it before coating or saucing, so the flavor will go directly on the meat.

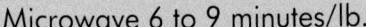

Microwave 6 to 9 minutes/lb.

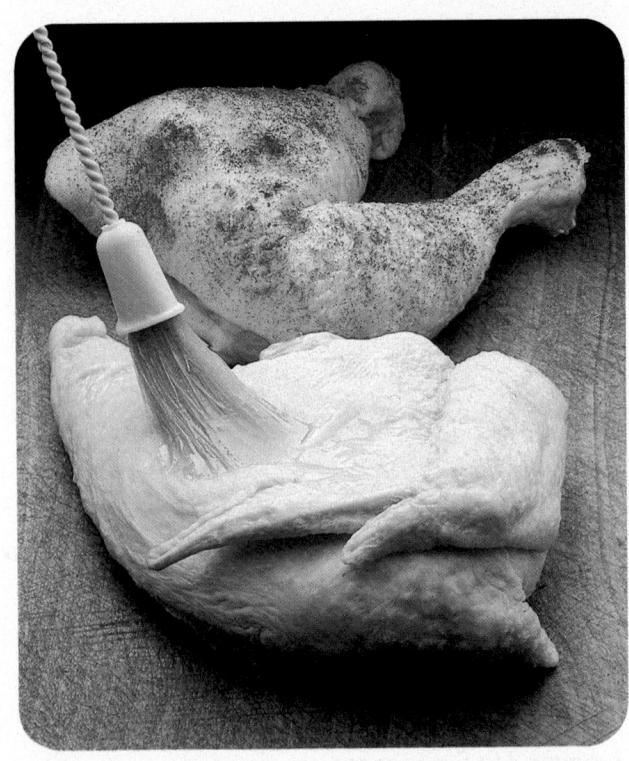

1. Brush chicken with melted butter and sprinkle with paprika for color, or use one of the browning techniques suggested on page 98.

2. Arrange chicken pieces in baking dish with meatiest portions to the outside of dish, where they will receive most energy. Cover with waxed paper. Microwave at HIGH (100%) for half the time.

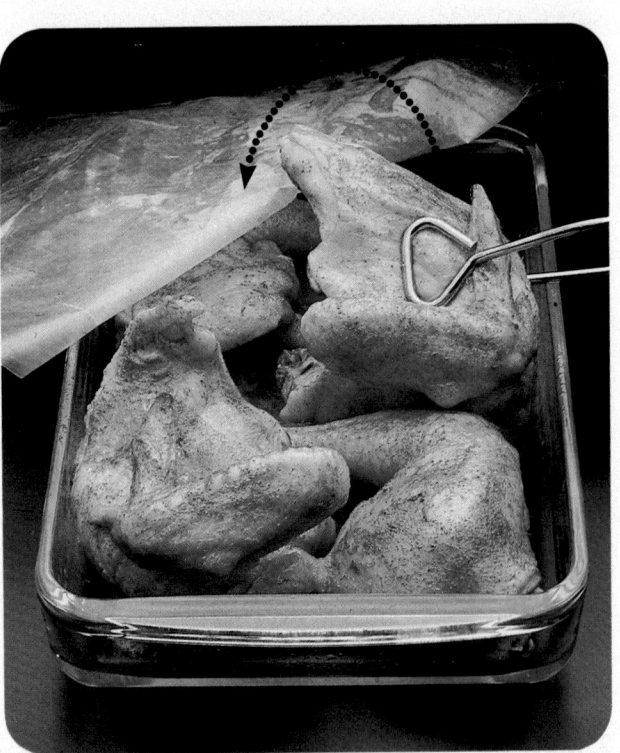

3. Turn chicken over or rearrange so less cooked parts are to outside of dish. Microwave remaining time until meat near the bone is no longer pink and juices run clear.

Hamburgers

Ground beef microwaves well at HIGH (100%) because it is porous and the fat is evenly distributed. The weight, thickness and number of hamburgers cooked affect microwaving time. This chart is for patties weighing ¼ pound.

Hamburgers need only a short standing time, during which they complete cooking and turn brown. The meat in these pictures was microwaved without a browning agent, but you may use one of those listed on page 17 for deeper color. If you wish a crusty surface, microwave patties in a browning dish. Directions for using the dish are on page 68; times are given in the chart on page 72.

Hamburgers	1st Side	2nd Side
2	2 min.	1½ - 2½ min.
4	2½ min.	2 - 3 min.
6	3½ min.	3¼ - 3½ min.

1. Elevate hamburgers on rack set in a rectangular baking dish, 12 × 8 inches or 10-inch square casserole. The rack keeps patties out of drippings. Cover with waxed paper.

2. Microwave the first side at HIGH (100%). Turn hamburgers over, as you would if cooking conventionally. Replace waxed paper. Microwave second side for minimum time.

3. Check for doneness. Patties will cook a little more and change in appearance as they stand 1 to 2 minutes, covered with waxed paper.

Meat Loaf

Meat loaf illustrates how the shape of foods influences cooking time. A meat loaf doesn't have to be loaf-shaped. It can be molded in a ring or baked as individual loaves. The ring shape and individual loaves are ideal for microwaving because energy can penetrate evenly from all sides.

    2 pounds lean ground beef
 1¼ cups tomato sauce, tomato juice or catsup
    1 cup quick or old-fashioned oats, dry bread
          crumbs or crushed dry cereal
    2 eggs, beaten
  ⅓ cup finely chopped onion
 1½ teaspoons salt

Topping:
  ⅔ cup tomato sauce, barbecue sauce or catsup

1. Combine all ingredients except topping. Form mixture into a ring in 9-inch pie plate or divide into six to eight 6-ounce custard cups.

2. Place pie plate in center of oven, or arrange custard cups around edge of carousel. Microwave at HIGH (100%) until internal temperature registers 150°, 14 to 18 minutes for ring shape, 11 to 16 minutes for individual loaves. If using oven other than Sharp Carousel, rotate after half the cooking time.

3. Pour topping over meat. Microwave at HIGH (100%) to heat sauce, 2 to 3 minutes. Let stand 3 to 5 minutes. Meat loaf will finish cooking and become firm.

Pot Roast

Pot roast demonstrates several techniques for tenderizing less tender cuts of beef. Pierce meat deeply with a fork; cook with a small amount of liquid in a tightly covered container to hold in steam. A lower power level gives meat time to tenderize without overheating. Standing time completes cooking and develops flavor. If you wish to add vegetables, you'll learn three more cooking principles: cut vegetables in small pieces; add them after half the time so they won't overcook; increase the total microwaving time to allow for greater volume.

2 to 3-pound beef chuck roast
1 envelope (1.5 ounces) spaghetti sauce mix
¼ cup water

Optional:

3 medium carrots, cut into 1-inch chunks
1 medium onion, cut into eighths
1 large potato, peeled and cut into eighths

Roast: 22 - 28 min./pound
Roast and Vegetables: 28 - 32 min./pound

Makes 4 to 6 servings

1. Pierce meat deeply and thoroughly on all sides with a fork. This allows steam and moisture to reach the interior. An acid liquid, such as tomato or lemon juice, wine, beer or vinegar, also helps tenderize meat.

2. Place meat, sauce mix and water in a 3-quart covered casserole, a baking dish covered with plastic wrap, or a cooking bag set in a casserole. To seal bag, tie end loosely with strip of plastic, leaving a small space for escaping steam.

3. Microwave at MEDIUM (50%) for half the time. Turn roast over; add vegetables, if desired. Microwave remaining time, or until meat is fork tender and splits at the fibers. Let stand, covered, 20 to 30 minutes, to tenderize further and develop flavor.

Tuna Casserole

This casserole illustrates several advantages of a microwave oven as well as some simple techniques. The frozen broccoli is thawed right in its package. The casserole is mixed, microwaved, and served in one dish for easy clean-up. A single stirring helps distribute heat. Microwaved casseroles do not crust or brown, so topping provides a crisp, colorful surface. Total microwaving time is about 12 to 15 minutes.

1 package (10 ounces) frozen chopped broccoli
7 ounces elbow macaroni, cooked and drained
1 can (12½ ounces) tuna
1 can (10¾ ounces) condensed cream of onion soup
1 can (5¼ ounces) evaporated milk
2 teaspoons brown mustard
1 can (3 ounces) French-fried onions

Makes 4 servings

1. Thaw broccoli in package until package feels warm, 4 to 5½ minutes. Drain broccoli well. Combine all ingredients except half the onion rings in a 3-quart casserole.

2. Microwave at HIGH (100%) 6 minutes. Stir from outside to center of casserole to shorten cooking time and equalize heat.

3. Sprinkle with remaining onion rings. Toppings are always added at the end of cooking so they will not be disturbed by stirring and will stay crisp. Microwave at HIGH (100%) until center is hot, 2 to 4 minutes.

Broccoli

In microwaving, the center of a dish receives least energy. Vegetables with tender ends can be arranged so the stalks, which need most cooking, are at the outside of the dish. Use a 10-inch cov-

ered square casserole or rectangular baking dish, 12×8 inches, covered with vented plastic wrap. Add salt to water; salt sprinkled directly on vegetables causes dry, dark spots.

1. To prepare a 1½-pound bunch of broccoli, divide it in about 8 pieces. Trim 1 inch from butt end and peel skin from 2 inches of stalks.

2. Dissolve ½ teaspoon salt in ½ cup water. Pour into casserole. Arrange broccoli with heads in center of dish. Cover. Microwave at HIGH (100%) until tender-crisp, 8 to 12 minutes. If using oven other than Sharp Carousel, rotate dish after half the time. Let stand, covered, 2 to 4 minutes.

Baked Potato

Potatoes are naturally moist and the skin serves as a cover to hold in steam. Be sure to prick the skin twice with a fork so excess steam can escape, or potatoes may burst. Line the carousel with a paper towel to absorb moisture.

1 potato	3 - 5 min.
2 potatoes	5 - 7½ min.
3 potatoes	7 - 10 min.
4 potatoes	10½ - 12½ min.

1. Space potatoes at least 1 inch apart around edge of carousel, so energy can penetrate from all sides. Microwave at HIGH (100%) following the times on the chart. Turn over after half the time. If using oven other than Sharp Carousel, rearrange for even cooking.

2. Remove potatoes from oven while they still feel slightly firm. Wrap in foil or place on counter and cover with casserole. Let stand 5 minutes. Potato on the left was cut open right after microwaving; notice the uncooked center. Potato on the right stood for 5 minutes and is cooked through.

Chili Cheese Dogs

Bread is porous and heats rapidly in the microwave oven. When overheated, it toughens. Small sausages and thin fillings can be heated with the bread, but stacks of meat or thick sausages should be heated first, then microwaved with bread for a brief warm-up.

In this recipe, MEDIUM-HIGH (70%) is used to heat the filling without overheating sensitive bread and cheese. Bread should be placed on paper napkins or towels to absorb moisture. Steam trapped between sandwich and the carousel would make bread soggy.

- 4 hot dog buns
- ½ cup chili
- 4 frankfurters
- 2 slices (1 ounce each) process American cheese, cut into 4 lengthwise strips

Makes 4 servings

1 to 4 hot dogs: Place wiener in bun; wrap each in a paper towel or napkin. Arrange on carousel. Microwave at HIGH (100%) until wiener is hot, 20 to 45 seconds each.

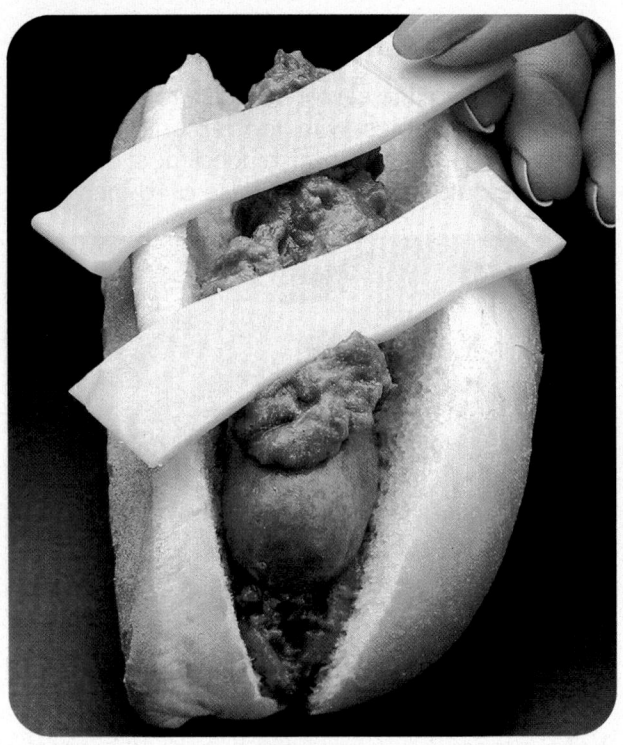

1. Split buns part way through. Spoon 1 tablespoon chili on each. Place frankfurters in buns. Top each frankfurter with another tablespoonful of chili and 2 strips of cheese.

2. Arrange 4 paper napkins or paper towels on carousel. Place filled buns on napkins, leaving an open center.

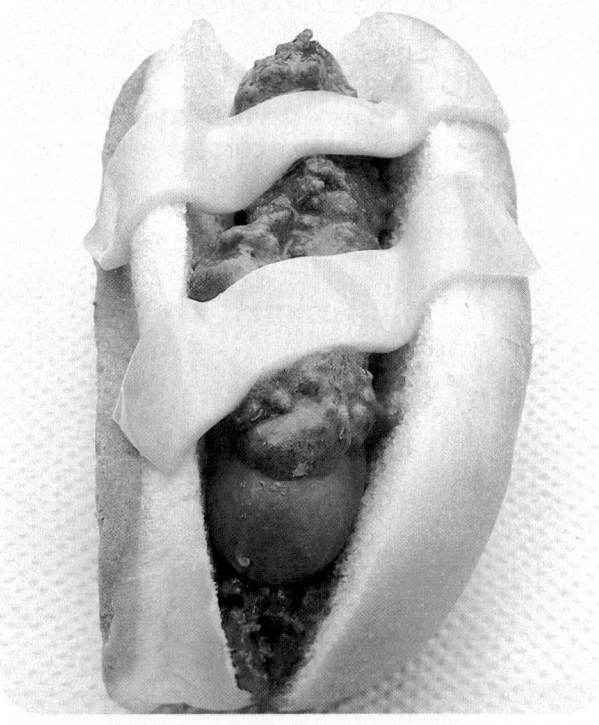

3. Microwave at MEDIUM-HIGH (70%) until filling is heated and cheese starts to melt, 2 to 5 minutes. If using oven other than Sharp Carousel, rearrange once or twice.

Broccoli

In microwaving, the center of a dish receives least energy. Vegetables with tender ends can be arranged so the stalks, which need most cooking, are at the outside of the dish. Use a 10-inch cov-ered square casserole or rectangular baking dish, 12 × 8 inches, covered with vented plastic wrap. Add salt to water; salt sprinkled directly on vegetables causes dry, dark spots.

1. To prepare a 1½-pound bunch of broccoli, divide it in about 8 pieces. Trim 1 inch from butt end and peel skin from 2 inches of stalks.

2. Dissolve ½ teaspoon salt in ½ cup water. Pour into casserole. Arrange broccoli with heads in center of dish. Cover. Microwave at HIGH (100%) until tender-crisp, 8 to 12 minutes. If using oven other than Sharp Carousel, rotate dish after half the time. Let stand, covered, 2 to 4 minutes.

Baked Potato

Potatoes are naturally moist and the skin serves as a cover to hold in steam. Be sure to prick the skin twice with a fork so excess steam can escape, or potatoes may burst. Line the carousel with a paper towel to absorb moisture.

1 potato	3 - 5 min.
2 potatoes	5 - 7½ min.
3 potatoes	7 - 10 min.
4 potatoes	10½ - 12½ min.

1. Space potatoes at least 1 inch apart around edge of carousel, so energy can penetrate from all sides. Microwave at HIGH (100%) following the times on the chart. Turn over after half the time. If using oven other than Sharp Carousel, rearrange for even cooking.

2. Remove potatoes from oven while they still feel slightly firm. Wrap in foil or place on counter and cover with casserole. Let stand 5 minutes. Potato on the left was cut open right after microwaving; notice the uncooked center. Potato on the right stood for 5 minutes and is cooked through.

Chili Cheese Dogs

Bread is porous and heats rapidly in the microwave oven. When overheated, it toughens. Small sausages and thin fillings can be heated with the bread, but stacks of meat or thick sausages should be heated first, then microwaved with bread for a brief warm-up.

In this recipe, MEDIUM-HIGH (70%) is used to heat the filling without overheating sensitive bread and cheese. Bread should be placed on paper napkins or towels to absorb moisture. Steam trapped between sandwich and the carousel would make bread soggy.

- 4 hot dog buns
- ½ cup chili
- 4 frankfurters
- 2 slices (1 ounce each) process American cheese, cut into 4 lengthwise strips

Makes 4 servings

> 1 to 4 hot dogs: Place wiener in bun; wrap each in a paper towel or napkin. Arrange on carousel. Microwave at HIGH (100%) until wiener is hot, 20 to 45 seconds each.

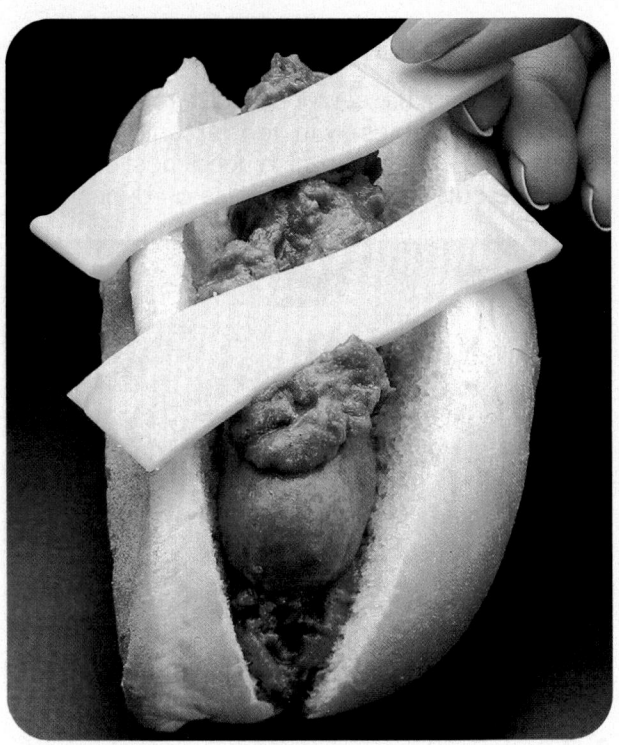

1. Split buns part way through. Spoon 1 tablespoon chili on each. Place frankfurters in buns. Top each frankfurter with another tablespoonful of chili and 2 strips of cheese.

2. Arrange 4 paper napkins or paper towels on carousel. Place filled buns on napkins, leaving an open center.

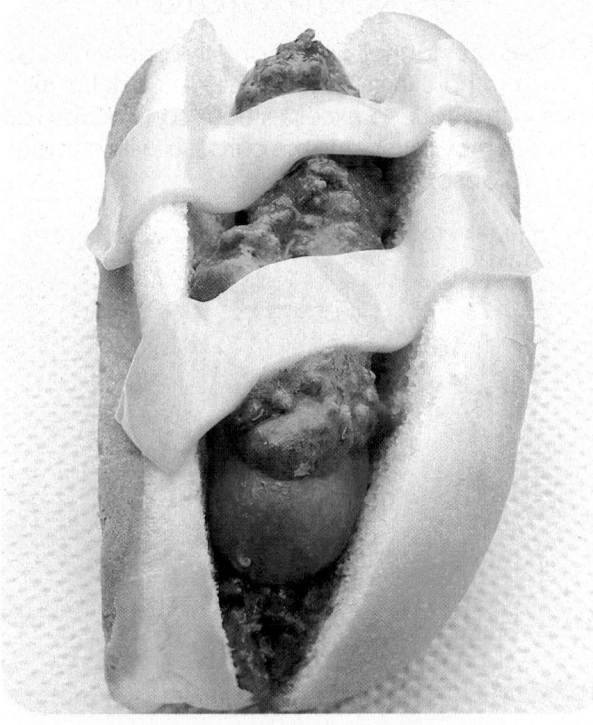

3. Microwave at MEDIUM-HIGH (70%) until filling is heated and cheese starts to melt, 2 to 5 minutes. If using oven other than Sharp Carousel, rearrange once or twice.

Baked Custard

Delicate baked custard is so simple to microwave it's a beginner's specialty. Scald the milk right in the measuring cup. Arrange cups of custard in a ring in the oven. In a microwave oven, you don't need the conventional pan of hot water to keep custard moist and tender.

Custard also demonstrates the advantage of a carousel. If using oven other than Sharp Carousel, rotate and rearrange the dishes every 2 minutes; remove any which set faster than the others.

1⅓ cups milk
 3 eggs
 ¼ cup sugar
 ¼ teaspoon salt
 ½ teaspoon vanilla
   Dash of ground nutmeg

Makes 4 servings

1. Microwave milk in 2-cup measure at HIGH (100%) until tiny bubbles appear around edges of cup, 2 to 3½ minutes.

2. Mix eggs, sugar, salt and vanilla in 1-quart bowl. Blend in milk. Divide into four 6-ounce custard cups; sprinkle with nutmeg.

3. Arrange cups in ring around outer edge of carousel. Microwave at MEDIUM-HIGH (70%) until custard resembles soft-set gelatin, 4 to 7 minutes. Center will become firm as custard cools. Chill several hours before serving.

Muffins from a Mix

Muffins show the way microwaved cakes and quick breads rise higher and cook faster than conventionally baked. The tops will not brown, so use colorful batters or sprinkle with a topping. Several suitable containers for muffins are pictured on page 167. These directions illustrate the use of paper baking cups as both liner and container. When muffins are microwaved in paper-lined dishes, remove them from dishes immediately after baking so steam trapped in bottom of dishes will not make muffins soggy.

1 package (13½ ounces) muffin mix

Makes 12 muffins

1. Stack 3 paper baking cups for each muffin. The outer cups can be used again, but help support muffin during microwaving. Prepare mix as directed on package. Fill cups only half full.

2. Arrange 6 at a time around edge of carousel. Microwave at HIGH (100%) 2½ to 4½ minutes. If using oven other than Sharp Carousel, rotate and rearrange after half the cooking time.

3. Dry tops mean muffins are baked; any moist spots will dry as muffins cool on wire rack. Bake remaining muffins.

CONVECTION MICROWAVE COOKING

What is Convection Cooking?

Professional chefs and bakers have used convection ovens for over 3 decades; in recent years, convection ovens have been introduced for use in the home. A convection oven differs from a conventional oven because in most of them the heating element is outside the oven cavity. The entire cavity can be used for cooking.

A high speed fan circulates air past the heat source and around the food. Even when the oven is not preheated, warm air begins to surround the food as soon as the oven is turned on. A convection oven cooks food with hot air, but because the air is moving, it heats food faster. Excessively hot air does not collect at the top of the oven, and cool air is moved away from the food and reheated.

Advantages of Convection Cooking

Moisture and flavor are sealed in quickly as circulating hot air browns the surface of food. There is less shrinkage and dripping of meat than in conventional cooking.

Preheating is not necessary for many foods, unless directed in the recipe.

Less time is needed to cook with the convection oven because circulating air heats food rapidly and evenly.

Fill the oven to capacity. Temperatures inside the convection oven are even, so the entire cavity can be used.

Some foods are best when cooked using convection heat alone, especially small, crisp items which cook in 15 minutes or less. Among the foods you'll bake with convection heat are appetizers, cream puffs, brownies, biscuits and rolls, cookies, puff pastry, fish sticks, muffins, crusts, pizza and soufflés.

Techniques

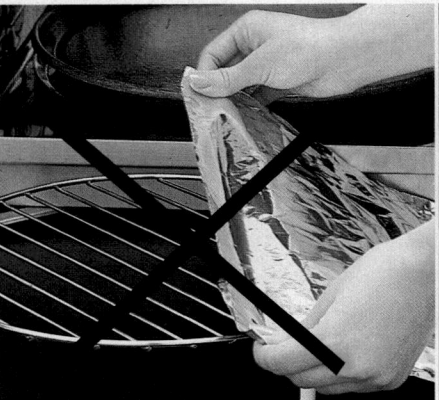

Cook many foods directly on carousel or on broiling trivet so they are surrounded by hot air. Use baking rack for 2 level cooking of cakes, muffins or cookies.

Do not cover turntable or rack with foil. It interferes with the circulation of air which cooks the food evenly.

Let food stand in oven 1 or 2 minutes if it is not done when checked after cooking time. Hot air in the oven will complete cooking without additional heating.

The Convection Microwave Team

Both microwave and convection ovens have advantages over conventional cooking; together they produce results neither one can achieve alone. Microwaving brings out the natural flavor of foods and keeps them moist or juicy, but most foods do not brown. Those which do brown, like roasts and turkeys, do not have a dry, crisp surface. The Convection Microwave oven browns and crisps food beautifully.

If cooked by convection alone, breads or cakes may overbrown or develop a thick crust before the inside is done. In the combination oven, convection heat seals and browns the outside perfectly while microwave energy makes sure the interior is done. Roasts and chickens can be cooked from the frozen state. You don't have to thaw them first. They won't spatter or smoke any more than if fresh or thawed, or be underdone on the inside.

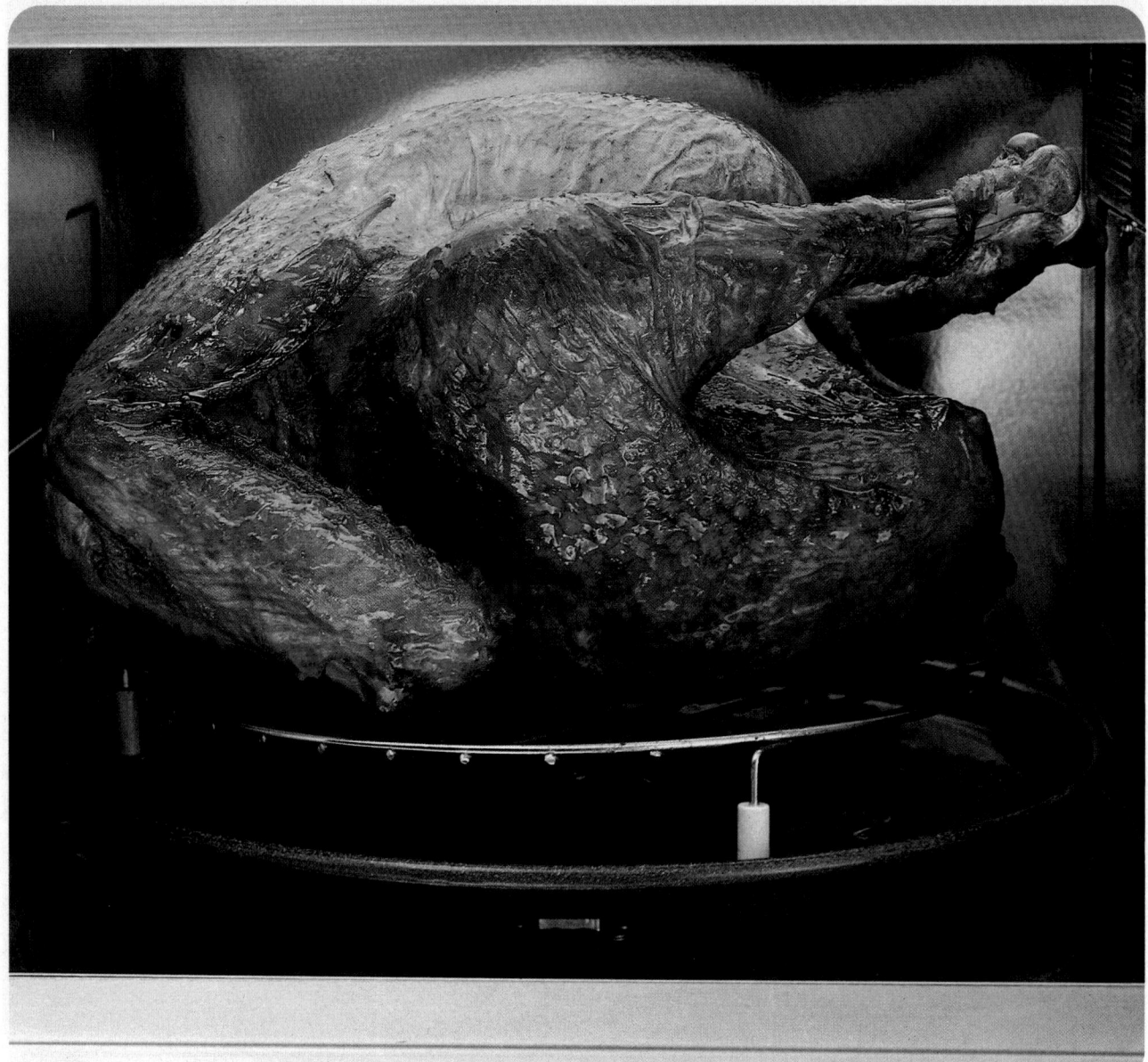

Turkey is an excellent example of what this team can do. The combination oven allows you to roast a larger turkey than is possible with microwaving alone. No turning over is needed. You don't have to baste, unless you want to give the bird a special seasoning. Just place the turkey on the broiling trivet, breast side up, and roast.

Convection Microwave Utensils

A wide variety of utensils may be used in convection and combination cooking. Many of them are also suitable for microwaving alone. Microwave-only paper and plastic products should not be used for combination cooking or placed in the oven while it is still hot from convection cooking.

Be sure to use hot pads when handling utensils. They become hot from convection and combination cooking.

The metal carousel is a utensil itself: a drip pan under the broiling trivet during roasting and broiling, or a baking sheet for breads and cookies.

Baking rack serves as a shelf for two-level cooking, such as layer cakes or cookies. Use it for convection and combination cooking, not for microwaving alone.

Metal and aluminum foil pans are safe for combination as well as convection cooking. During the convection cycle heat transferred from the pan cooks the bottom and sides of food. During the microwave cycle, energy penetrates from the top.

Oven glass is excellent for convection, combination and microwave cooking. Stoneware and pottery utensils designed for use in ovens may be used if they are also microwave-safe. See the dish test on page 8.

Glass ceramic (Pyroceram®) casseroles go from oven to table. They are microwave-safe and resist the heat of surface elements as well as ovens.

Ovenable paper is designed for use in both microwave and conventional ovens up to 400°, so it's suitable for convection or combination cooking too. Other paper products used for microwaving alone, such as paper napkins and toweling cannot be used with convection heat.

Thermoset-filled polyester plastics are heat resistant to temperatures of 400° to 425° as well as microwave-safe. They are sold as dual purpose utensils and can be used. Do not use any other plastics for combination and convection cooking.

Dual safe microwave/conventional thermometers may be used in the oven during combination cooking. Other thermometers should only be used outside the oven, since microwave thermometers are not heat resistant and conventional types are not microwave-safe.

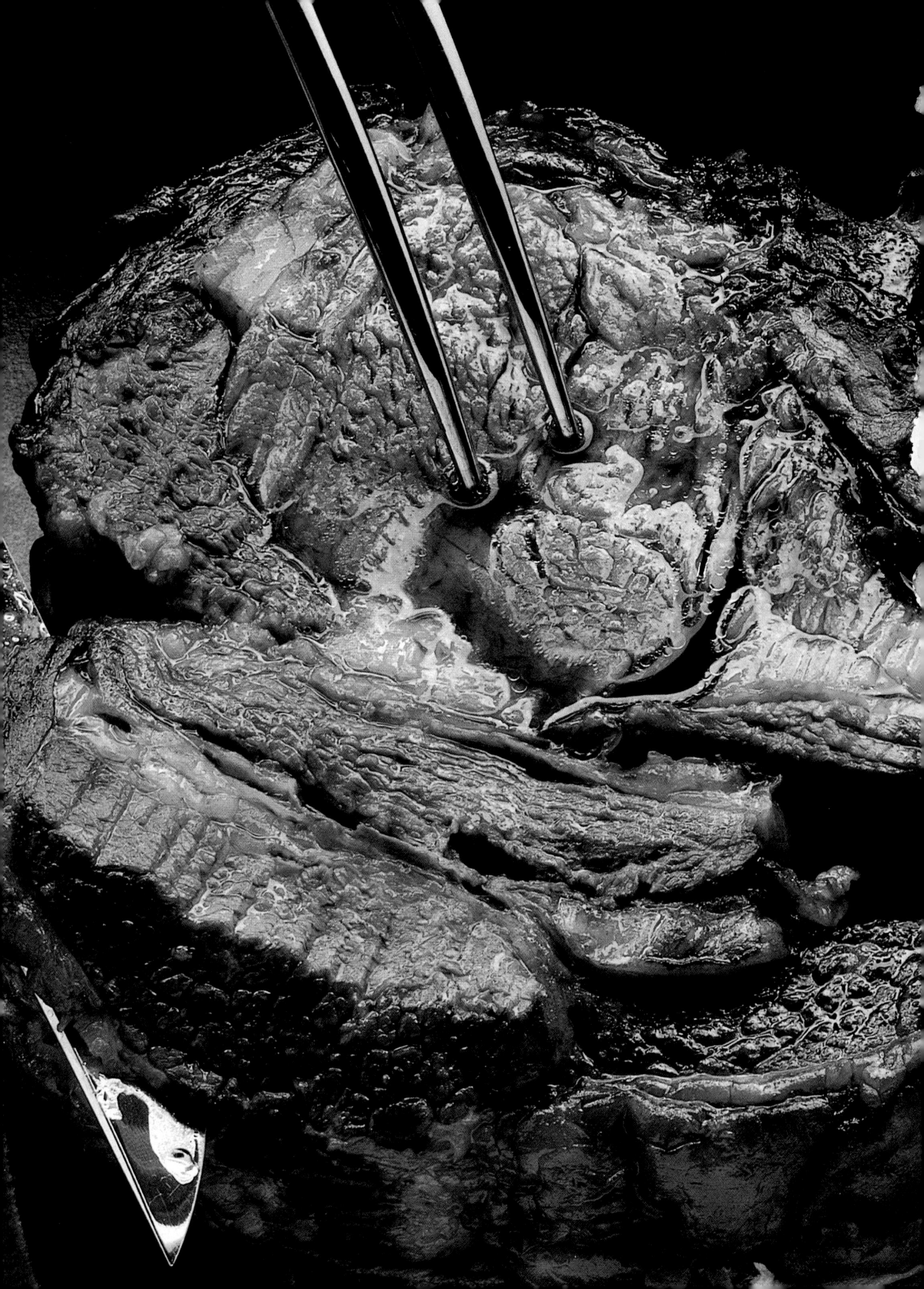

CONVECTION MICROWAVE MEATS & MAIN DISHES

Meat and poultry roasted or broiled in the convection microwave oven have superb flavor. They're brown and crisp on the outside, juicier than conventionally roasted, and ready in much less time. Frozen roasts, steaks and chickens can be cooked without preliminary thawing.

On the MIX settings, microwave energy pulses on and off, so food cooks with hot air and microwave energy at the same time. The oven temperature is preset, but can be changed for complete flexibility. The SLOW COOK setting is designed for foods which cook longer than 99 minutes and 99 seconds at 300° or less. Try baked beans or marinated chuck steak.

Directions for roasting Standing Rib Roast are on pages 14c and 16c.

Broiling Techniques

Set oven for maximum cooking time on BROIL. It automatically heats to 450°. Season meat on both sides, if desired. Slash fat at 1-inch intervals to prevent curling. When audible signal tells you oven is ready, place meat on broiling trivet.

Cook for the minimum time recommended in the chart; then test for doneness. Time varies with the thickness or weight of meat, and is longer for frozen meat. Turning meat over is not necessary, as moving air cooks it on both sides.

Spray trivet and turntable with non-stick vegetable spray for easy clean-up. Do not cover trivet with foil, as it blocks the flow of warm air which cooks the food.

Broil food in advance, if desired, then slice. Individual servings may be reheated as needed by microwaving at MEDIUM (50%), following directions on page 33.

Convection Broiling Chart

Cut	Weight/Thickness		Fresh	Convection Time Frozen
Beef				
Rib	¾-1 in. 7-8 oz. each	Rare: Medium: Well Done:	10-13 min. 14-16 min. 17-20 min.	15-18 min. 19-21 min. 22-25 min.
Steaks: Sirloin, Porterhouse, T-Bone	1-1½ in.	Rare: Medium: Well Done:	10-13 min. 14-18 min. 19-25 min.	14-18 min. 20-23 min. 25-28 min.
Chuck Steak	1 in.	Rare: Medium: Well Done:	12-14 min. 15-18 min. 19-23 min.	20-22 min. 23-25 min. 26-30 min.
London Broil	1-1¼ in. 2½-3 lbs.	Rare: Medium:	23-25 min. 26-30 min.	30-33 min. 35-40 min.
Hamburgers	¼ lb. each	Medium: Well Done:	13-15 min. 18-20 min.	18-20 min. 22-24 min.
Pork				
Chops: loin or center	¾-1 in.	Well Done:	16-20 min.	25-30 min.
Bacon	Regular sliced Thick sliced		4-5 min. 7-8 min.	8-9 min. 9-10 min.
Sausage Brown 'n Serve	Patties: ½ in., 8 oz.		8-10 min.	11-12 min.
Fresh	Links: 8 oz. Links: 1 lb.		8-10 min. 7-8 min.	11-12 min. 12-14 min.
Ham slice, fully cooked	¾ in.		10-12 min.	15-17 min.
Frankfurters	1 lb.		5-7 min.	8-10 min.
Lamb				
Chops: rib, loin or center	¾ in. 3-4 oz. each	Medium: Well Done:	12-14 min. 15-17 min.	22-24 min. 25-30 min.
Chicken				
Broiler-Fryer, halved, quartered or cut-up	1-3 lbs.		25-35 min.	35-50 min.
Fish				
Fillets	¼-¾ in.		6-7 min.	12-14 min.
Steaks	¾ in.		12-14 min.	17-20 min.

Roasting Techniques

Preheating the oven is not necessary for roasted meat and poultry. You don't even need a pan because the carousel will catch the drippings. For moist, tender, perfectly done meat in a fraction of the conventional time, just place the meat in the oven and cook, following the temperature and time in chart on page 16c.

Roasts and chickens may be cooked from the frozen state without being separately thawed. Be sure to shield edges and thin or bony sections. For frozen roasts, set the oven at HIGH MIX, 325°, and remove meat when internal temperature is 20° lower than finished temperature desired. Internal temperature of frozen meat rises more during standing than fresh.

Season meat and place directly on the carousel or on the metal broiling trivet, which holds meat out of its juices. The carousel catches the drippings.

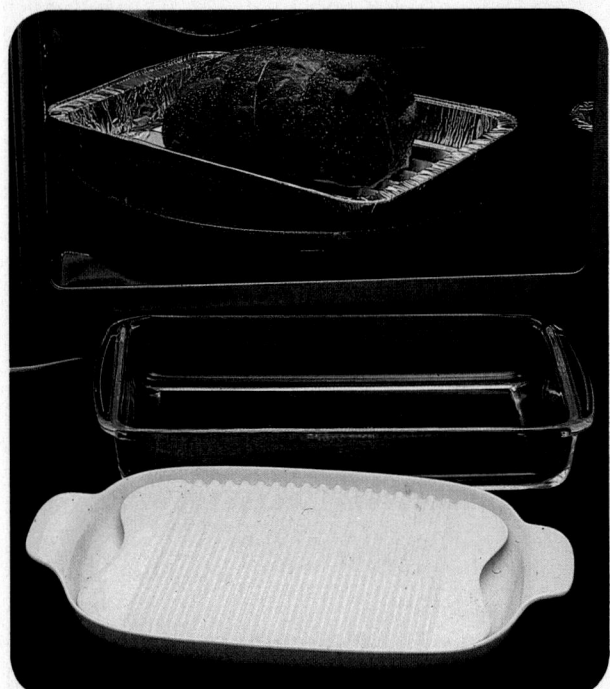

Optional utensils are metal or foil roasting pans, an oven glass baking dish or 10-inch pyroceram casserole. Elevate meat on a heat-resistant rack, if desired, and place utensil on carousel.

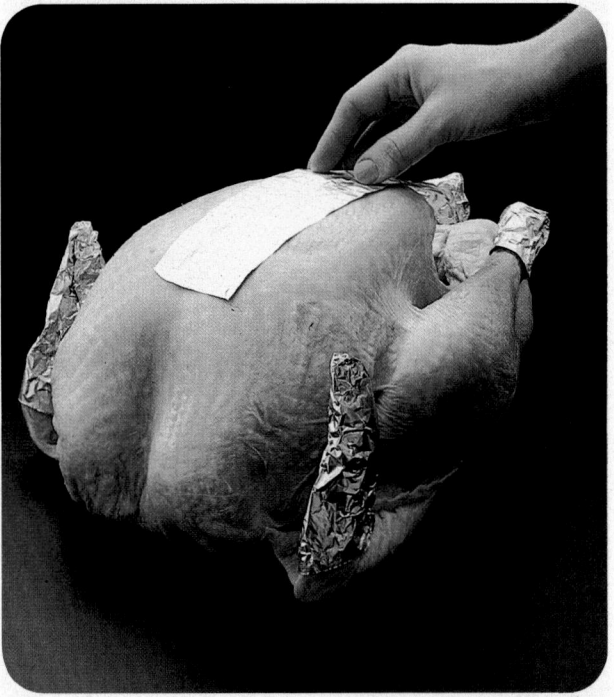

Shield thin or bony areas of roasts or breast, wing tips and legs of birds to prevent overbrowning, especially if meat is frozen. Be sure foil does not touch trivet. Remove shielding from fresh meat after half the time, and from frozen meat after three-fourths of the time.

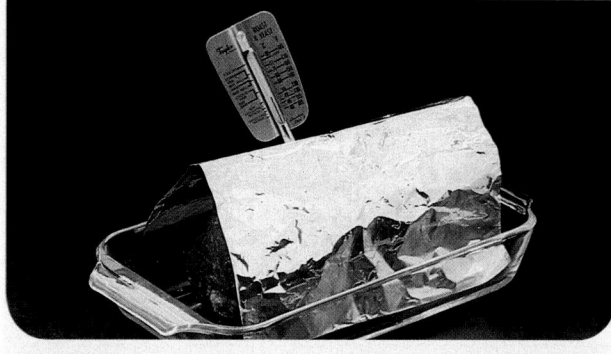

Check doneness after minimum time using a meat thermometer. If meat is not done, cook 5 minutes longer and check again. Remove roast from oven when internal temperature is 10° lower than the finished temperature desired. Let stand, tented with foil, 5 to 10 minutes before carving.

Dual safe microwave/conventional meat thermometer may be inserted in fresh meat before cooking or in frozen meat after half the cooking time. Other thermometers should only be used outside the oven.

Roast meat in oven glass baking dish or shallow pyroceram casserole when you wish to make gravy. When meat is done, let it stand on carving board. Microwave gravy in the same dish.

Roast less tender cuts of beef in heat resistant and microwave oven-safe covered casserole, or in cooking bag set in a baking dish. Covering helps tenderize meat. You may also use the SLOW COOK setting.

Combination Roasting Chart

Cut		Fresh	Frozen	Internal Temp. After Standing (Fresh or Frozen)
Beef				
Roasts (tender cuts)	Rare:	12-14 min./lb. at HIGH MIX, 375°	15-17 min./lb. at HIGH MIX, 325°	140°
	Medium:	13-15 min./lb. at HIGH MIX, 375°	18-20 min./lb. at HIGH MIX, 325°	150°
	Well Done:	14-17 min./lb. at HIGH MIX, 375°	21-23 min./lb. at HIGH MIX, 325°	160°
Roasts (less tender cuts)	Rare:	12-15 min./lb. at HIGH MIX, 375°	15-17 min./lb. at HIGH MIX, 325°	140°
	Medium:	13-17 min./lb. at HIGH MIX, 375°	21-23 min./lb. at HIGH MIX, 325°	150°
	Well Done:	14-18 min./lb. at HIGH MIX, 375°	23-25 min./lb. at HIGH MIX, 325°	160°
Veal				
Roast (boned, rolled, tied)	Well Done:	14-16 min./lb. at HIGH MIX, 375°	19-21 min./lb. at HIGH MIX, 325°	165°-170°
Breast (stuffed)	Well Done:	11-13 min./lb. at HIGH MIX, 375°		170°
Pork				
Roasts (boned, rolled, tied or bone-in)	Well Done:	14-16 min./lb. at HIGH MIX, 375°	18-20 min./lb. at HIGH MIX, 325°	185°
Smoked Ham		7-9 min./lb. at HIGH MIX, 350°		140°
Lamb				
Leg, Roasts	Rare:	10-12 min./lb. at HIGH MIX, 375°	15-17 min./lb. at HIGH MIX, 325°	130°
	Medium:	12-14 min./lb. at HIGH MIX, 375°	17-19 min./lb. at HIGH MIX, 325°	145°
	Well Done:	14-16 min./lb. at HIGH MIX, 375°	19-21 min./lb. at HIGH MIX, 325°	160°
Poultry				
Chicken		9-13 min./lb. at HIGH MIX, 375°	14-16 min./lb. at HIGH MIX, 375°	185°
Turkey (stuffed or unstuffed)		7-10 min./lb. at HIGH MIX, 375°	Sharp does not recommend roasting frozen turkey	185°

Pot Roast With Vegetables ►

4 to 5-pound round or chuck pot roast
½ teaspoon salt
½ teaspoon garlic powder
½ teaspoon dried thyme leaves
⅛ teaspoon pepper
4 potatoes, peeled and quartered
3 onions, quartered
2 carrots, sliced
¾ cup water
2 tablespoons brown bouquet sauce

Makes 8 servings

1. Place meat in 4-quart casserole. Pat seasoning into meat. Add vegetables. Combine water and browning sauce; pour into casserole dish. Cover.

2. Roast 20 minutes per pound on HIGH MIX, 375°, or until internal temperature reaches 140°.

Meatloaf

1½ pounds ground beef
1 egg
1 small onion, chopped
1 carrot, grated
1 stalk celery, finely chopped
½ cup seasoned bread crumbs
¼ cup catsup
½ teaspoon dried thyme leaves
¼ teaspoon garlic powder
⅛ teaspoon pepper
¼ pound boiled ham, sliced
¼ pound Swiss cheese, sliced

Makes 4 to 6 servings

1. Thoroughly combine all ingredients except ham and cheese. On a sheet of wax paper, press mixture into a 9 × 12 inch rectangle.

2. Layer sliced ham on meat, then cheese. Roll up, starting at narrow end. Seal ends to form loaf. Place seam side down in loaf pan, 9 × 5 inches. Roast 25 minutes on HIGH MIX, 375°, or until internal temperature reaches 150°.

Steak Roulade ▲

¼ cup red wine
¼ cup soy sauce
¼ cup vegetable oil
1½ pound flank steak
 1 medium onion, diced
 1 stalk celery, diced
½ green pepper, diced
½ cup sliced mushrooms
 2 tablespoons margarine or butter
½ cup seasoned bread crumbs

Makes 4 servings

1. Combine wine, soy sauce and oil in large dish. Add steak and marinate several hours.

2. Combine remaining ingredients, except bread crumbs, in small bowl. Microwave at HIGH (100%) until soft, 4 to 5 minutes. Stir in crumbs.

3. Remove meat from marinade. Spread filling evenly over meat. Roll meat up, starting at narrow end. Tie securely with string. Roast 30 minutes on HIGH MIX, 375°, or until internal temperature reaches 130°.

Leg of Lamb

¼ cup margarine or butter, softened
½ teaspoon garlic powder
½ teaspoon dried thyme leaves
½ teaspoon dried oregano leave
½ teaspoon dried parsley flakes
 2 tablespoons lemon juice
 1 small onion, chopped
 4 to 5-pound leg of lamb

Makes 4 to 6 servings

1. Combine butter, garlic powder, thyme, oregano and parsley. Add lemon juice and onion, making a paste. Spread over lamb.

2. Roast 14 to 16 minutes per pound on HIGH MIX, 375°, or until internal temperature reaches 130°.

Pineapple Pork Roast

1 cup pineapple preserves
¼ cup prepared mustard
1 tablespoon prepared horseradish
1 tablespoon soy sauce
3 to 5-pound pork roast

Makes 4 to 6 servings

1. Combine all ingredients except pork roast. Spread glaze over roast. Baste once during cooking time.

2. Roast 14 to 16 minutes per pound on HIGH MIX, 375°, or until internal temperature reaches 175°.

Stuffed Pork Chops

4 pork chops, 1¼ inches thick
1 cup chopped apple
½ cup soft bread crumbs
½ cup chopped walnuts
¼ cup chopped onion
¼ cup raisins
1 egg
1 teaspoon dried parsley flakes
½ teaspoon dried thyme leaves
¼ teaspoon ground sage
⅛ teaspoon pepper

Makes 4 servings

1. Make pocket in each chop. Combine remaining ingredients; mix well. Stuff each chop with one-fourth of the mixture. Place chops directly on turntable or round pizza pan.

2. Roast 30 minutes on HIGH MIX, 375°, or until meat next to bone is no longer pink.

Convert your own casserole recipes.

Use HIGH MIX, 375° for 25 to 30 minutes, or until thoroughly heated.

Macaroni and Ham Casserole

1½ cups medium white sauce (page 142)
1½ cups shredded Cheddar cheese
½ teaspoon curry powder
4 cups cooked macaroni
2 cups cooked ham, cubed
1 package (10 ounces) frozen peas, thawed
½ cup shredded Cheddar cheese

Makes 4 servings

1. Prepare one and a half recipes of medium white sauce. Add 1½ cups cheese and the curry powder. Microwave at HIGH (100%) until cheese melts, about 1 minute. Combine sauce, macaroni, ham and peas in a 2-quart casserole. Sprinkle with ½ cup cheese.

2. Roast 30 minutes on HIGH MIX, 375°, or until thoroughly heated.

Layered Casserole

1¼ cups water
¾ cup uncooked long grain rice
1 pound ground beef
1 package (10 ounces) frozen whole kernel corn
1 can (15 ounces) tomato sauce
2 tablespoons water
¼ teaspoon garlic powder
¼ teaspoon salt
⅛ teaspoon pepper
½ cup chopped onion
½ cup chopped green pepper
1 package (9 ounces) frozen green beans, thawed
4 slices bacon, cut up

Makes 4 servings

1. Combine 1¼ cups water and rice in 2-quart casserole. Microwave at HIGH (100%) 5 minutes. Reduce power to MEDIUM-HIGH (70%). Microwave 5 minutes; set aside.

2. Place ground beef in 1-quart casserole. Microwave at HIGH (100%) until meat loses pink color, about 5 minutes; drain.

3. Pour corn over rice. Combine tomato sauce, water and spices; pour one-third over corn. Layer onion, green pepper, beans and ground beef over rice and corn. Pour remaining sauce over layers. Top with bacon. Roast 20 to 25 minutes on HIGH MIX, 375°, or until thoroughly heated.

◄ Hearty Pizza

¾ pound ground beef
  Pizza Sauce (below)
3 cups all-purpose flour
1 package active dry yeast
1 teaspoon salt
¾ cup milk
¼ cup water
¼ cup vegetable oil
1 egg
2 cups shredded mozzarella cheese
  (about 8 ounces)

Makes 12- or 14-inch pizza

1. Place ground beef in medium bowl. Microwave at HIGH (100%) until beef loses pink color, 4 to 6 minutes, stirring to break up beef after half the cooking time. Drain and set aside. Prepare Pizza Sauce. Set aside.

2. Mix flour, yeast and salt in large bowl. Stir in milk, water, oil and egg to make a pliable dough. Turn dough onto lightly floured surface. Knead until smooth, about 2 minutes. Place in well-greased large bowl; turn greased side up. Cover with clean, moist towel. Place in oven at 100° until double in size, about 40 minutes. (Dough is ready if an indentation remains when touched.)

3. Remove dough from oven. Preheat oven to 425°. Punch down dough. With well-greased fingers, pat dough in greased 12- or 14-inch round pizza pan. Pinch dough to form edge. Bake 12 to 14 minutes, or until crust is golden brown. Top crust with ground beef, Pizza Sauce and cheese. Bake 10 to 15 minutes, or until heated through.

Pizza Sauce

1 medium onion, chopped
1 clove garlic, minced
1 tablespoon vegetable oil
1 can (16 ounces) peeled tomatoes
1 can (16 ounces) tomato purée
1 teaspoon salt
⅛ teaspoon pepper

Makes about 1½ cups

1. Combine onion, garlic and oil in medium bowl. Microwave at HIGH (100%) until vegetables are tender, about 2 minutes. Stir in tomatoes, tomato puree, salt and pepper.

2. Microwave at HIGH (100%) until bubbly, about 5 minutes. Reduce power to MEDIUM (50%). Microwave until thickened, 8 to 10 minutes.

Tamale Casserole

1 pound lean ground beef
1 medium onion, chopped
1 small green pepper, chopped
2 cans (8 ounces each) tomato sauce
1 clove garlic, minced
1 teaspoon chili powder
1 teaspoon taco seasoning mix
½ teaspoon sugar
¼ teaspoon salt
¼ teaspoon pepper
  Golden Corn Bread (below)
½ cup shredded Cheddar cheese
  (about 2 ounces)
¼ cup sliced pitted black olives

Makes 4 to 6 servings

1. Mix ground beef, onion and green pepper in 1½- to 2-quart casserole. Microwave at HIGH (100%) 5 minutes, stirring to break up beef after half the cooking time. Stir in tomato sauce, garlic, chili powder, taco seasoning mix, sugar, salt and pepper. Microwave at HIGH (100%) 5 minutes. Reduce power to MEDIUM-HIGH (70%). Microwave 5 minutes.

2. Prepare Golden Corn Bread; pour over beef mixture. Bake 25 minutes on HIGH MIX, 375°, or until corn bread is golden. Sprinkle with cheese and olives. Cool 5 minutes before serving.

Golden Corn Bread

½ cup yellow cornmeal
½ cup all-purpose flour
2 tablespoons baking powder
1 tablespoon sugar
¼ teaspoon salt
½ cup milk
1 egg
2 tablespoons melted shortening

1. Combine cornmeal, flour, baking powder, sugar and salt in medium bowl.

2. Stir in milk, egg and shortening. Beat mixture until almost smooth.

Note: Corn bread mix can be substituted for the Golden Corn Bread.

Sausage Kabobs ◄

Barbecue Sauce (below)
2 pounds Italian sausage
1 pound large fresh mushrooms
2 large green peppers, cut into chunks
2 medium onions, cut into wedges
1 pint cherry tomatoes

Makes 4 servings

1. Prepare Barbecue Sauce. Set aside. Prick sausage in several places with fork. Microwave at MEDIUM-HIGH (70%) 10 minutes; remove sausage from oven.

2. Cut sausage into 2-inch pieces. Thread alternately with vegetables on 8 wooden or metal skewers. Place on broiling trivet. Brush with Barbecue Sauce. Broil 20 minutes, basting frequently with Barbecue Sauce.

Note: Skewers up to 12 inches can be used.

Barbecue Sauce

1 medium onion, chopped
1 tablespoon vegetable oil
1 cup beef broth
1 can (6 ounces) tomato paste
⅓ cup vinegar
3 tablespoons packed brown sugar
3 tablespoons Worcestershire sauce
2 tablespoons prepared mustard
2 teaspoons salt
½ teaspoon pepper

Makes about 1½ cups

1. Place onion and oil in medium bowl. Microwave at HIGH (100%) until onion is tender, 1 to 2 minutes. Blend in remaining ingredients.

2. Microwave at HIGH (100%) until bubbly, about 5 minutes. Reduce power to MEDIUM (50%). Microwave until thickened, about 5 minutes, stirring occasionally during cooking time.

Steak Kabobs ▲

¼ cup sugar
¼ cup soy sauce
¼ cup white wine
1 tablespoon vegetable oil
1 teaspoon ground ginger
¼ teaspoon salt
2 pounds lean top beef round steak, cut into 1-inch cubes
2 large green peppers, cut into chunks
2 medium tomatoes, cut into quarters
1 can (8 ounces) pineapple chunks, drained

Makes 4 servings

1. Mix sugar, soy sauce, wine, oil, ginger and salt in medium bowl. Stir in steak cubes; cover. Marinate at room temperature 1 hour or at least 4 hours in refrigerator.

2. Remove steak cubes from marinade; reserve marinade. Thread steak cubes alternately with remaining ingredients on 8 wooden or metal skewers. Place on broiling trivet. Broil 7 to 9 minutes, or until desired doneness, brushing with marinade after half the time.

Note: Skewers up to 12 inches can be used.

Honey Chicken ▲

2½ to 3-pound broiler-fryer chicken, cut up
¼ cup honey
¼ cup sherry
2 tablespoons catsup
2 tablespoons soy sauce
½ teaspoon ground ginger
¼ teaspoon garlic powder

Makes 4 servings

1. Arrange chicken pieces on metal pizza pan. Combine remaining ingredients in small bowl. Microwave at HIGH (100%) 1 minute. Pour over chicken pieces.

2. Roast 35 minutes on HIGH MIX, 375°, or until chicken next to bone is no longer pink.

Broiled Chicken

1 cup dry white wine
1 medium onion, chopped
1 tablespoon dried thyme leaves
½ teaspoon salt
½ teaspoon garlic powder
⅛ teaspoon pepper
2½ to 3-pound broiler-fryer chicken, cut up

Makes 4 servings

1. Combine all ingredients except chicken. Place chicken skin side down in large dish. Pour marinade over chicken. Marinate 2 hours.

2. Preheat oven to 450°. Remove chicken from marinade; reserve marinade. Place chicken pieces on broiling trivet. Broil until chicken next to bone is no longer pink, about 30 minutes.

3. Pour mariande into small bowl. Microwave at HIGH (100%) until onion is soft, about 2 minutes. Pour over chicken pieces.

◄ Glazed Stuffed Cornish Hens

1 cup chopped pecans
¾ cup apricot preserves
¼ cup margarine or butter, melted
3 tablespoons orange juice concentrate
1 tablespoon lemon juice
1 cup seasoned stuffing cubes
½ cup water
2 Cornish hens (1½ pounds each)

Makes 2 to 4 servings

1. Combine pecans, preserves, melted butter, orange juice concentrate and lemon juice. Combine half the sauce mixture with stuffing cubes and water. Stuff cavity of each bird. Truss birds.

2. Pour half of the remaining sauce over hens. Brush with remaining sauce halfway through cooking time.

3. Roast 12 minutes per pound on HIGH MIX, 375°, or until meat next to bone is no longer pink.

Roast Chicken

1 teaspoon ground ginger
½ teaspoon ground coriander
Dash pepper
5 to 6-pound roasting chicken
2 tablespoons margarine or butter
½ cup minced onion
½ cup plain yogurt
½ cup half-and-half
1 teaspoon turmeric
½ teaspoon salt

Makes 4 to 6 servings

1. Combine ginger, coriander and pepper; rub into chicken. Tie legs of chicken; place on roasting rack in roasting pan.

2. Place butter in a medium bowl. Microwave at HIGH (100%) until melted, 30 to 45 seconds. Blend in remaining ingredients. Reserve one-fourth cup of the mixture; set aside. Spread remaining mixture over chicken.

3. Roast 10 to 12 minutes per pound on HIGH MIX, 375°, or until chicken next to bone is no longer pink. Combine pan drippings and reserved sauce. Microwave at HIGH (100%) until hot, about 1 minute. Serve with chicken.

Poultry Pie

Filling:
3 cups diced, cooked boneless chicken or turkey
1 package (10 ounces) frozen peas, thawed
1 can (10¾ ounces) cream of mushroom soup
½ cup milk
2 tablespoons chopped pimiento
½ teaspoon dried oregano leaves
½ teaspoon dried marjoram leaves
½ teaspoon salt
¼ teaspoon dried thyme leaves
¼ teaspoon garlic powder
⅛ teaspoon pepper

Crust:
1 cup all-purpose flour
1¼ teaspoons baking powder
½ teaspoon salt
¼ cup margarine or butter
3 to 5 tablespoons milk

Makes 8 servings

1. Combine filling ingredients in a 9-inch deep dish pie pan; set aside.

2. Combine flour, baking powder and salt in medium bowl. Cut in butter until mixture resembles coarse crumbs. Add enough milk to form a soft dough. Roll out on lightly floured surface to fit top of dish. Fit dough onto dish. Trim, seal and flute. Cut small slits in crust.

3. Place on broiling trivet. Bake 25 to 30 minutes on LOW MIX, 375°, or until thoroughly heated.

Mustard and Mayonnaise Chicken

2½ to 3-pound broiler-fryer chicken, cut up
¼ cup spicy prepared mustard
¼ cup mayonnaise

Makes 4 to 5 servings

1. Arrange chicken pieces skin side up on metal pizza pan or directly on turntable. Combine mustard and mayonnaise; spread on chicken pieces.

2. Roast 35 minutes on HIGH MIX, 375°, or until chicken next to bone is no longer pink.

Deviled Ham-Filled Dutch Pancake

Deviled Ham Filling (below)
4 eggs
¼ cup plus 2 tablespoons all-purpose flour
¼ teaspoon salt
½ cup milk
2 tablespoons plus 2 teaspoons margarine
   or butter, melted
½ cup shredded Cheddar cheese
   (about 2 ounces)
2 tablespoons snipped parsley

Makes 6 servings

1. Preheat oven to 425°. Prepare Deviled Ham Filling. Set aside. Heat pie plate, 9 × 1¼ or 10 × 1½ inches, until hot. Meanwhile, beat eggs in small bowl until blended. Mix flour and salt; gradually beat into eggs until smooth. Stir in milk. Stir in 2 tablespoons margarine. Using 2 teaspoons margarine, grease inside of hot pie plate (margarine will sizzle). Pour egg mixture into pie plate.

2. Bake at 425° until pancake has risen, forming large cup, about 20 minutes. Prick center of pancake several times with fork. Reduce heat to 325°. Bake until golden brown, about 5 minutes. Fill immediately with Deviled Ham Filling. Sprinkle with cheese and parsley. Cut in wedges to serve.

Spicy Shrimp ▲

¼ cup white wine
¼ cup water
3 tablespoons soy sauce
2 tablespoons sugar
1 tablespoon vegetable oil
2 teaspoons dried parsley flakes
⅛ to ¼ teaspoon ground ginger
   Dash of hot pepper sauce
1 pound jumbo raw shrimp, shelled and
   deveined

Makes 4 servings

1. Mix all ingredients except shrimp in medium bowl. Stir in shrimp; cover. Marinate at room temperature 45 minutes or 3 hours in refrigerator.

2. Remove shrimp from marinade; reserve marinade. Place shrimp on carousel or round pizza pan. Broil 6 to 8 minutes, brushing with marinade after half the time.

3. Microwave remaining marinade at HIGH (100%) 2 minutes. Serve over rice or as a dipping sauce with appetizers, if desired.

Deviled Ham Filling

¼ cup margarine or butter
2 medium onions, chopped (about 1 cup)
8 ounces fresh mushrooms, sliced
1½ tablespoons all-purpose flour
1 teaspoon dry mustard
1 teaspoon salt
¼ teaspoon pepper
1 cup chicken broth
1½ cups (6 ounces) fully cooked ham,
   cut into thin strips
2 large tomatoes, cut into quarters and
   seeds removed

1. Place margarine and onions in medium bowl. Microwave at HIGH (100%) until onions are tender, about 3 minutes. Add mushrooms. Microwave at HIGH (100%) 2 minutes, stirring once. Blend in flour, mustard, salt and pepper.

2. Microwave at HIGH (100%) 2 minutes. Stir in chicken broth. Microwave at HIGH (100%) 5 minutes, stirring occasionally. Stir in ham and tomatoes. Microwave at HIGH (100%) until heated through, 2 to 3 minutes.

Cheese Soufflé ▲

¼ cup margarine or butter
¼ cup all-purpose flour
½ teaspoon salt
⅛ teaspoon cayenne
1½ cups milk
2 cups shredded Cheddar cheese
  (about 8 ounces)
6 eggs, separated

Makes 4 servings

1. Place margarine in large bowl. Microwave at HIGH (100%) until melted, about 1 minute. Blend in flour, salt and cayenne. Gradually stir in milk. Microwave at MEDIUM-HIGH (70%) until slightly thickened, about 6 minutes, stirring every 2 minutes. Add cheese. Microwave at MEDIUM-HIGH (70%) 2 minutes; stir to blend.

2. Preheat oven at 325°. Beat egg yolks. Stir a small amount of hot sauce gradually into egg yolks; return to sauce, blending well. Cool slightly.

3. Beat egg whites until soft peaks form. With rubber spatula fold egg whites into cheese sauce, half at a time, just until blended. Pour into greased 2-quart soufflé dish. Bake 35 minutes on LOW MIX, 325°, or until top is puffed and golden and center is set. Serve immediately.

Broiled Tomatoes

½ cup mayonnaise or salad dressing
¼ cup grated Parmesan cheese
1 teaspoon dried basil leaves
½ teaspoon dried onion flakes
2 medium tomatoes, cut into halves
  Salt and pepper

Makes 4 servings

1. Mix mayonnaise, cheese, basil and onion flakes in small bowl; set aside. Scoop out fleshy part of tomatoes; discard seeds. Stir tomato pulp into mayonnaise mixture.

2. Sprinkle tomato halves with salt and pepper; spoon mayonnaise-tomato mixture into each. Place on broiling trivet or carousel. Broil 10 minutes, or until mayonnaise-tomato mixture is puffed and golden brown.

Frittata ▲

- ¾ cup diced green pepper
- ¾ cup diced mushrooms
- ¾ cup diced zucchini
- ¾ cup diced onion
- ½ cup diced pimiento
- 2 tablespoons vegetable oil
- 6 eggs
- 2 packages (8 ounces each) cream cheese
- ¼ cup milk
- 2 cups cubed bread (3 slices)
- 1½ cups shredded Cheddar cheese
- 1 teaspoon salt
- ½ teaspoon garlic powder
- ¼ teaspoon pepper

Makes 6 to 8 servings

1. Combine vegetables and oil in medium bowl; cover. Microwave at HIGH (100%) until vegetables are tender, about 5 minutes. Drain liquid.

2. Beat eggs with cream cheese and milk until smooth. Mix in remaining ingredients. Pour into buttered 9-inch spring form pan.

3. Bake 30 minutes on LOW MIX, 350°, or until set in center. Cool 10 to 20 minutes. Cut into wedges.

Spinach Pie

- 1 cup chopped onion
- 2 tablespoons margarine or butter
- 2 packages (10 ounces each) frozen chopped spinach, thawed and drained
- 1 container (15 ounces) ricotta cheese
- 2 cups feta cheese, crumbled
- 5 eggs
- 2 tablespoons all-purpose flour
- 1 teaspoon dried basil leaves
- ½ teaspoon salt
- ½ teaspoon dried oregano leaves
- ⅛ teaspoon pepper
- 1 can (8 ounces) refrigerator crescent rolls
- 2 tablespoons margarine or butter, melted

Makes 8 servings

1. Place onion and butter in large mixing bowl. Microwave at HIGH (100%) until onion is tender, 1 to 2 minutes. Blend in remaining ingredients except crescent rolls and butter.

2. Spread mixture into square baking dish, 10 × 10 inches. Shape crescent rolls into four rectangles; place on top of mixture. Brush with melted butter.

3. Bake 30 minutes on HIGH MIX, 375°, or until thoroughly heated.

Broccoli Kugel ►

3 tablespoons margarine or butter, melted
½ pound cooked egg noodles
1 package (10 ounces) chopped broccoli, thawed and drained
3 ounces cream cheese
1 cup cottage cheese
½ cup dairy sour cream
2 eggs, slightly beaten
½ teaspoon salt
½ teaspoon vanilla

Makes 8 servings

1. Combine half the butter, the noodles and broccoli in square baking dish, 8 × 8 inches. Combine remaining ingredients except the remaining butter in medium bowl; add to noodles and mix well. Brush with remaining butter.

2. Bake 30 minutes on LOW MIX, 350°, or until thoroughly heated.

Broccoli Quiche

1 baked 9-inch pie shell
1 medium onion, chopped
5 eggs, beaten
2 cups shredded Swiss cheese
2 cups shredded mozzarella cheese
1 can (5 ounces) evaporated milk
1 package (10 ounces) frozen chopped broccoli, thawed and drained
¼ teaspoon ground nutmeg
¼ teaspoon salt
⅛ teaspoon pepper

Makes 4 to 6 servings

1. Place onion in small dish. Microwave at HIGH (100%) until tender, about 2 minutes.

2. Combine onion and remaining ingredients. Pour into prepared pie shell. Place on broiling trivet.

3. Bake 30 minutes on LOW MIX, 350°. If wooden pick inserted in center does not come out clean, let stand in oven a few minutes to complete cooking.

CONVECTION MICROWAVE BAKING & DESSERTS

Combination cooking produces fine textured breads and moist, tender cakes with just the right amount of browning and crisping. Directions for baking Strawberry Puff Ring are on page 39c.

Bread Techniques

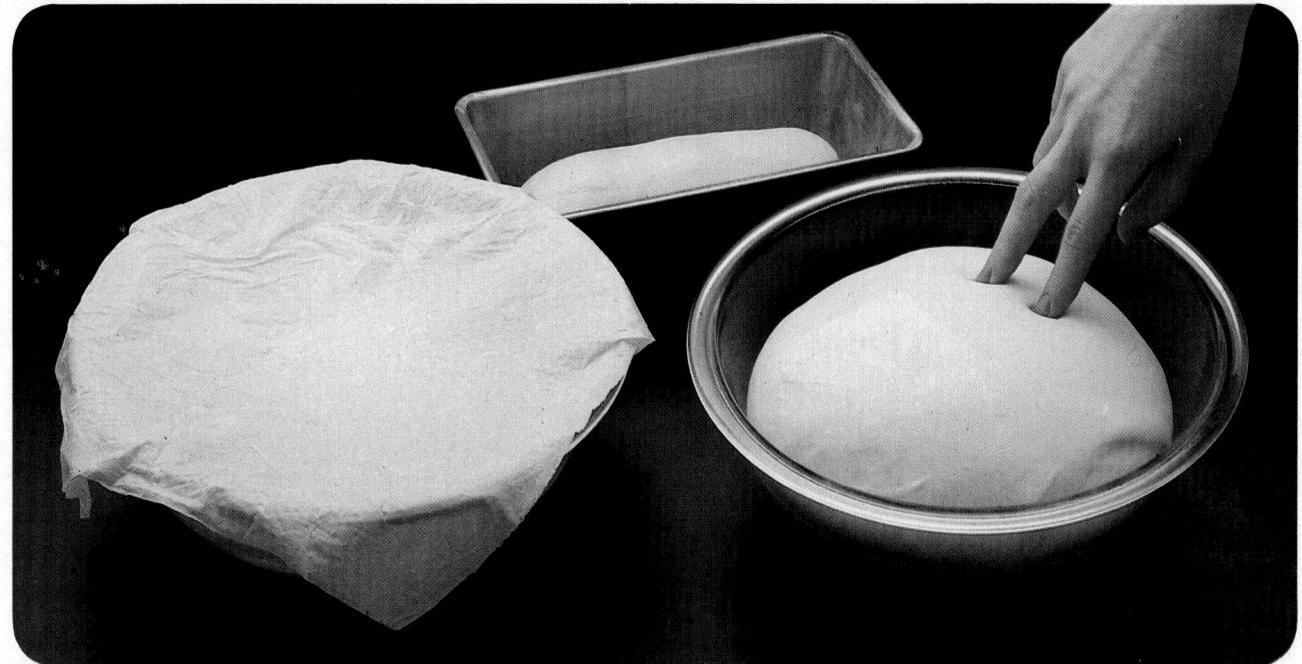

Proofing dough. Use your own recipe or frozen dough. Place in well-greased bowl or loaf pan; cover with damp cloth. Place in oven at 100° for 30 to 45 minutes. Frozen dough will take longer, 1 to 1½ hours. Dough is doubled when impressions remain after fingers are pressed ½ inch into dough.

Preheating of oven is not necessary. Bake loaf 20 minutes at LOW MIX, 350°. After baking, bread should be golden brown and sound hollow when tapped. Do not let bread stand in oven; remove from pans immediately to cool on wire rack.

Braid or other shape. Remove carousel from oven. Shape bread; place directly on carousel. No preheating is needed. Bake for minimum time in your conventional recipe, on LOW MIX, 350°.

Cake Techniques

Layer Cakes. Use a mix or your own conventional recipe. No preheating of oven is needed. Bake 20 to 25 minutes on LOW MIX, 350°. If not done, let stand in oven a few minutes to complete cooking.

Tube Cakes. Do not preheat oven. Bake mix cakes for minimum time in package directions or your own recipe for half the recommended time, using LOW MIX, 350°. If arcing occurs with fluted tube pan, place a heat-and-microwave-safe dish or plate between pan and carousel.

Angel Food. Do not preheat oven. Bake your own recipe or a mix for 25 minutes on LOW MIX, 350°.

Loaf Cakes or Quick Breads. Do not preheat oven. Bake a mix for the minimum time directed on package, or your own recipe for half the recommended time, using LOW MIX, 350°. Test for doneness. If loaf is not done, let stand in oven a few minutes to complete cooking.

Pie Techniques

Pie Shell. Use mix, frozen pie dough, or your recipe for single crust pie. Prick crust with fork. Preheat oven to 425°. Place pie shell on broiling trivet; bake with convection heat 8 to 10 minutes, or until lightly browned. Cool and fill.

Double Crust or Crumb Top Pies. Prepare pie as you would for conventional baking; make slits in top of two crust pie. Preheat oven to 400°. Place pie on broiling trivet. Bake double crust or lattice pies 25 to 30 minutes on HIGH MIX, 400°; crumb top pies 18 to 20 minutes on HIGH MIX, 400°.

Custard Pies. Prebake and cool pie shell as directed above. Fill with uncooked custard. Without preheating, bake pie on broiling trivet for 30 minutes on LOW MIX, 325°. If custard is not set, let stand in oven a few minutes to complete cooking.

Frozen Prepared Pies. Do not preheat oven. Bake 30 minutes. Use HIGH MIX, 375° for fruit pies and LOW MIX, 325° for custard pies.

Combination Baking Chart

Item	Procedure
Cakes: Your recipe or mix	
Layer Cakes	LOW MIX, 350° for 20 to 25 minutes.
Tube Cakes (except Angel Food)	LOW MIX, 350° for half the recommended time.*
Angel Food	LOW MIX, 350° for 25 minutes.
Loaf Cakes or Quick Breads	LOW MIX, 350° for half the recommended time.
Bar Cookies: Your recipe or mix	LOW MIX, 350° for two-thirds the recommended time, or until wooden pick inserted in center comes out clean.
Pies	
Single Crust: Baked before filling, your recipe, mix or frozen prepared	Prick crust with fork. Preheat oven to 425°. Bake on broiling trivet 8 to 10 minutes, or until lightly browned. Let cool before filling.
Double Crust	Preheat oven to 400°. Bake on broiling trivet 25 to 30 minutes on HIGH MIX, 400°.
Crumb Top	Preheat oven to 400°. Bake on broiling trivet 18 to 20 minutes on HIGH MIX, 400°.
Custard Pie	Prebake, following directions for single crust; cool. Fill with desired uncooked custard. Bake on broiling trivet 30 minutes on LOW MIX, 325°. If custard is not set, let stand in oven a few minutes.
Variety Pies (Pecan, Chess, etc.)	Bake on broiling trivet 25 to 30 minutes on LOW MIX, 350°.
Frozen prepared pies	Bake 30 minutes. Use HIGH MIX, 375° for fruit pies and LOW MIX, 325° for custard pies.
Breads	
Loaf: Your recipe or frozen, thawed and proofed	LOW MIX, 350°. 1 to 2 loaves, 20 to 25 minutes; 3 to 4 loaves, 25 to 30 minutes.
Braid or other shape	Remove metal turntable from oven. Place bread directly on metal turntable. LOW MIX, 350° for two-thirds the conventional time.

*If arcing occurs while using a fluted tube pan, place a heat-resistant dish (Pyrex pie plate, glass pizza tray or dinner plate) between the pan and the turntable.

Convection Baking Chart

Item	Baking Time and Temperature
Appetizers: Brown and serve, pastry	Follow package directions.
Biscuits: Your recipe, mix or refrigerator	Follow recipe or package directions.
Cookies: Drop, rolled, refrigerator, spritz, molded	Follow recipe or package directions.
Cream Puffs	Follow recipe directions.
Fish Sticks: Frozen	Follow package directions.
Muffins: Your recipe or mix	Follow recipe or package directions.
Pizza: Your recipe or frozen	Follow recipe or package directions.
Puff Pastry: Your recipe or frozen	Follow recipe or package directions.
Rolls: Your recipe, package or refrigerator.	Follow recipe or package directions.

Caraway Rolls ➤

1 package active dry yeast
¼ cup warm water
1 cup cottage cheese
2 tablespoons sugar
1 tablespoon caraway seeds
1 teaspoon salt
¼ teaspoon baking soda
1 egg, slightly beaten
2 cups all-purpose flour

Makes 12 rolls

1. Dissolve yeast in warm water in large bowl. Microwave cottage cheese at HIGH (100%) until cheese is lukewarm, about 20 seconds; add to yeast mixture. Stir in sugar, caraway seeds, salt, soda and egg. Slowly add flour, mixing until dough cleans bowl.

2. Cover with damp cloth. Place in oven. Let rise at 100° until double in bulk, 30 to 45 minutes. Stir down dough. Divide among 12 greased medium muffin cups. Let rise at 100° until double in bulk, about 20 minutes.

3. Bake 15 minutes on LOW MIX, 350°, or until tops spring back when touched lightly with finger.

Zucchini Muffins

1½ cups all-purpose flour
½ cup sugar
1 teaspoon baking powder
½ teaspoon ground cinnamon
½ teaspoon salt
1 cup grated zucchini
½ cup chopped walnuts
½ cup raisins
1 egg
⅓ cup vegetable oil

Makes 12 muffins

1. Combine dry ingredients in medium bowl. Mix in remaining ingredients until just moistened. Fill 12 greased muffin cups ⅔ full.

2. Bake 20 minutes on LOW MIX, 400°, or until tops spring back when touched lightly with finger.

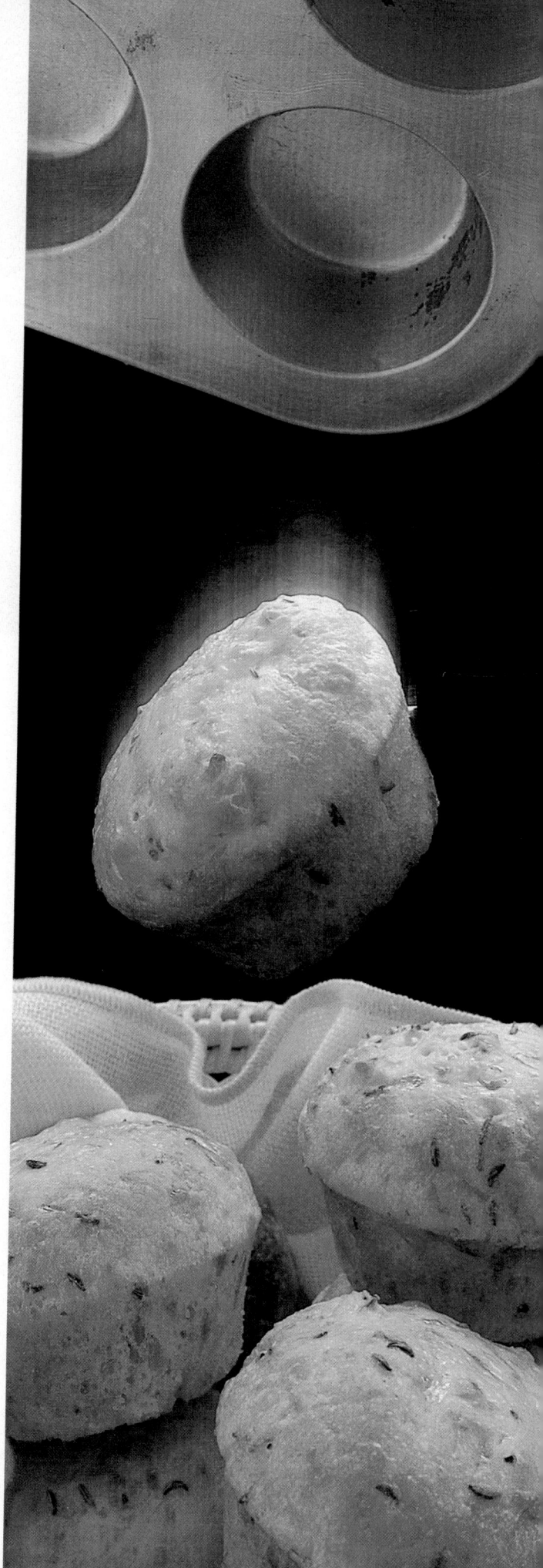

Biscuits ▲

5 cups all-purpose flour
3 tablespoons baking powder
3 tablespoons sugar
1 teaspoon salt
1 teaspoon baking soda
1 cup vegetable shortening
2 packages active dry yeast
2 to 4 tablespoons warm water
2 cups buttermilk

Makes 6 to 7 dozen

1. Combine dry ingredients. Cut in shortening until mixture resembles coarse crumbs. Dissolve yeast in warm water. Add dissolved yeast and buttermilk to dry ingredients; mix well. Roll out desired amount on lightly floured surface to a little over ¼ inch thick. Cut with floured 2-inch biscuit cutter.

2. Preheat oven to 400°. Place biscuits on lightly greased pan. Let rise 10 minutes. Bake at 400° for 10 to 12 minutes, or until golden brown.

NOTE: Dough can be refrigerated for one week in an air-tight plastic bag.

Beer Muffins

4 cups buttermilk baking mix
1 can (12 ounces) beer
2 tablespoons sugar

Makes 12 muffins

1. Preheat oven to 400°. Combine all ingredients in large bowl. Spoon batter into twelve greased muffin cups.

2. Bake 15 minutes at LOW MIX, 400°, or until golden brown.

Ham and Cheese Crescents

2 packages (8 ounces each) refrigerator crescent rolls
¾ cup apricot preserves
1 tablespoon spicy prepared mustard
¼ pound sliced ham
8 slices American cheese

Makes 16 servings

1. Preheat oven to 375°. Separate rolls into triangles. Combine preserves and mustard; spread on dough. Place ½ slice of cheese and ½ piece of ham on base of each triangle. Roll up starting at wide end. Repeat with remaining rolls, ham and cheese. Place on two metal pizza pans.

2. Bake at 375° for 10 minutes, or until golden brown.

Onion-Cheese Bread ►

- 1 medium onion, chopped (about ½ cup)
- 1 tablespoon margarine or butter
- 1½ cups biscuit baking mix
- ½ cup milk
- 1 egg, well beaten
- ½ cup shredded sharp Cheddar cheese (about 2 ounces)
- 2 tablespoons snipped parsley or 1 tablespoon dried parsley flakes
- 2 tablespoons margarine or butter
- ½ cup shredded sharp Cheddar cheese (about 2 ounces)

Makes 6 to 8 servings

1. Combine onion and 1 tablespoon margarine in small bowl. Microwave at HIGH (100%) until onion is tender, about 2 minutes. Set onion aside.

2. Preheat oven at 400°. Mix baking mix, milk and egg until just moistened in medium bowl. Stir in onion, ½ cup cheese and the parsley. Spread in greased square baking pan, 8 × 8 inches. Dot with 2 tablespoons margarine; sprinkle with ½ cup cheese. Bake until wooden pick inserted in center comes out clean, about 15 minutes.

Orange Nut Bread

- 2 cups all-purpose flour
- 2 teaspoons baking powder
- 1 teaspoon salt
- ½ cup packed brown sugar
- ½ cup orange marmalade
- 1 egg, well beaten
- ¼ cup milk
- ¼ cup orange juice
- 1 tablespoon grated orange peel
- 2 tablespoons margarine or butter, melted
- ½ cup chopped walnuts

Makes 8 to 10 servings

1. Mix flour, baking powder and salt in large bowl. Mix in brown sugar, marmalade, egg and milk until smooth. Stir in orange juice, orange peel and margarine until just mixed. Stir in nuts. Pour into greased loaf pan, 8 × 4 inches.

2. Bake 25 to 30 minutes on LOW MIX, 350°. If wooden pick inserted in center does not come out clean, let stand in oven a few minutes to complete cooking. Cool 5 minutes; remove from pan. Cool completely on wire rack.

Monkey Bread ▲

- 5 cups all-purpose flour
- 3 packages active dry yeast
- ¼ cup sugar
- 1 teaspoon salt
- 1½ cups milk
- ⅓ cup margarine or butter
- 1 egg
- ¾ cup margarine or butter, melted

Makes 1 loaf

1. Mix 1½ cups flour, the yeast, sugar and salt in large mixing bowl. Set aside. Microwave milk and ⅓ cup margarine at MEDIUM-HIGH (70%) until very warm (125°), about 5 minutes. Pour over flour mixture. Beat in egg, scraping bowl occasionally. Beat in 1 cup flour. Stir in remaining 2½ cups flour with a wooden spoon until thoroughly blended. Grease top of dough. Place in oven at 100° until double in size, 30 to 45 minutes. (Dough is ready if an indentation remains when touched.)

2. Turn dough onto lightly floured surface. Knead until smooth. Divide dough in half. Roll each half into rectangle, 18 × 12 inches. Cut into ¾-inch strips, then cut crosswise into 3-inch pieces. Dip each piece in melted margarine. Place randomly in tube pan, 10 × 4 inches. Place in oven at 100° until double in size, about 1 hour. Place on broiling trivet. Bake 20 minutes on LOW MIX, 350°, or until golden brown. Serve warm.

Round-Up Bread

- ⅔ cup water
- ½ cup flaked coconut
- ½ cup finely ground cooked beef (from leftover roast)
- ¼ cup sugar
- 2 packages active dry yeast
- 1 cup lukewarm water (105 to 115°)
- 2 tablespoons melted shortening
- 2 tablespoons molasses
- 1½ teaspoons salt
- 1 cup whole wheat flour
- ½ cup all-bran cereal
- 3 cups all-purpose flour

Makes 1 loaf

1. Mix ⅔ cup water, the coconut, beef and sugar in small bowl. Microwave at HIGH (100%) until boiling, 1 to 2 minutes. Cool. Dissolve yeast in ¼ cup of the lukewarm water in large bowl. Stir in remaining ¾ cup lukewarm water, the shortening, molasses, salt, wheat flour, cereal and 1 cup all-purpose flour. Stir in cooled meat mixture. Mix in remaining 2 cups all-purpose flour to form stiff dough.

2. Turn dough onto lightly floured surface. Knead until smooth, about 7 minutes. (Dough will be heavy.) Shape into round loaf. Place on well greased 12-inch round pizza pan; cover. Place in oven at 100° until double in size, about 1 hour.

3. Bake 30 minutes on LOW MIX, 350°. Check for doneness (bread will sound hollow when bottom is tapped). If not done, let stand in oven a few minutes to complete cooking.

Preserve Cake ▾

3 cups all-purpose flour
1 teaspoon baking soda
½ teaspoon ground allspice
½ teaspoon ground cinnamon
½ teaspoon ground nutmeg
2 cups sugar
¾ cup margarine or butter, softened
4 eggs
1 cup buttermilk
½ teaspoon vanilla
2 cups preserves (combine 2 or more flavors)
2 cups chopped pecans

Makes 10 to 12 servings

1. Mix flour, baking soda, allspice, cinnamon and nutmeg. Set aside. Beat sugar and margarine until light and fluffy. Add eggs, 1 at a time, beating well after each. Stir in flour mixture alternately with buttermilk, beating well after each addition until smooth. Mix in vanilla; fold in preserves and pecans.

2. Pour into greased tube pan, 10 × 4 inches. Bake 50 minutes on LOW MIX, 350°. If wooden pick inserted in center does not come out clean, let stand in oven a few minutes to complete cooking. Cool 10 minutes; remove from pan. Cool completely on wire rack.

Strawberry Puff Ring

½ cup water
2 tablespoons plus 1½ teaspoons margarine
   or butter
½ cup all-purpose flour
3 eggs
2 cups prepared vanilla pudding or 2 cups
   sweetened whipped cream
1 pint strawberries, rinsed, hulled and sliced
   Powdered sugar

Makes 6 to 8 servings

1. Place water and margarine in medium bowl. Microwave at HIGH (100%) until boiling, about 2 minutes. Blend in flour until smooth. Microwave at HIGH (100%) 1 minute. Add eggs, 1 at a time, beating well after each. Preheat oven to 400°. Drop dough by tablespoonfuls in 8-inch circle onto greased round pizza pan or carousel.

2. Bake 25 minutes at 400°. Prick puff with sharp knife in several places to allow steam to escape. Let stand in oven 5 minutes; remove from oven to cool. Cut cooled puff ring in half. Spoon pudding into bottom half of ring; top with strawberries. Replace top half. Sprinkle with powdered sugar.

◄ Nut Cake With Mocha Frosting

    8 eggs
 1½ cups sugar
    2 cups hazelnuts or walnuts
   ¼ cup all-purpose flour
 1½ tablespoons baking powder

Frosting:
    1 pint heavy cream
   ½ cup plus 2 tablespoons sugar
   ¼ cup plus 1 tablespoon chocolate flavor
        drink mix
 2½ teaspoons vanilla
    1 teaspoon instant coffee

Makes 8 to 10 servings

1. Grease and flour two 9-inch round cake pans; line with wax paper. Combine eggs and sugar in blender; blend until light and fluffy. Add nuts; blend until finely chopped. Add flour and baking powder; blend until just mixed. Pour into prepared pans. Bake 25 minutes on LOW MIX, 350°. If wooden pick inserted in center does not come out clean, let stand in oven a few minutes to complete cooking. Cool.

2. For frosting, combine remaining ingredients in medium bowl. Beat until stiff. Frost cake and chill. Cake must be refrigerated.

Poppy Seed Bundt Cake

   ¾ cup margarine or butter
 1½ cups sugar
   ¾ cup half-and-half
    3 eggs
    2 tablespoons poppy seeds
 1½ teaspoons vanilla
 2¼ cups all-purpose flour
 1½ teaspoons baking powder
   ¾ teaspoon salt

Makes 8 to 10 servings

1. Cream butter and sugar until light and fluffy. Add half-and-half, eggs, poppy seeds and vanilla; mix well. Gradually beat in dry ingredients. Pour into greased 9-inch fluted tube pan.

2. Bake 30 minutes on LOW MIX, 350°. If wooden pick inserted in center does not come out clean, allow to stand 5 minutes in oven. Cool 10 minutes, remove from pan. Cool completely on wire rack.

Cheese Cake ▲

Crust:
- 1¼ cups all-purpose flour
- ¾ cup margarine or butter
- ¼ cup sugar
- 1 egg yolk
- Grated lemon peel from ½ lemon

Filling:
- 4 packages (8 ounces each) cream cheese
- 1¼ cups sugar
- 2 tablespoons all-purpose flour
- 4 eggs
- 1 egg yolk
- 2 tablespoons heavy cream
- Grated lemon peel from ½ lemon

Makes 12 servings

1. Combine crust ingredients in small bowl; beat until well mixed. Refrigerate, covered, for 1 hour.

2. Preheat oven to 400°. Press one-third flour mixture into bottom of 9-inch spring form pan. Bake at 400° for 8 minutes; cool. Mainiain oven temperature at 350°.

3. In large bowl, beat cream cheese until smooth. Slowly beat in sugar. Add flour and remaining ingredients. Beat 5 minutes. Press remaining dough around side of pan to within 1-inch of top; do not bake. Pour cream cheese mixture into pan.

4. Bake 35 minutes on LOW MIX, 350°. Let cheese cake remain in oven 30 minutes. Remove; cool in pan.

Blueberry Pizza

- 1¼ cups sugar
- ⅔ cup margarine or butter
- 3 eggs
- ¾ teaspoon vanilla
- ¼ teaspoon almond extract
- 2¼ cups all-purpose flour
- 1 teaspoon baking powder
- ½ teaspoon baking soda
- ¼ teaspoon salt
- 1 can (21 ounces) blueberry pie filling

Makes 12 servings

1. Cream sugar and butter until light and fluffy. Beat in eggs one at a time. Add flavorings. Combine dry ingredients; gradually add butter mixture. Beat until smooth. Reserve ¾ cup batter.

2. Spread remaining batter into 12-inch metal pizza pan. Spread pie filling over dough. Drop remaining batter by tablespoonfuls over filling.

3. Preheat oven to 350°. Bake at 350° for 30 minutes. Microwave at MEDIUM-HIGH (70%) 5 minutes, or until golden brown.

◄Coconut Oatmeal Pie

3 eggs, well beaten
1 cup packed brown sugar
⅔ cup granulated sugar
⅔ cup quick cooking oats
⅔ cup shredded coconut
½ cup milk
2 tablespoons margarine or butter, melted
1 teaspoon vanilla
½ cup broken pecans
1 9-inch unbaked pie shell

Makes 9-inch pie

1. Preheat oven to 450°. Combine all ingredients except pecans in large bowl. Add pecans; mix well. Pour into pie shell.

2. Place pie on broiling trivet. Bake at 450° for 8 minutes. Lower temperature to 375°. Bake 15 minutes on LOW MIX, 375°, or until set.

Coconut Custard Pie

1 9-inch baked pie shell
½ cup shredded coconut
2½ cups milk
½ cup sugar
3 eggs
1 teaspoon vanilla
¼ teaspoon salt
¼ teaspoon ground nutmeg

Makes 9-inch pie

1. Sprinkle coconut on bottom of pie shell. Combine remaining ingredients; mix well. Pour mixture into pie shell.

2. Place pie on broiling trivet. Bake 30 minutes on LOW MIX, 325°. If custard is not set, let stand in oven a few minutes to complete cooking.

Harvest Fruit Pie ▲

Crust:
2 cups all-purpose flour
1 teaspoon salt
1 teaspoon ground cinnamon
⅔ cup plus 2 tablespoons vegetable
   shortening
4 to 5 tablespoons cold water

Filling:
¾ cup sugar
¼ cup all-purpose flour
½ teaspoon ground cinnamon
½ teaspoon ground nutmeg
3 cups sliced, peeled apples
3 cups sliced, peeled pears
2 tablespoons margarine or butter
1 tablespoon milk
1 tablespoon sugar

Makes 9-inch pie

1. Preheat oven to 400°. Combine flour, salt and cinnamon in medium bowl. Cut in shortening. Sprinkle in water 1 tablespoon at a time, until flour is moistened. Gather dough into ball; divide in half. Roll each half into 9-inch circle. Ease one circle into 9-inch pie pan.

2. Combine sugar, flour, cinnamon and nutmeg; mix with apples and pears. Turn into pastry-lined pan; dot with butter. Cover with top crust. Brush crust with milk; sprinkle with 1 tablespoon sugar. Trim, seal and flute. Cut small slits in top crust.

3. Place on broiling trivet. Bake 35 minutes on LOW MIX, 400°, or until juice begins to bubble through slits in crust.

Peach Kuchen

1 cup all-purpose flour
1 tablespoon sugar
¼ teaspoon salt
¼ teaspoon baking powder
¼ cup margarine or butter
4 to 5 medium peaches, peeled and sliced or
   1 package (20 ounces) frozen peaches,
   thawed and drained
¼ cup sugar
1 teaspoon ground cinnamon
1 cup dairy sour cream
1 egg yolk, slightly beaten
1 teaspoon vanilla

Makes 8 servings

1. Combine flour, 1 tablespoon sugar, salt and baking powder in medium bowl; mix well. Using a pastry blender, cut in butter until mixture resembles coarse crumbs. Turn mixture into baking pan, 8 × 8 inches. Pat evenly over bottom and one-fourth way up the sides.

2. Arrange peaches on top of flour mixture. Combine sugar and cinnamon, sprinkle over peaches. Combine sour cream, egg yolk and vanilla; pour over peach mixture.

3. Bake 30 minutes on LOW MIX, 375°, or until juice begins to bubble. Cool; cut into squares.

Sour Cream Pound Cake ▲

- 4 cups all-purpose flour
- 2 teaspoons baking powder
- 1 teaspoon baking soda
- ½ teaspoon salt
- 2 cups sugar
- 1 cup margarine or butter, softened
- 4 eggs
- 1 teaspoon vanilla
- 2 cups dairy sour cream
- ½ cup sugar
- ¼ cup finely chopped walnuts
- 2 tablespoons ground cinnamon

Makes 10 to 12 servings

1. Mix flour, baking powder, baking soda and salt in medium bowl. Set aside. Beat 2 cups sugar and the margarine until light and fluffy. Add eggs, 1 at a time, beating well after each. Mix in vanilla. Stir in flour mixture alternately with sour cream, beating after each addition until smooth. Set aside.

2. Combine ½ cup sugar, the nuts and cinnamon. Pour half of batter into well greased tube pan, 10 x 4 inches; sprinkle with half of filling. Repeat with remaining batter and filling.

3. Bake 40 minutes on LOW MIX, 350°. If wooden pick inserted in center does not come out clean, let stand in oven a few minutes to complete cooking. Cool 10 minutes; remove from pan. Cool completely on wire rack.

Chocolate Meringue Pie ►

- ¾ cup sugar
- 2 tablespoons cornstarch
- 2 cups milk
- 2 squares (1 ounce each) unsweetened chocolate
- 3 eggs, separated
- 2 tablespoons margarine or butter
- 1 tablespoon grated orange peel
- 1 9-inch baked pie shell
- ½ teaspoon cream of tartar
- 6 tablespoons sugar

Makes 9-inch pie

1. Mix sugar and cornstarch in medium bowl. Stir in milk. Add chocolate squares. Microwave at HIGH (100%) until smooth and thick, 6 to 8 minutes, stirring after 3 minutes. Stir a small amount of chocolate mixture into egg yolks; return to hot chocolate mixture, blending well. Microwave at MEDIUM-HIGH (70%) 3 minutes, stirring once. Stir in margarine and orange peel until margarine is melted. Pour into pie shell. Set aside.

2. Preheat oven to 425°. Beat egg whites and cream of tartar until foamy. Beat in sugar, 1 tablespoon at a time; continue beating until stiff and glossy. Spoon meringue onto chocolate filling; spread over filling, carefully sealing meringue to edge of crust. Bake 8 to 10 minutes, or until meringue is brown.

Baked Fruit ▲

- 1 tablespoon margarine or butter
- ½ cup cake or cookie crumbs
- 2 cups canned fruit halves, well drained (any combination of apricots, peaches or pears), reserve ½ cup juice
- 3 tablespoons margarine or butter
- ¼ cup packed brown sugar
- ½ cup flaked coconut
- ½ cup cake or cookie crumbs
- ½ to 1 teaspoon curry powder

Makes 6 servings

1. Grease shallow baking dish with 1 tablespoon margarine. Spread ½ cup crumbs in baking dish. Arrange fruit hollow side up over crumbs. Dot with 3 tablespoons margarine. Sprinkle with brown sugar, coconut and ½ cup crumbs. Mix reserved fruit juice and curry; pour evenly over top. Cover.

2. Bake 10 minutes on HIGH MIX, 450°, or until golden brown. Serve warm.

Carousel Crackles

- 1 cup semi-sweet chocolate chips
- 1 cup packed brown sugar
- ⅓ cup vegetable oil
- 2 eggs
- 1 teaspoon vanilla
- 1 cup all-purpose flour
- 1 teaspoon baking powder
- ¼ teaspoon salt
- ½ cup finely chopped walnuts
- ½ cup powdered sugar

Makes 4 dozen

1. Place chocolate chips in large mixing bowl. Microwave at HIGH (100%) until melted, about 2 minutes. Blend in brown sugar and oil. Add eggs, 1 at a time, beating well after each. Stir in vanilla. Combine flour, baking powder and salt; stir into chocolate mixture. Mix in nuts. Chill dough at least 1 hour.

2. Preheat oven to 350°. Drop dough by rounded teaspoonfuls into powdered sugar; roll to coat. Place 2 inches apart on greased carousel or round pizza pan. Bake 10 to 12 minutes at 350°. Remove from carousel; cool on wire rack.

Peanut Butter Cookies ►

- ½ cup peanut butter
- ½ cup granulated sugar
- ½ cup packed brown sugar
- ¼ cup margarine or butter
- ¼ cup vegetable shortening
- 1 egg
- 1¼ cups all-purpose flour
- ¾ teaspoon baking soda
- ½ teaspoon baking powder

Makes 3 dozen

1. Combine peanut butter, sugars, butter, shortening and egg; beat until smooth. Blend in flour, baking soda and baking powder.

2. Shape dough into ¾-inch balls. Place 2 inches apart on lightly greased baking pan. With fork, flatten in crisscross pattern.

3. Preheat oven to 375°. Bake 12 minutes at 375°, or until set but not hard.

Chocolate Chip Bars

- 2¼ cups all-purpose flour
- 1 teaspoon baking soda
- ½ teaspoon salt
- ¾ cup granulated sugar
- ¾ cup packed brown sugar
- ½ cup margarine or butter
- ½ cup vegetable oil
- 1 teaspoon vanilla
- 2 eggs
- 1 package (12 ounces) chocolate chips
- 1 cup chopped nuts

Makes 32 bars

1. Combine flour, soda and salt; set aside. Cream together granulated sugar, brown sugar, butter, oil and vanilla. Beat until creamy. Beat in eggs. Gradually add flour mixture; mix well. Stir in chocolate chips and nuts.

2. Spread mixture into 2 ungreased 8 × 8 inch square pans. Bake 25 to 30 minutes on LOW MIX, 350°, or until wooden pick inserted in center comes out clean. Let cool in pans. Cut into 32 squares.

Sesame Snacks ▲

2 ounces sesame seeds
1 cup sugar
½ teaspoon vanilla

Makes about 8 ounces

1. Spread sesame seeds on round pizza pan or carousel. Bake about 15 minutes at 450°, or until light brown. Set aside. Place sugar in shallow baking pan. Bake 20 minutes at 450°, or until sugar is melted, occasionally stirring outer edge of sugar into center to keep from burning sugar.

2. Immediately stir in sesame seeds and vanilla. Using a greased spatula, spread evenly on well greased baking sheet. Cool. Break into pieces.

Mixed Bag

2 cups honey graham cereal
1 can (6½ ounces) salted peanuts
1 cup raisins
1 cup dried banana chips
3 tablespoons margarine or butter
3 tablespoons honey
1 teaspoon ground ginger
¼ teaspoon salt
4 cups popped popcorn
1 cup flaked coconut

Makes about 9 cups

1. Mix cereal, peanuts, raisins and banana chips in large bowl. Pour into greased rectangular baking dish, 12 × 8 inches or 10-inch casserole. Set aside. Place margarine, honey, ginger and salt in 1-cup measure. Microwave at HIGH (100%) until margarine is melted, about 1 minute. Pour over cereal mixture; tossing lightly until thoroughly coated.

2. Bake at 300° for 15 minutes, stirring after half the cooking time. Mix popcorn and coconut in same large bowl. Stir in cereal mixture until thoroughly mixed. Store in airtight container.

Note: Ingredient amounts can be varied to taste.

Reheating

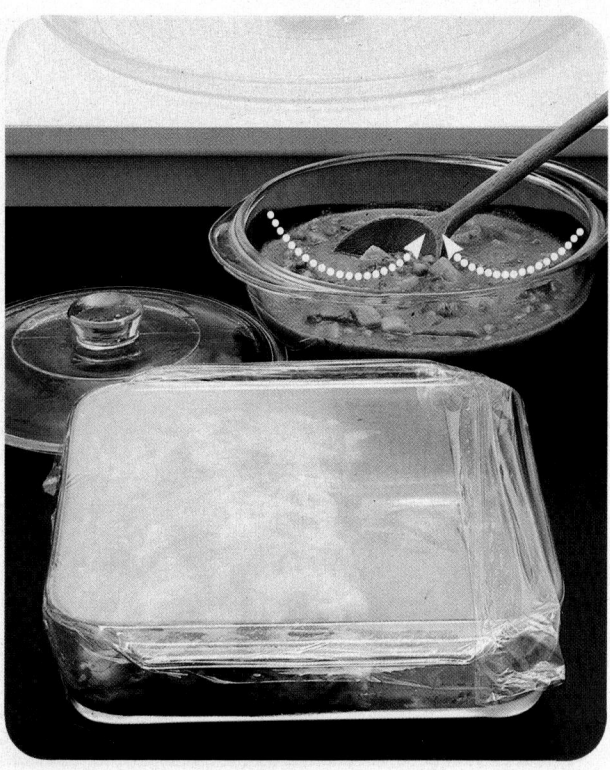

Foods reheated in the microwave oven taste freshly cooked, not reheated. Suit the power level to the food. A bowl of leftover vegetables can be reheated at HIGH (100%), while lasagna, which contains sensitive cheese and cannot be stirred, should be reheated at MEDIUM (50%).

Casseroles. Cover dish tightly. Stir several times during cooking, especially if casserole has been refrigerated. If casserole cannot be stirred, reheat at MEDIUM (50%) and rotate dish if using oven other than Sharp Carousel.

Meats. Medium to thin slices reheat best. Cover meat with sauce, gravy or paper towel. Top with waxed paper to hold in heat. Microwave at MEDIUM (50%) about 45 seconds to 1 minute per serving. If using oven other than Sharp Carousel, rotate dish when reheating more than one serving.

Reheating (continued)

Plates of food. Arrange food with thickest parts of meat and bulky vegetables to outside of plate. Place quick-to-heat foods in center. Spread single serving of a main dish in even layer on plate. Cover with waxed paper or plastic wrap. Reheat until underside of plate feels warm in the center.

Vegetables. Wrap large, whole vegetables in plastic wrap. Cover dishes of vegetables tightly and stir during cooking, if possible. If using oven other than Sharp Carousel, rotate or rearrange foods which cannot be stirred.

Pie. Place whole pie in glass pie dish or slice of pie on serving plate. Reheat whole pie at MEDIUM-HIGH (70%) 5 to 7 minutes, and one slice 30 seconds at HIGH (100%).

Reheating Chart

Item	Starting Temperature	Microwave Time	Procedure
Plate of food 1 serving of meat, 2 servings of vegetables	Room temp.	MED.-HIGH (70%) 1½-3 min.	Meaty portions and bulky vegetables to outside. Cover with waxed paper.
Meat (chicken pieces, chops, hamburgers, meat loaf slices) 1 serving 2 servings	Refrigerated Refrigerated	MED.-HIGH (70%) 1-2 min. 2½-4½ min.	Cover loosely.
Meat Slices (beef, ham, pork, turkey) 1 or more servings	Refrigerated Room temp.	MEDIUM (50%) 1-3 min./serving 45 sec.-1 min./serving	Cover with gravy or waxed paper. Check after 30 sec./serving.
Stirrable Casseroles and Main Dishes 1 serving 2 servings 4-6 servings	Refrigerated Refrigerated Refrigerated	HIGH (100%) 2-4 min. 4-6 min. 6-8 min.	Cover. Stir after half the time.
Non-Stirrable Casseroles and Main Dishes 1 serving 2 servings 4-6 servings	Refrigerated Refrigerated Refrigerated	MEDIUM (50%) 5-8 min. 9-12 min. 13-16 min.	Cover with waxed paper.
Vegetables 1 serving (½ cup) 2 servings (1 cup)	Refrigerated Refrigerated	HIGH (100%) ¾-1½ min. 1½-2½ min.	Cover. Stir after half the time.
Rolls Dinner or Breakfast 1 roll 2 rolls 4 rolls	Room temp. Room temp. Room temp.	HIGH (100%) 8-12 sec. 11-15 sec. 18-22 sec.	Wrap single rolls in paper towel. For several rolls, line plate with paper towel; cover rolls with another towel.
Pie Whole 1 slice	Refrigerated Refrigerated	MED.-HIGH (70%) 5-7 min. HIGH (100%) 30 sec.	

Thawing Frozen Foods

Thawing food, especially meats, with the microwave oven is not only faster than any other method, it can also give better results.

Once frozen meat is thawed, it begins to lose its juices. With a microwave oven, you can thaw meat just before you plan to cook it, for highest juiciness and quality.

Microwave thawing doesn't take a lot of fuss, but some attention is needed to make sure that parts of the meat do not start to cook before the center is thawed. MEDIUM-LOW (30%) is fast enough to be convenient, but gentle enough to give good results. At MEDIUM (50%) meat thaws in about one-third less time, but needs more attention.

Place plastic or paper-wrapped package of frozen food directly in oven. To speed thawing, remove wrappings as soon as possible and cover food with waxed paper to hold in heat. Foil-wrapped foods must be unwrapped.

Break up or separate ground beef, cubed meat, chicken pieces, or fish fillets after one-third of thawing time. Remove any thawed pieces. Place remainder in baking dish to complete thawing.

Turn over flat roasts, steaks, chops, whole chickens or Cornish hens after half the time. If package contains several steaks or chops, separate as soon as possible and place in baking dish.

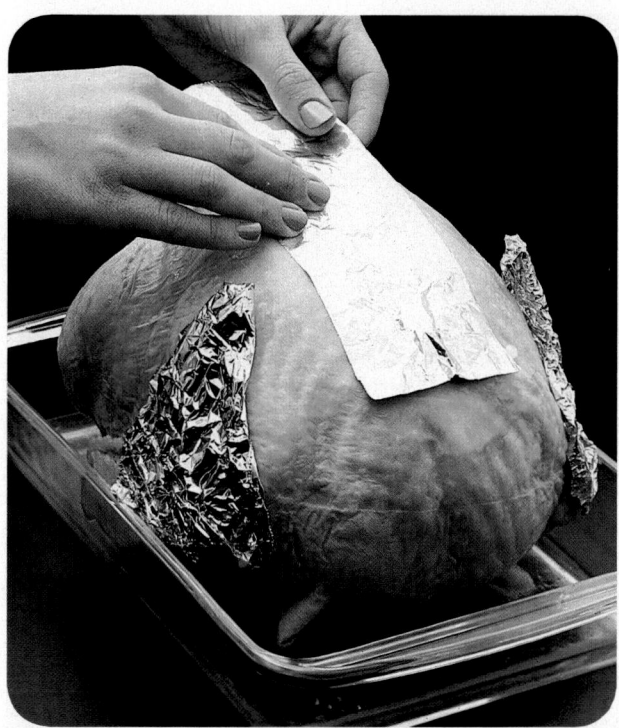

Remove wrapping from turkey so you can feel warm spots as it thaws. Metal clamps holding legs need not be removed. Start breast side down; shield warm areas and turn over after each one-fourth of time.

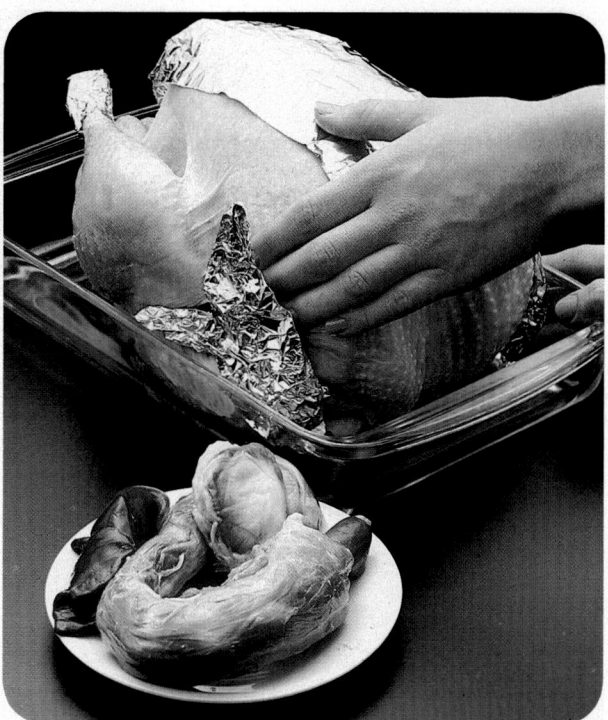

Let turkey stand 20 to 30 minutes after thawing, until giblets and neck can be removed and breast meat under wings is completely thawed. Remove metal clamps, if desired. Turkey may be micro-waved with clamps if they are difficult to remove.

Turn over large roasts after each one-fourth of thawing time. As you turn, touch meat for warm areas and shield these with small pieces of foil. Let roast stand 10 minutes after first half of time and 10 to 20 minutes after second half.

Thaw meats and poultry only until they can be pierced to the center with a skewer. Surface or cavity should feel cool but not icy. Cook as soon as possible to prevent loss of juices.

Thawing Frozen Foods Chart

Procedure: Place plastic or paper-wrapped packages of frozen food directly in oven. Remove wrappings as soon as possible, then place in baking dish. Cover with waxed paper. Continue thawing.

Power Level: MEDIUM-LOW (30%)

Cut	Microwave Time	Standing Time	Special Instructions
BEEF			
Rib Roast (Standing & Rolled) Rump Roast, Sirloin Tip Roast, Beef Eye or Round	9-14 min./lb.	5-10 min.	Turn over after half the time. Shield as needed.
Corned Beef	11½-15½ min./lb.	20-30 min.	Turn over after half the time. Shield as needed.
Tenderloin, Chuck Roast, Steaks: Top Round, Sirloin, Round	7-10 min./lb.	5-10 min.	Turn over after half the time. Shield as needed.
Steaks: Porterhouse, T-Bone, Cubed, Flank, Rib	5½-8½ min./lb.	5-10 min.	Turn over after half the time. Shield as needed.
Beef Ribs	5-10 min./lb.	10-15 min.	Separate and rearrange once.
Stew Meat	5-10 min./lb.	5-10 min.	Separate and rearrange once.
Ground Beef	5-8 min./lb.	5-10 min.	Break apart, remove any thawed pieces as soon as possible. Place remainder in baking dish.
Beef Liver	9-12 min./lb.	5-10 min.	Separate and rearrange once.
PORK			
Loin Roast	11-15 min./lb.	20-30 min.	Turn over after half the time. Shield as needed.
Tenderloin	8½-13½ min./lb.	10-15 min.	Turn over after half the time. Shield as needed.
Chops	6½-11 min./lb.	5-10 min.	Separate and turn over once.
Ribs	7-12 min./lb.	10-15 min.	Separate and rearrange once.
Ground Pork	5½-9½ min./lb.		Break apart, remove any thawed pieces as soon as possible. Place remainder in baking dish.

Cut	Microwave Time	Standing Time	Special Instructions
LAMB			
Leg Roast, Shoulder Roast	9-15 min./lb.	15-20 min.	Turn over after half the time. Shield as needed.
Rib & Loin Chops	7-12½ min./lb.	5-10 min.	Separate and turn over once.
Sirloin Chops	7-12½ min./lb.	10-15 min.	Separate and turn over once.
VEAL			
Roasts	14½-19½ min./lb.	20-30 min.	Let stand 20 minutes after half the time. Turn over. Shield as needed.
Chops, Cutlets	6-11 min./lb.	10-15 min.	Separate and turn over once.
Ground Veal	5-8 min./lb.		Break apart, remove any thawed pieces as soon as possible. Place remainder in baking dish.
POULTRY			
Whole Turkey	6-10 min./lb.	20-30 min.	Follow directions on page 37.
Half-Turkey, Turkey Breast	5-10 min./lb.	5-10 min.	Breast side down. Turn over after half the time. Shield as needed. Rinse in cool water after thawing.
Turkey Pieces	7-11 min./lb.	5-10 min.	Turn over after half the time. Shield as needed. Rinse in cool water after thawing.
Whole Chicken	5½-10 min./lb.	5-10 min.	Breast side down. Turn over after half the time. Shield as needed.
Chicken Quarters & Pieces, Boneless Breasts	5-10 min./lb.	5-10 min.	Separate and rearrange once.
Duck	8-11 min./lb.	10-15 min.	Breast side down. Turn over after half the time. Shield as needed.
Cornish Hens	9-12½ min./lb.	5-10 min.	Breast side down. Turn over after half the time. Shield as needed.
FISH			
Fillets & Steaks, Whole Small Fish	7-10 min./lb.	5-10 min.	Separate and rearrange once.
Scallops	5-9 min./lb.		Separate and rearrange once.
Shrimp	4½-8 min./lb.		Separate and rearrange once.

Convenience Foods

With a microwave oven, convenience foods can be ready to serve in far less time than it takes conventionally. Most heat-and-eat convenience foods provide microwaving instructions on the packages. These instructions are usually for HIGH (100%), which is on all microwave ovens.

Microwaving can also shorten the time needed for foods which are usually thawed several hours at room temperature. MEDIUM-LOW (30%) is gentle enough to thaw cakes, brownies and cream pies without melting the delicate frostings or fillings. Let these foods stand to complete thawing.

TV Dinners. Remove lid from foil pan. If dinner includes a cake-like dessert, set this aside in a custard cup. Return tray to box and place in center of carousel. Microwave at HIGH (100%) until heated through, following times in chart on opposite page. Cook dessert at HIGH (100%), 1 to 4 minutes. Sprinkle with cinnamon-sugar, if desired.

Frosted Cakes. Place cake on serving plate. Microwave at MEDIUM-LOW (30%), until a wooden pick inserted in center of cake meets little resistance. Watch closely; if frosting starts to soften, remove cake from oven. Let cake stand 15 to 25 minutes. When using oven other than Sharp Carousel, rotate dish 2 to 3 times.

Cream Pies. Remove pie from foil pan to pie dish or serving plate. Microwave at MEDIUM-LOW (30%) until a wooden pick inserted in center of filling meets no resistance. Let pie stand 5 minutes before serving. If using oven other than Sharp Carousel, rotate dish 2 or 3 times.

Convenience Foods Chart

Item	Package Size	Microwave Time	Procedure
Brownies	13 oz.	MED.-LOW (30%) 1½-3½ min./lb.	Remove from pan. Place on paper towel-lined plate. Test by inserting wooden pick in center; there should be little or no resistance. Ovens other than Sharp, rotate after half the time.
Cheesecake	11¼ oz. 19 oz. 26 oz.	MED.-LOW (30%) 1-3½ min. 1½-4 min. 3½-7 min.	Remove from pan. Place on plate. Test by inserting wooden pick in center; there should be little or no resistance. Let stand 10-15 min. Ovens other than Sharp, rotate every 30-45 sec.
Coffee Cakes	6½-13 oz.	MEDIUM (50%) 1-4 min.	Remove from package. Place on paper towel-lined plate. Test by inserting wooden pick in center; there should be little or no resistance. Let stand 2-5 min.
Cream Pies	13-22½ oz.	MED.-LOW (30%) ¾-2 min./lb.	Follow photo directions on opposite page.
Frosted Layer Cakes	10-13 oz. 15½-17 oz. 21 oz.	MED.-LOW (30%) 1-3½ min. 1½-4 min. 3½-6 min.	Follow photo directions on opposite page.
Pound Cake	10¾ oz. 16 oz.	MED.-LOW (30%) ¾-1½ min. 1-2 min.	Remove all wrappings. Place on plate. Test by inserting wooden pick in center; there should be little or no resistance and cake should feel warm. Let stand 5 min. Ovens other than Sharp, rotate once or twice.
TV Dinners	5-7 oz. 10¾-19 oz.	HIGH (100%) 2½-7½ min. 8-13 min.	Follow photo directions on opposite page.

Recipe Conversion

Many conventional recipes can be adapted to microwave cooking with few changes other than a shortened cooking time. Your best guide is a microwave recipe for a similar type of food. Compare the amount and type of main bulky ingredients and liquid. If they are similar, use the container, cooking techniques, power level and time recommended in the microwave recipe to convert your conventional recipe.

Watch the food carefully, and check for doneness after the minimum time. If longer cooking is needed, add more time in small amounts. Be sure to allow standing time for foods which require it.

At the beginning of each section of this book, you'll find directions for microwaving specific foods and suggestions for recipe conversion.

Moist foods, like chicken, seafood, ground beef, vegetables, fruits and saucy main dishes or casseroles convert well. Dry or crusty foods may have a moist surface when microwaved.

Techniques like covering, steaming and stirring, are common to both conventional and microwave cooking. A recipe which calls for these techniques should convert easily and give excellent results when microwaved.

No change in ingredients should be needed for foods which are heated rather than cooked, such as dips, spreads, and some casseroles, or foods which are brought to a boil but not simmered, like white sauce or pudding.

42

Conventional | Microwave

Reduce liquid in recipes which call for raw ingredients, simmering, or baking longer than is needed to heat foods through. Little evaporation occurs during microwaving. Use two-thirds the liquid and add more, if needed, as you cook.

Omit fat needed to brown foods and prevent sticking in conventional cooking. A small amount of butter or olive oil may be used for flavor.

Use less salt or highly flavored seasonings, like garlic, chili, curry powder or sage. After microwaving, correct seasoning to taste. Small amounts of mild herbs and spices need not be changed.

Conventional

Microwave

Cut less tender meat, like stewing beef, and dense vegetables, like potatoes and carrots, in smaller pieces than you would for conventional stews and soups. Small, uniform pieces microwave rapidly and evenly.

Recipe Conversion (continued)

HIGH (100%)

Reduced Power

Power level depends on the type of food to be microwaved. To speed cooking, use HIGH (100%) for casseroles which can be stirred, and tender meats, like chicken or ground beef, which are cooked with a sauce of tomatoes, broth or wine. Lower power levels are required for less tender meats, heat-sensitive foods like eggs, cream, cheese, and layered casseroles.

Substitute quick-cooking rice for raw rice, or canned kidney beans for dried, when these ingredients are combined with foods which would overcook in the time needed to rehydrate dry foods.

Add delicate or quick-cooking ingredients, like seafood and cheese, toward the end of microwaving, to avoid toughening them.

Top casseroles with bread or crouton crumbs, canned onion rings, crushed potato or corn chips, or a mixture of crumbs and Parmesan cheese. Add topping after the final stirring to keep surface crisp.

Cooking time depends on the quantity and type of food, so a comparable microwave recipe is your most accurate guide. Microwaving time may be one-fourth to one-third of conventional time. Check for doneness frequently and add more time in small amounts.

Ingredients: Double, except liquid
Time: Increased one-half

Ingredients: Cut in half
Time: Cut one-third

Original Recipe

Change dish size and time when you change the yield of a microwave recipe. Whether you double a recipe, or cook half of it, level of food should be the same depth as the original microwave recipe. If food is spread too thinly, it will overcook or dry out. It will boil over if dish is too full. To double recipe, double the ingredients, then decrease liquid by one-fourth to one-third; increase time by one-half to two-thirds. For half a recipe, use half the ingredients, cut time by one-third.

Menu Planning

The first consideration in planning any menu is to provide balanced nutrition. The meal should include protein, vegetables and fruits, cereals or starchy vegetables, and dairy products.

Next comes appetite appeal. The foods should look and taste good together. A meal of foods which are all bland, soft, or the same color may be nutritious, but it will be uninteresting.

Finally, you'll want all the food to be hot and ready to serve at the same time, without a lot of last-minute fuss. With a well-planned conventional meal, you start one food, then go on to another. Microwave meals are prepared in the same way, with the added advantage that many foods can be reheated easily without loss of flavor or quality. These directions, and the menus which follow, show you how to prepare an entire meal with your microwave. If necessary, you can also use other cooking appliances to supplement your microwave oven.

1. Start by microwaving foods which need to be chilled or cooled to room temperature. Often, this will be a dessert which can be made early in the day, or even the night before.

2. Prepare in advance any food which you plan to reheat before serving. Mix an appetizer dip or spread for last-minute heating, or precook potatoes for twice-baked potatoes.

3. Microwave meats, main dishes or vegetables with long standing times. While this dish is in the oven, you can get another one ready to cook.

4. Let the first food stand. Tent a roast loosely with foil; wrap or cover other foods tightly. Most foods with long standing times will stay hot for an additional 20 to 45 minutes after standing is completed.

5. Use the standing time of one food to microwave another. While this food is in the oven, you might set the table or prepare a salad.

6. Reheat any foods prepared in advance; or microwave quick-cooking foods with short standing times. Warm rolls just before serving.

7. During the meal, or while clearing the table, you can microwave a hot dessert sauce, thaw convenience brownies, or warm pie.

Dinner in Half an Hour

Fillet of Sole in Lemon Parsley Butter, page 119
Baked Potatoes, page 29
Italian Zucchini, page 159
Tossed Salad
Chocolate Almond Fondue, page 189

This meal is attractive enough to serve for a special occasion, yet the microwaving time is only about 30 minutes. The dessert is assembled before dinner, but is microwaved just before serving.

1. Start microwaving potatoes. Wash and chill the lettuce; prepare ingredients for fondue.

2. Wrap potatoes in foil to stand and hold. They will stay hot up to an hour. Melt butter for fillets.

3. Microwave zucchini the first 4 to 6 minutes while you prepare fillets for cooking.

4. Microwave fish. Drain zucchini and toss with seasoning.

5. Reheat zucchini and toss salad when fish is done.

6. Heat fondue while clearing the table for dessert.

Company Dinner

Stuffed Mushrooms, page 61
Glazed Baked Ham, page 89
Parsley Potatoes, page 155
Sautéed Green Beans, page 154
Waldorf Salad
Crème de Menthe Pie, page 183

The stuffed mushrooms may be served as an appetizer or as an accompaniment to the ham. You may stuff them in advance and heat just before serving. If they are refrigerated, add an extra minute to the heating time. When you serve the mushrooms as an appetizer, you may interrupt cooking of the ham in order to heat them.

1. Prepare and refrigerate Crème de Menthe Pie early in the day.

2. Stuff mushrooms. Prepare and microwave potatoes. Set aside to reheat just before serving.

3. Start ham about an hour before serving time. While it bakes the first 15 minutes, clean green beans and mix glaze.

4. Decorate, glaze and finish cooking ham. Prepare salad while ham is cooking.

5. Set ham aside, covered with foil; it will keep warm 20 to 30 minutes.

6. Microwave beans, then reheat potatoes while beans stand.

Easy Casserole Supper

Fiesta Tamale Pie, page 85
Lettuce with Avocado Dressing
Peaches with Raspberry Sauce,
  page 188

The meat, vegetables and bread for this supper are all in one dish. Use canned peaches in the dessert to make things even easier. While the pie is cooking, you'll have plenty of time to prepare the salad and assemble the dessert.

1. Thaw raspberries about 30 to 45 minutes before serving time.

2. Prepare corn muffin mixture while microwaving meat for pie.

3. Microwave Tamale Pie while you chop an avocado coarsely and toss it with oil and vinegar dressing to coat.

4. Place peaches in serving dishes, drain raspberries and mix sauce. Set aside. Top casserole with cheese.

5. Toss lettuce with marinated avocado, adding more dressing if needed.

6. Microwave raspberry sauce and assemble dessert just before serving.

Sunday Chicken Dinner

Oven Fried Chicken, page 104
Acorn Squash with Cranberry Filling,
  page 157
Wilted Spinach Salad, page 158
Cheesecake, page 176

This menu takes advantage of the fact that squash stays hot well beyond the necessary 5 minutes standing time. Make the dessert in advance, and assemble the rest of the meal while the chicken is cooking.

1. Prepare cheesecake early in the day and refrigerate.

2. Microwave bacon about an hour before serving time; set aside to drain. Start squash.

3. Coat chicken with crumbs; set aside on waxed paper. Let squash stand. Microwave onions for salad.

4. Cook chicken while you wash the spinach. Mix cranberry sauce and salad dressing.

5. Set chicken aside to keep warm. Cut and seed squash while heating cranberry sauce.

6. Fill and reheat squash. Cook salad dressing; toss with spinach.

APPETIZERS

With a microwave oven you can serve tempting hot appetizers as an impromptu snack or planned-and-prepared in advance. Your party can be as easy and entertaining for the hosts as it is for the guests. Your microwave oven is also a cool and efficient way to toast nuts, soften cream cheese, freshen crackers, or reheat conventionally baked cream puffs.

Chicken Kabobs

- 1 pound boned chicken breasts, skinned and cut into 1-inch cubes
- ¼ cup soy sauce
- 2 teaspoons sugar
- ½ teaspoon salt
- ⅛ teaspoon garlic powder
- ⅛ teaspoon ground ginger
  Dash of pepper
- 1 green pepper, cut into ½-inch cubes
- 4 ounces mushrooms (about 15 medium mushrooms), halved
- 2 tablespoons honey

Makes about 30 kabobs

1. Mix chicken pieces, soy sauce, sugar, salt, garlic powder, ginger and pepper. Let stand 10 to 20 minutes. Drain, reserving soy sauce mixture.

2. Alternate 1 green pepper cube, 1 chicken cube and 1 mushroom half on round wooden toothpicks. Place kabobs on single layer of paper toweling around outer edge of carousel or on roasting rack. Stir honey into reserved soy sauce mixture; brush each kabob generously.

3. Microwave, uncovered, at HIGH (100%) until chicken is tender and green peppers are tender-crisp, 3½ to 6½ minutes, brushing each kabob with soy sauce mixture after half the cooking time. If using oven other than Sharp Carousel, rotate after half the cooking time.

Variation: Substitute 1 can (15 ounces) pineapple chunks (juice pack), drained, for mushrooms.

Microwaving Appetizers

Recipe Conversion

Recipes for dips, spreads and canapés which are heated, rather than cooked, need no change in ingredients. Mix them in a microwave-safe serving dish and heat, using one of these recipes as a guide to microwaving time and power level.

Reduce the amount of liquid by one-fourth to one-half when preparing saucy cocktail wieners or ham tidbits. Use just enough to cover the meat. For bacon-wrapped appetizers, use raw bacon to wrap raw fillings. With cooked or canned fillings, microwave bacon for half its cooking time before assembling the appetizers. At serving time, microwave either type of appetizer until the bacon is crisp and brown.

Microwave and serve appetizers in a microwave oven-proof dish or paper plate to speed serving and simplify clean-up. Cook some foods directly on the carousel with a lining of paper toweling to absorb moisture and spatters.

Prepare most of these recipes early in the day, or even the day before a party; then cook or heat them just before serving.

Mix spreads and toppings in advance. Do not assemble canapés until ready to heat or the crisp bases will become soggy. Heat crackers and breads on paper toweling to absorb excess moisture from steam trapped under them.

Arrange individual pieces, like rumaki and stuffed mushrooms or tomatoes on paper toweling in a ring around the outer edge of the carousel. If you do not have a Sharp Carousel™ Microwave Oven, rotate and rearrange pieces after half the cooking time to help them cook evenly.

Use HIGH (100%) for most appetizers. Small pieces heat rapidly and evenly.

Reduce the power level when cooking foods which need time to develop flavor, and cheese, which attracts microwave energy and may become stringy or tough at high temperatures.

◄ Marinated Chicken Wings

12 chicken wings
1 cup dry sherry
½ cup soy sauce
1 teaspoon ground ginger
¼ teaspoon garlic powder
¼ teaspoon onion powder

Makes 24 appetizers

1. Separate chicken wings at joints into 3 parts each, discarding tip. Mix sherry, soy sauce, ginger, garlic powder and onion powder. Combine chicken and sherry mixture in medium bowl or plastic bag. Cover and refrigerate overnight, stirring once or twice during marinating time.

2. Drain chicken. Arrange on double layer of paper toweling around outer edge of carousel or on roasting rack. Microwave at MEDIUM-HIGH (70%) until juices run clear, 18 to 22 minutes. If using oven other than Sharp Carousel, rearrange wings twice during cooking time.

◄ Cheese Toasties

4 slices bacon
1 cup shredded Cheddar cheese
  (about 4 ounces)
1 tablespoon mayonnaise or salad dressing
1 tablespoon finely chopped onion
1 teaspoon milk
½ teaspoon Worcestershire sauce
¼ teaspoon dry mustard
  Dash of paprika
  Dash of garlic powder
2 English muffins, split and crisply toasted

Makes 16 appetizers

1. Place bacon on triple thickness of paper toweling. Cover with paper towel. Microwave at HIGH (100%) until bacon is evenly browned, 3 to 4 minutes; set aside. If using oven other than Sharp Carousel, rotate bacon after half the cooking time.

2. Mix cheese, mayonnaise, onion, milk, Worcestershire sauce, mustard, paprika and garlic powder. Spread 2 tablespoons on each muffin half. Crumble 1 piece of bacon on top of each.

3. Place muffins around outer edge of carousel, leaving center empty, or on double thickness of paper toweling on dinner plate. Microwave at MEDIUM-HIGH (70%) until cheese melts, 1 to 2 minutes. If using oven other than Sharp Carousel, rotate dinner plate and rearrange muffins after half the time. Cut each muffin half into 4 wedges.

Miniature Pizzas

¼ cup catsup
1 teaspoon dried oregano leaves
1 teaspoon wine vinegar
½ teaspoon onion powder
¼ teaspoon sugar
⅛ teaspoon pepper
2 English muffins, split and crisply toasted
½ cup chopped pepperoni
¼ cup shredded mozzarella cheese
    (about 1 ounce)
4 teaspoons grated Parmesan cheese

Makes 16 appetizers

1. Mix catsup, oregano, vinegar, onion powder, sugar and pepper. Spread one-fourth on each muffin half. Top each with one-fourth of the pepperoni. Place 1 tablespoon mozzarella on each muffin half; sprinkle with Parmesan. Place on single layer of paper toweling on carousel or on double layer of paper toweling on dinner plate.

2. Microwave at HIGH (100%) until cheese is melted and filling is heated through, 45 seconds to 1 minute 45 seconds. If using oven other than Sharp Carousel, rotate dinner plate and rearrange muffins after half the cooking time. Cut each muffin half into 4 wedges.

◄ Spicy Cocktail Meatballs

- 1 pound ground beef
- 1 envelope (1¼ ounces) taco seasoning mix
- 1 egg
- 1 can (4 ounces) whole green chilies, chopped
- ½ cup chopped onion
- 1 tablespoon margarine or butter
- 2 tablespoons all-purpose flour
- ½ cup milk
- 1½ cups shredded Cheddar cheese (about 6 ounces)
- ½ cup shredded Monterey Jack cheese (about 2 ounces)
- 2 tablespoons coarsely chopped tomato

Makes 20 to 30 meatballs

1. Mix ground beef, taco seasoning mix and egg. Shape into 1-inch balls; place in single layer in 10-inch square casserole. Microwave at HIGH (100%) until meatballs are firm and lose their pink color, 7 to 10 minutes, stirring once or twice during cooking. Drain; cover and set aside.

2. Combine green chilies, onion and margarine in 2-quart casserole. Microwave at HIGH (100%) until onions are tender, 2 to 3 minutes. Blend in flour; stir in milk until smooth. Microwave at HIGH (100%) until thickened, 3 to 4 minutes, stirring once or twice during cooking.

3. Stir in Cheddar cheese, Monterey Jack cheese and tomato. Microwave at MEDIUM-HIGH (70%) until cheese is melted and smooth, 1 to 2 minutes, stirring once or twice with a wire whisk. Add meatballs to cheese sauce. Place in chafing dish and serve hot.

Oysters in Blankets

- 1 can (8 ounces) oysters, drained
- 12 to 14 slices bacon

Makes 24 to 28 appetizers

1. If oysters are large, cut into halves to make 24 to 28. Cut bacon slices into halves. Wrap each oyster in a piece of bacon; secure with wooden pick. Line carousel with triple thickness of paper toweling. Place bacon-wrapped oysters around outer edge of carousel or on baking sheet lined with paper toweling. Cover with paper toweling.

2. Microwave at HIGH (100%) until bacon is evenly browned, 12 to 18 minutes. If using oven other than Sharp Carousel, rotate baking sheet quarter turn every 2 to 3 minutes.

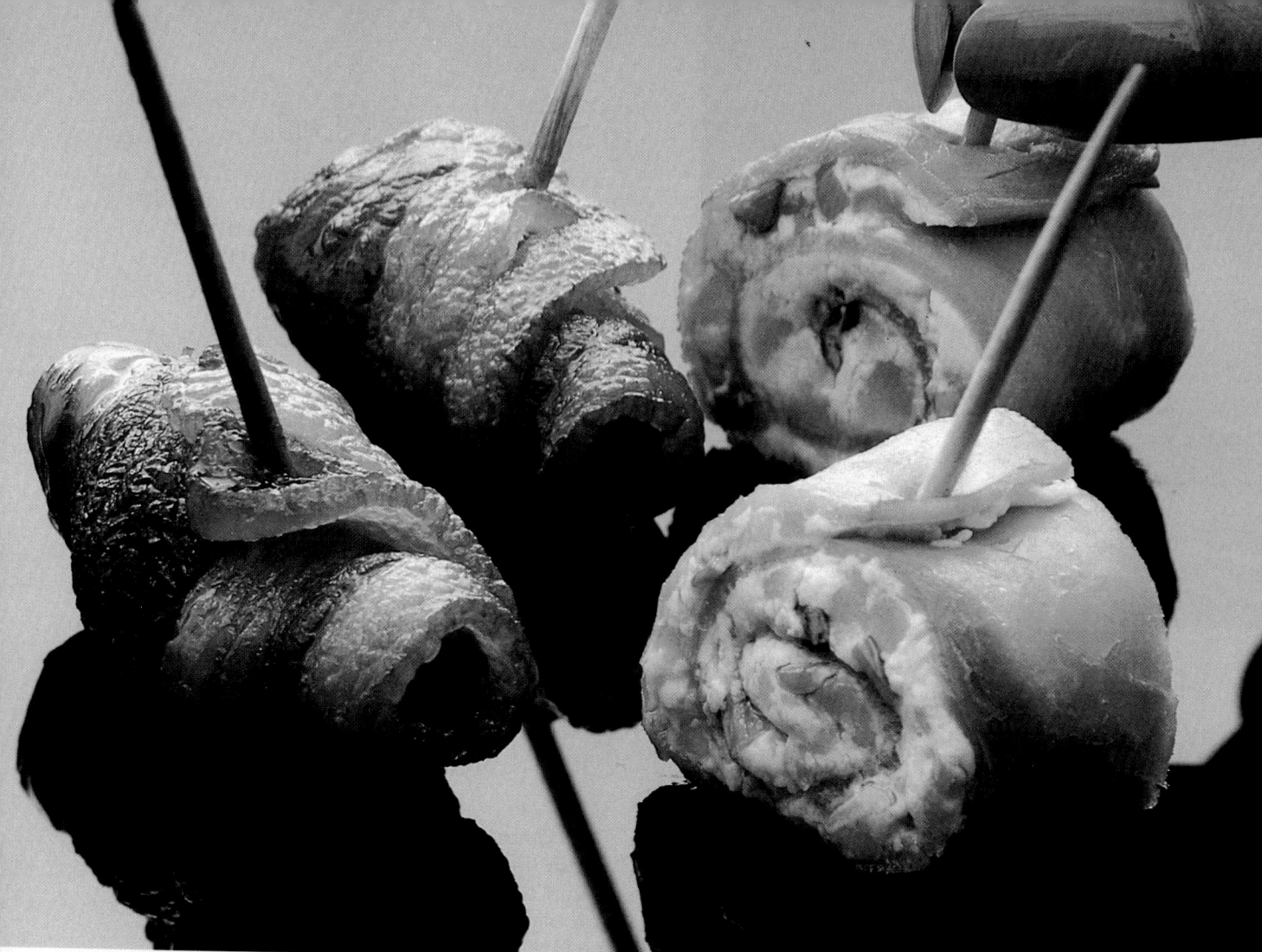

Rumaki ▲

1 cup soy sauce
½ cup packed brown sugar
⅛ teaspoon ground ginger
12 to 13 slices bacon
½ pound chicken livers
1 can (8 ounces) water chestnuts, drained
and halved

Makes 25 appetizers

1. Mix soy sauce, brown sugar and ginger in square baking dish, 8 × 8 inches. Cut bacon slices and chicken livers into halves. Wrap a piece of chicken liver and a water chestnut in each bacon piece. Secure with wooden pick. Place in marinade. Refrigerate, covered, 2 hours; drain.

2. Place rumaki on double layer of paper toweling around outer edge of carousel or on baking sheet lined with paper toweling. Microwave at HIGH (100%) 5 minutes. Reduce power to MEDIUM-HIGH (70%). Microwave until bacon is evenly browned, 12 to 18 minutes. If using oven other than Sharp Carousel, rotate baking sheet quarter turn every 3 to 5 minutes.

Ham Roll-Ups ▲

1 package (3 ounces) cream cheese
½ cup shredded Cheddar cheese
(about 2 ounces)
1 tablespoon chopped green onion
½ teaspoon prepared mustard
4 slices fully cooked ham

Makes 16 appetizers

1. Microwave cream cheese in small bowl at HIGH (100%) until softened, 10 to 15 seconds. Stir in Cheddar cheese, green onion and mustard.

2. Spread cheese mixture on ham slices. Roll ham from narrow end. Cut each roll into 4 pieces; secure with wooden pick. Place on paper toweling on carousel or large dinner plate. Microwave at HIGH (100%) 45 seconds to 1 minute 30 seconds. If using oven other than Sharp Carousel, rotate plate half turn after half the time.

Directions for Bacon-Wrapped Pineapple are in Learn While You Cook, page 20.

Hot Cheese Dip ▲

1 package (8 ounces) process American
   cheese loaf, cubed
¼ cup finely chopped green pepper
¼ cup milk
2 drops red pepper sauce

Makes 1½ cups

1. Mix all ingredients in 1-quart casserole.

2. Microwave at MEDIUM-HIGH (70%) until
cheese melts, 5 to 6 minutes, stirring to blend well
once or twice during cooking. Serve with corn
chips or snack crackers, if desired.

Variation: Add 2 cans (6½ ounces each) minced
clams, drained, with other ingredients. Microwave
as above.

Hot Roquefort Dip

1 package (8 ounces) cream cheese
½ cup crumbled Roquefort cheese
   (about 2 ounces)
3 tablespoons milk
1 tablespoon dried parsley flakes
1 tablespoon finely minced onion
1 teaspoon horseradish
½ teaspoon Worcestershire sauce
¼ cup finely chopped walnuts

Makes about 1½ cups

1. Combine all ingredients except chopped walnuts in small bowl.

2. Microwave at MEDIUM (50%) until heated
through, 3 to 5 minutes, stirring after half the cooking time. Sprinkle with walnuts. Serve with snack
crackers, if desired.

Hot Crabmeat Dip

1 package (8 ounces) cream cheese
2 cans (6½ ounces each) crabmeat, rinsed,
   drained and cartilage removed
¼ cup mayonnaise or salad dressing
2 tablespoons lemon juice
1 tablespoon minced green onion
1 teaspoon Worcestershire sauce
⅛ teaspoon cayenne pepper

Makes about 2 cups

1. Place cream cheese in medium bowl. Microwave at MEDIUM (50%) until softened, 1 to 2
minutes, stirring once. Shred crabmeat; stir into
cream cheese with remaining ingredients.

2. Microwave at MEDIUM (50%) until dip is
heated through, 4 to 7 minutes. If using oven
other than Sharp Carousel, stir twice during
cooking time. Serve hot with fresh vegetables or
wheat crackers, if desired.

Clam Stuffed Tomatoes

1 pint cherry tomatoes or 28 1- to 1½-inch
   tomatoes
¼ cup finely chopped onion
¼ cup chopped green pepper
2 tablespoons margarine or butter
1 clove garlic, minced
2 cans (6½ ounces each) minced clams,
   drained
⅓ cup seasoned bread crumbs
2 tablespoons grated Parmesan cheese
½ teaspoon dried oregano leaves
   Paprika

Makes about 28 appetizers

1. Cut stem ends off tomatoes; scoop out seeds
with a small spoon. Set aside.

2. Mix onion, green pepper, margarine and garlic
in medium bowl. Microwave at HIGH (100%) until
onion is tender, 2 to 3 minutes. Mix in remaining
ingredients except paprika. Spoon 1 tablespoon
of mixture into each tomato. Sprinkle with paprika.

3. Place in a single layer on paper toweling around
outer edge of carousel or in 10-inch square casserole. Microwave at HIGH (100%) until tomatoes are tender, 1 to 2 minutes. If using oven other
than Sharp Carousel, rotate casserole and rearrange tomatoes after half the cooking time.

Directions for Nachos are in Learn While You
Cook, page 21.

Stuffed Mushrooms ►

8 ounces fresh mushrooms (about 12
  1½-inch mushrooms)
3 slices bacon, chopped
⅓ cup finely chopped green onions
½ teaspoon salt
¼ teaspoon pepper
2 to 4 drops red pepper sauce
1 tablespoon all-purpose flour
¼ cup whipping cream
2 tablespoons shredded Cheddar cheese

Makes about 12 appetizers

1. Wash mushrooms. Remove stems and chop fine. Place mushroom caps on paper toweling on carousel or dinner plate. Microwave at MEDIUM-HIGH (70%) 1 minute. Drain and set aside. Place bacon in medium bowl. Microwave at HIGH (100%) until crisp, 2½ to 3 minutes. Drain. Add chopped mushroom stems, onions, salt, pepper and red pepper sauce. Microwave at HIGH (100%) until mushrooms and onions are tender, 2 to 3½ minutes.

2. Blend in flour; stir in cream until smooth. Reduce power to MEDIUM-HIGH (70%). Microwave until thickened and smooth, 2 to 3 minutes, stirring once or twice during cooking. Stir in cheese.

3. Fill each mushroom cap with bacon mixture. Place around outer edge of 9-inch pie plate or dinner plate. Microwave at HIGH (100%) until cheese melts, 1 to 1½ minutes. If using oven other than Sharp Carousel, rotate plate half turn after half the cooking time.

Party Mix ►

¼ cup margarine or butter
2 tablespoons Worcestershire sauce
3 to 5 drops red pepper sauce
2 cups bite-sized shredded corn squares
2 cups bite-sized shredded wheat squares
2 cups bite-sized shredded rice squares
1 cup salted nuts
1 cup thin pretzel sticks

Makes 8 cups

1. Combine margarine, Worcestershire sauce and red pepper sauce in small bowl. Microwave at HIGH (100%) until margarine melts, 1 to 2 minutes. Stir to blend.

2. Combine remaining ingredients in 3-quart casserole. Add margarine mixture, tossing to blend. Microwave at HIGH (100%) until cereal is well coated and crisp, 5 to 6 minutes, stirring every minute. Spread evenly onto paper toweling-lined tray or cookie sheet. Cool.

MEATS & MAIN DISHES

Fast defrosting and cooking are advantages of your microwave oven, but they are not the only ones. Microwaving meats and main dishes brings out their natural flavor and keeps them juicy. To cook with confidence, follow the directions in this section and be sure to allow standing time. For many meat dishes, standing is part of the cooking process. As it stands, the food continues to cook gently without additional heat.

Directions for microwaving Rolled Rib Roast are on pages 64 and 72.

Microwaving Meats: Tender Roasts

Browning mixtures are unnecessary, because the time needed to microwave a roast is long enough to develop browning.

Season meat with garlic, herbs or spices as you would conventionally, but do not salt until after microwaving, as salt drains juices.

Place roasts, fat side down, on a microwave roasting rack, set in a baking dish. Elevating the roast prevents its steaming in the drippings.

Shield roast with foil if needed to protect areas which might overcook because of their shape or position in the oven. Be sure the shields will not touch oven walls as the carousel turns.

Tender Roasts: Shielding

Wrap foil around the tail of standing rib. Shield shank end of a lamb leg so foil covers 2 inches of meat. Protect ends and 1 inch down sides of beef or pork tenderloins.

Remove shields from lamb or pork roasts when meat is turned over after half the cooking time. Keep beef shielded for two-thirds of cooking.

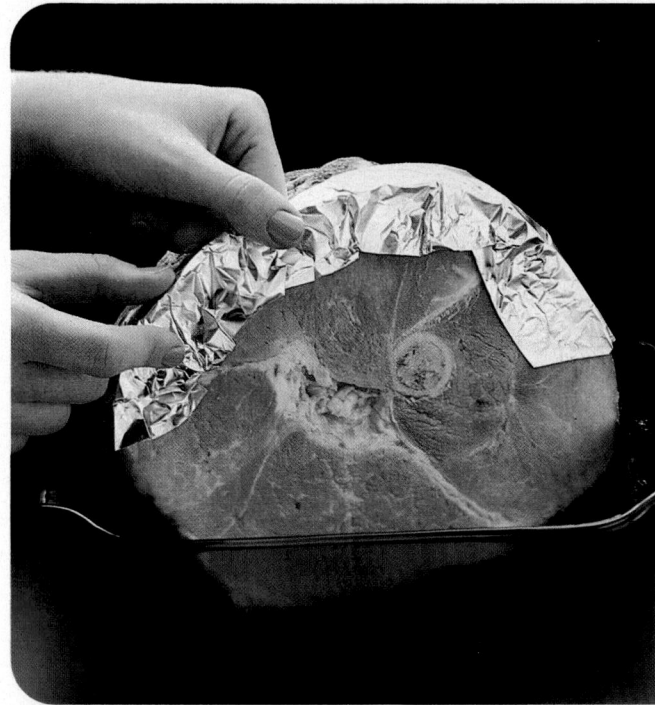

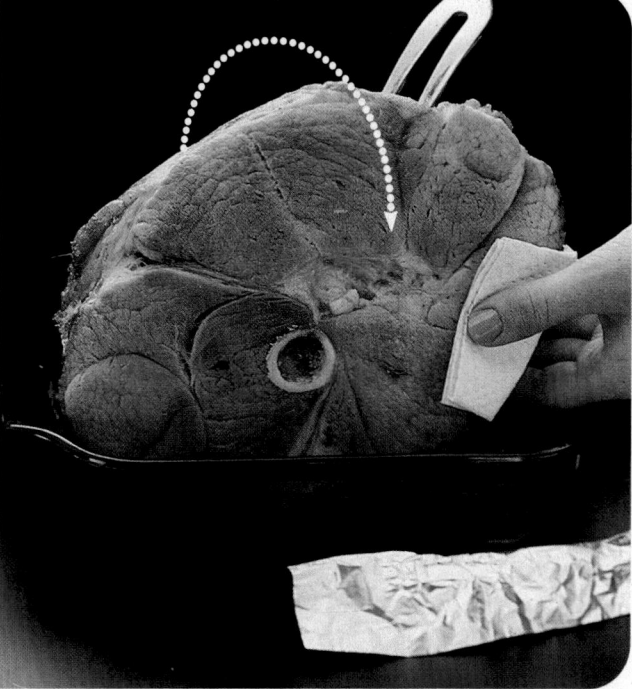

Mold strips of foil over the upper edges of a boneless roast or the cut side of a half ham. When the roast is turned over, reposition the shielding on top of the meat. In this way, the edges which receive most energy will be protected throughout cooking.

Tender Roasts: Microwaving and Standing

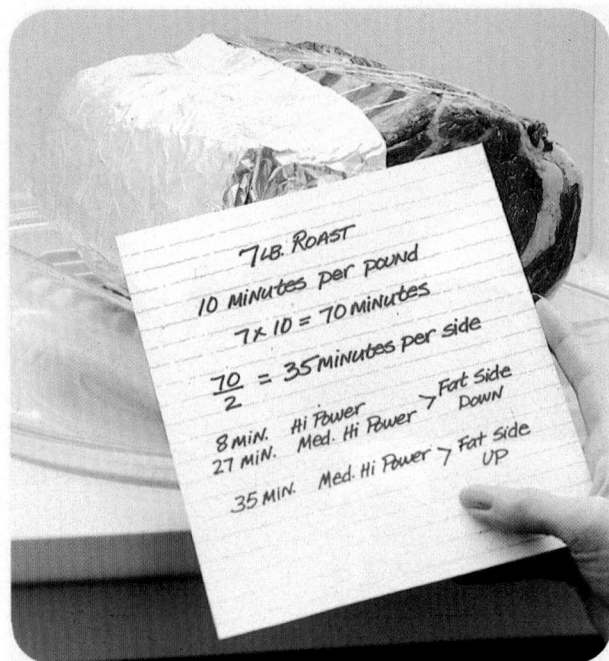

Estimate the total cooking time and divide in half. Following the chart on page 72, start the roast at HIGH (100%), then reduce power to MEDIUM-HIGH (70%) or MEDIUM (50%) and microwave remaining part of first half of cooking time.

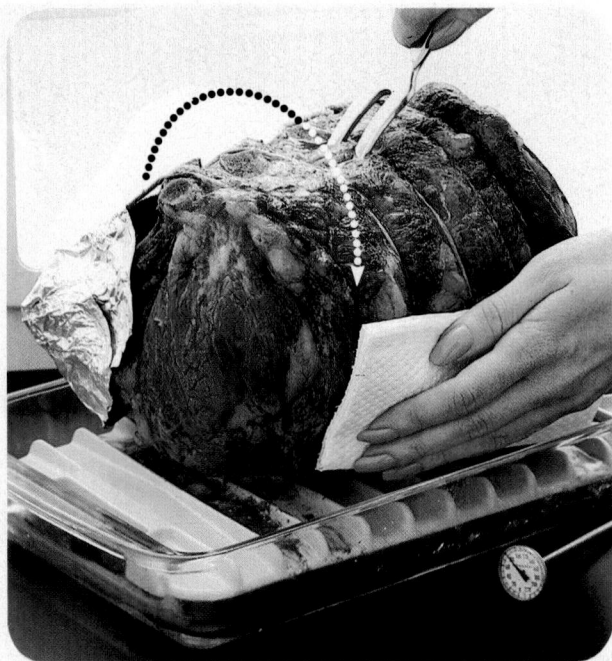

Turn roast over. Insert temperature probe or microwave thermometer as directed on following page. Continue cooking until the sensor indicates the desired removal temperature. Internal temperature is the most accurate way of determining doneness. Do not use a conventional thermometer inside the microwave oven.

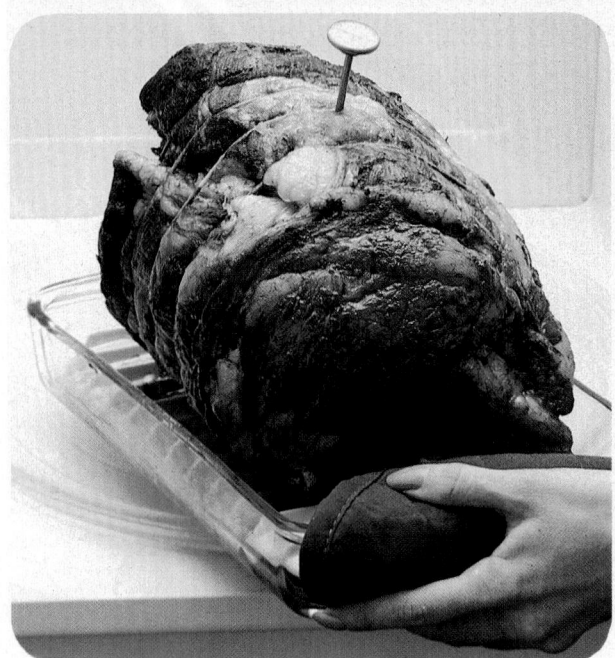

Remove roast from oven when internal temperature is 10° to 20° lower than desired finished temperature, following the chart on page 72.

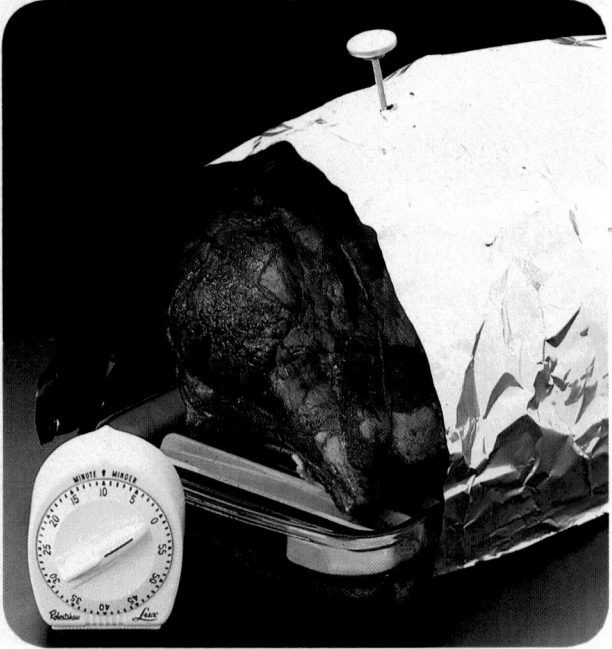

Cover loosely with foil and let stand 10 to 15 minutes. During standing, the roast continues to cook, internal temperature rises, and meat firms up for carving.

Tender Roasts: Probe Placement

Gauge distance from outside to center of meat by holding sensor at the proper angle and marking the point where it touches edge of roast with your fingers. Angle the probe or microwave thermometer in thin roasts so that it is supported by the meat with the point in the center of the roast.

Insert probe or microwave thermometer into the middle of a boneless roast so the tip rests in the center of the meatiest muscle, not in fat.

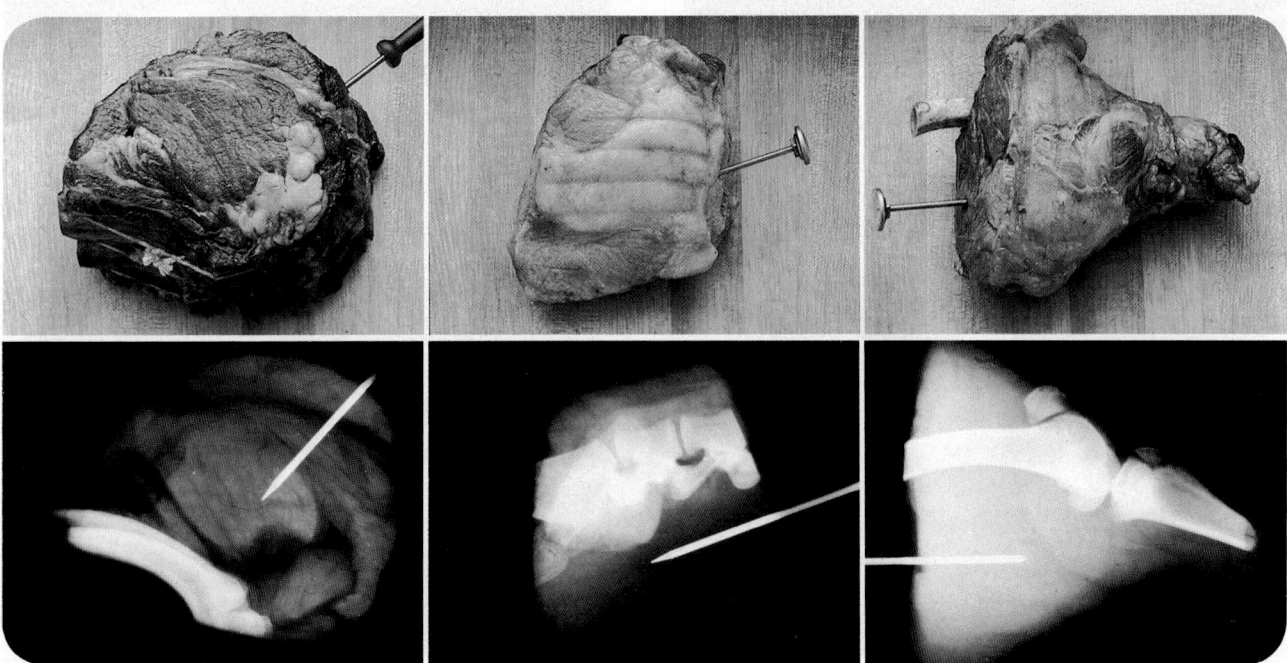

X rays show where to place the sensor in bone-in roasts so that the tip is in the meatiest area and does not touch bone or fat, which reach different temperatures than meat and give inaccurate readings. With loin and leg roasts, insert the sensor from the round bone end.

Microwaving Meats: Browning Dish

Microwave tender steaks, lamb chops or hamburgers in a browning dish or griddle to give them a crisp surface and brown color.

Slash the fat on steaks or chops at 1-inch intervals to prevent curling. Preheat utensil at HIGH (100%) as manufacturer directs.

Place meat in dish. Following chart on page 72, microwave the first side at HIGH (100%).

Turn meat over. Microwave the second side for remaining time; remove from dish immediately to prevent further cooking.

Microwaving Meats: Less Tender Cuts

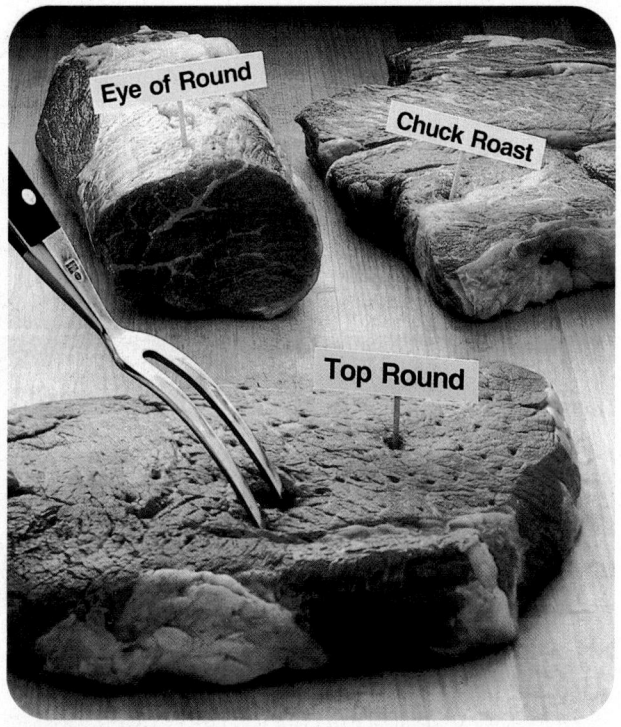

Tenderize less tender cuts of beef before microwaving. Pierce thick cuts thoroughly with a fork so steam can penetrate to interior of meat.

Pound thin cuts with a meat mallet or the edge of a saucer to break up long, tough fibers.

Microwave less tender beef in a covered utensil, using MEDIUM (50%). A marinade or cooking liquid containing beer, wine or tomatoes helps tenderize beef as well as flavor it.

Cook until fork tender, then let meat stand, tightly covered, to tenderize further and develop flavor. See Learn While You Cook, page 27 for Pot Roast.

Microwaving Main Dishes

Give chops and sausages an attractive color with a sauce, topping or browning mixture.

MEDIUM-HIGH (70%)

MEDIUM (50%)

Use MEDIUM-HIGH (70%) to equalize temperature in saucy veal, lamb chops and cubes, and to avoid popping of sausages. To prevent drying or toughening of pork chops, microwave at MEDIUM (50%).

Arrange chops with meatiest portions to the outside of the dish, where they receive most energy.

Turn over or rearrange chops after half the time. If using oven other than Sharp Carousel, rotate the dish 2 or 3 times during cooking.

HIGH (100%)

Reduced Power

Combined Settings

Select HIGH (100%) to microwave ground beef unless it is combined with cheese, cream, or other heat-sensitive ingredients, which require lower power. Start spaghetti sauce or chili at HIGH (100%), then reduce power to MEDIUM-HIGH (70%), and microwave uncovered to thicken sauce and develop flavor.

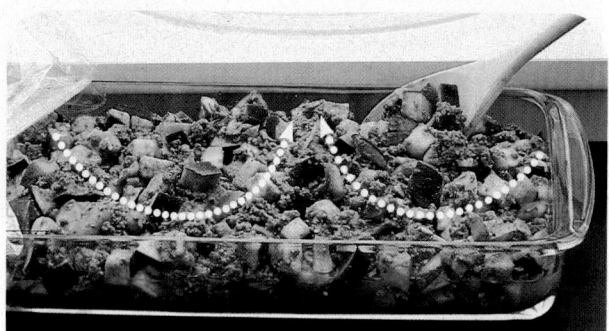

Stir casseroles and saucy mixtures once or twice during microwaving to distribute heat evenly and speed cooking. Add toppings after final stirring.

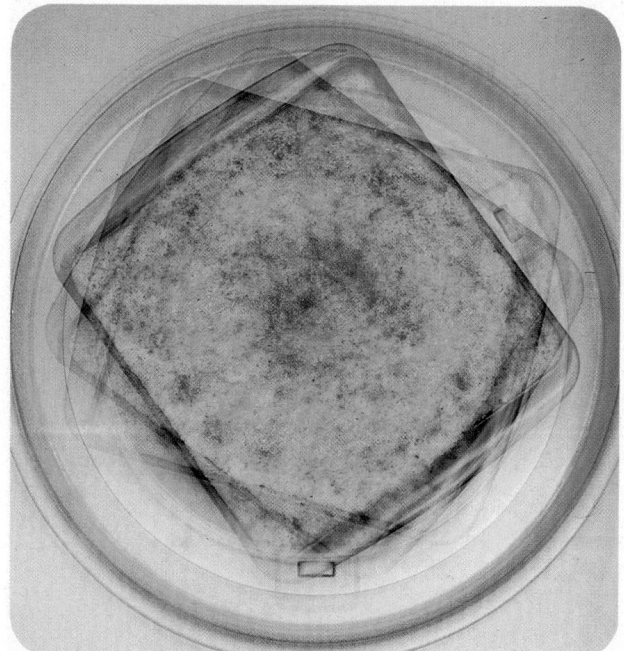

Moving foods in the energy pattern helps evenly cook those foods which cannot be stirred. Rotate and rearrange them if using an oven other than Sharp Carousel.

Recipe Conversion

Tender meats which you dry roast or grill conventionally can be microwaved on a roasting rack or browning utensil. Cuts which you normally braise or stew should be microwaved with liquid in a covered container. Some conventional pot roasts call for enough liquid to cover the meat; use only the amount needed for gravy.

To convert main dishes and casseroles, choose recipes for moist or saucy foods which call for covering, stirring or steaming. For changes in ingredients and cooking techniques, follow the directions in Recipe Conversion, page 42.

Cooking time depends on quantity, size of pieces, and type of ingredients. Casseroles made with precooked ingredients may take as little as one-fourth the time. Your best guide is a microwave recipe for a similar amount and type of food.

Meat Roasting Chart

Cut	Microwave Time: Start	Microwave Time: Finish	Internal Temp. at Removal	Internal Temp. after Standing
BEEF				
Standing or Rolled Rib	HIGH (100%) Less than 4 lbs.: 5 min. More than 4 lbs.: 8 min.	MED.-HIGH (70%) Rare: 7-10 min./lb. Med.: 7½-10½ min./lb. Well Done: 8-11½ min./lb.	120° 135° 150°	140° 150° 160°
Tenderloin	HIGH (100%) Less than 2 lbs.: 3 min. More than 2 lbs.: 5 min.	MED.-HIGH (70%) Rare: 6-8½ min./lb. Med.: 7-10 min./lb. Well Done: 8-11 min./lb.	120° 135° 150°	140° 150° 160°
Chuck Roast (cook in ¼ cup liquid, covered) 2-3 lbs.		MEDIUM (50%)		
Without vegetables		22-28 min./lb.		
With 3-4 cups cut-up vegetables		28-32 min./lb.		
Eye of Round 2-3 lbs.		MEDIUM (50%) 27-32 min./lb.		
Hamburger (to brown for casserole) 1 lb.	HIGH (100%) 2-3 min. (Stir to break up)	HIGH (100%) 2-3 min.		
Meat Loaf 1½ lbs. hamburger		HIGH (100%) 13-19 min.	150°	155°-160°
Hamburgers (¼ lb. each) 2 patties 4 patties 6 patties	1st Side HIGH (100%) 2 min. 2½ min. 3½ min.	2nd Side HIGH (100%) 1½-2½ min. 2-3 min. 3¼-3½ min.		

Cut	Microwave Time: Start	Microwave Time: Finish	Internal Temp. at Removal	Internal Temp. after Standing
PORK				
Loin Roast				
Bone-in or	HIGH (100%)	MED.-HIGH (70%)		
Boneless	5 min.	9½-12½ min./lb.	175°	185°
Tenderloin				
	HIGH (100%)	MED.-HIGH (70%)		
	3 min.	9-12½ min./lb.	175°	185°
Canadian Bacon				
(¼-in. thick)		MED.-HIGH (70%)		
2 slices		¾-1¼ min.		
4 slices		1½-2½ min.		
6 slices		2½-3½ min.		
8 slices		3-4½ min.		
Ham				
Canned		MEDIUM (50%)		
		6-9 min./lb.	130°	135°-140°
Boneless Rolled		MEDIUM (50%)		
		10½-15 min./lb.	130°	135°-140°
Bone-in,	HIGH (100%)	MEDIUM (50%)		
fully cooked	5 min.	11½-15½ min./lb.	130°	135°-140°
Bone-in,	HIGH (100%)	MEDIUM (50%)		
partially cooked	5 min.	15-19 min./lb.	160°	170°
LAMB				
Shoulder Roast				
	HIGH (100%)	MED.-HIGH (70%)		
	Less than 4 lbs.:	Med.: 7½-11½ min./lb.	135°	145°-150°
	3 min.	Well Done:		
	More than 4 lbs.:	8½-13 min./lb.	150°	160°-165°
	5 min.			
Leg or Sirloin				
	HIGH (100%)	MED.-HIGH (70%)		
	5 min.	Med.: 6½-10½ min./lb.	135°	150°
		Well Done:		
		7½-11½ min./lb.	150°	165°
Chops				
(1-in. thick)	Preheated browning dish			
	1st Side	2nd Side		
2 chops	1 min.	½-1½ min.		
4 chops	1 min.	1½-2½ min.		

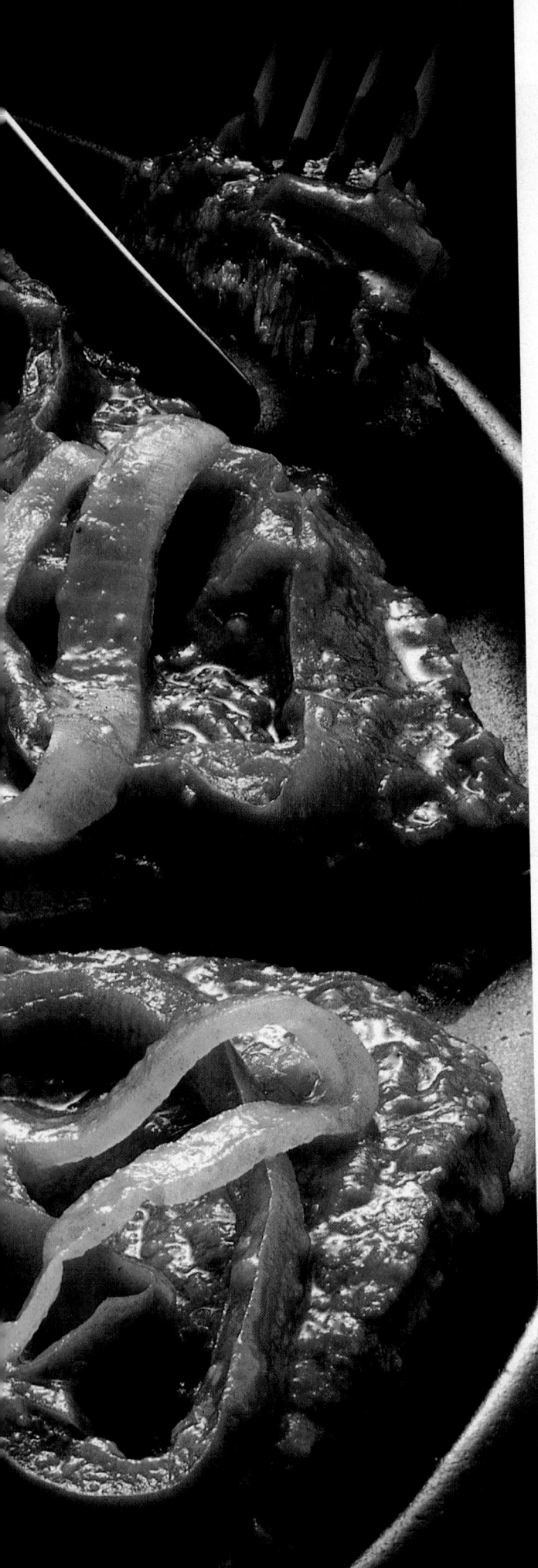

◄ Swiss Steak

2 pounds boneless beef round steak
¼ cup all-purpose flour
1 teaspoon salt
¼ teaspoon pepper
1 cup thinly sliced celery
1 medium onion, thinly sliced and
    separated into rings
1 medium green pepper, thinly sliced
1 can (10¾ ounces) condensed tomato soup
⅔ cup water
1 tablespoon Worcestershire sauce

Makes 6 to 8 servings

1. Trim round steak; pound well. Cut into 6 to 8 pieces. Mix flour, salt and pepper. Coat beef with flour mixture. Place meat and any remaining flour mixture in rectangular baking dish, 12 × 8 inches or 10-inch square casserole.

2. Combine celery, onion and green pepper in small bowl. Microwave at HIGH (100%) until vegetables are tender, 3 to 5 minutes. Mix with remaining ingredients. Pour over beef.

3. Microwave, covered, at HIGH (100%) 5 minutes. Reduce power to MEDIUM (50%). Microwave until beef is tender, 40 to 50 minutes, rearranging pieces after half the cooking time.

Short Ribs in Beer

3 pounds beef short ribs, cut into 3-inch
    pieces
1 can (12 ounces) beer
2 stalks celery, thinly sliced
1 medium onion, thinly sliced and
    separated into rings
1 medium bay leaf
½ teaspoon salt
¼ teaspoon garlic salt
⅛ teaspoon pepper

Makes 3 to 4 servings

1. Place all ingredients in 5-quart casserole. Microwave, covered, at HIGH (100%) 5 minutes.

2. Reduce power to MEDIUM (50%). Microwave 25 minutes. Stir. Microwave, covered, at MEDIUM (50%) until beef is tender, 25 to 35 minutes. Let stand 10 minutes.

Directions for Pot Roast are in Learn While You Cook, page 27.

Cut	Microwave Time: Start	Microwave Time: Finish	Internal Temp. at Removal	Internal Temp. after Standing
PORK				
Loin Roast				
Bone-in or Boneless	HIGH (100%) 5 min.	MED.-HIGH (70%) 9½-12½ min./lb.	175°	185°
Tenderloin				
	HIGH (100%) 3 min.	MED.-HIGH (70%) 9-12½ min./lb.	175°	185°
Canadian Bacon (¼-in. thick)				
2 slices		MED.-HIGH (70%) ¾-1¼ min.		
4 slices		1½-2½ min.		
6 slices		2½-3½ min.		
8 slices		3-4½ min.		
Ham				
Canned		MEDIUM (50%) 6-9 min./lb.	130°	135°-140°
Boneless Rolled		MEDIUM (50%) 10½-15 min./lb.	130°	135°-140°
Bone-in, fully cooked	HIGH (100%) 5 min.	MEDIUM (50%) 11½-15½ min./lb.	130°	135°-140°
Bone-in, partially cooked	HIGH (100%) 5 min.	MEDIUM (50%) 15-19 min./lb.	160°	170°
LAMB				
Shoulder Roast				
	HIGH (100%) Less than 4 lbs.: 3 min.	MED.-HIGH (70%) Med.: 7½-11½ min./lb. Well Done:	135°	145°-150°
	More than 4 lbs.: 5 min.	8½-13 min./lb.	150°	160°-165°
Leg or Sirloin				
	HIGH (100%) 5 min.	MED.-HIGH (70%) Med.: 6½-10½ min./lb. Well Done:	135°	150°
		7½-11½ min./lb.	150°	165°
Chops (1-in. thick)	Preheated browning dish 1st Side	2nd Side		
2 chops	1 min.	½-1½ min.		
4 chops	1 min.	1½-2½ min.		

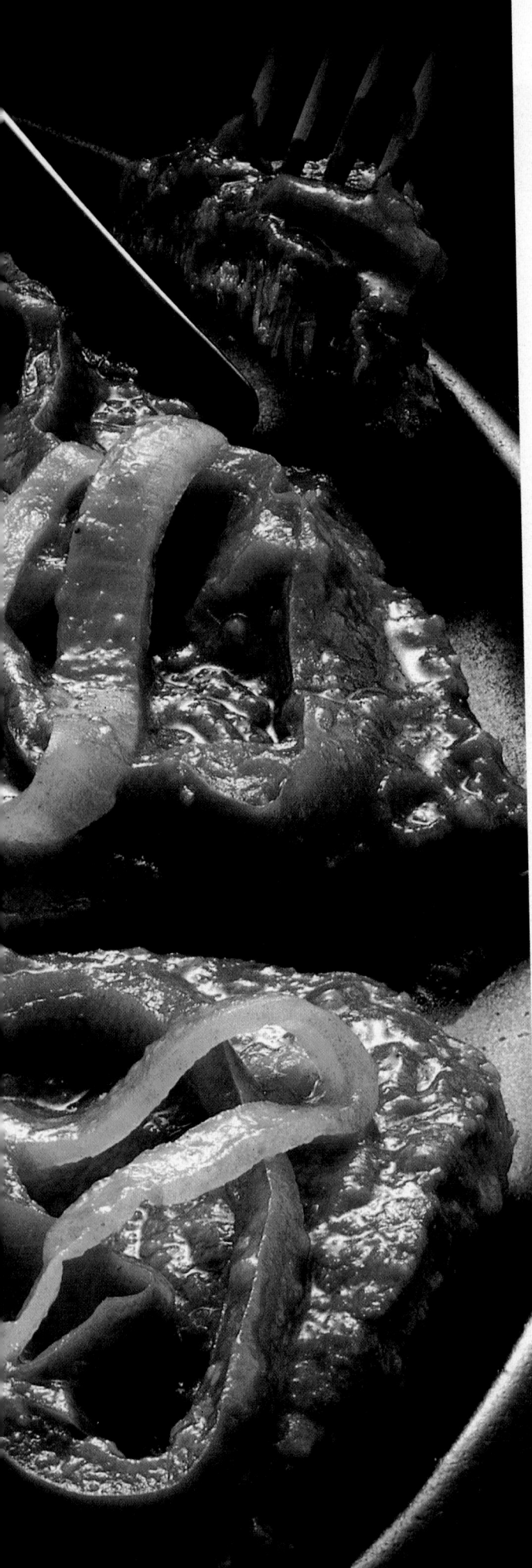

◄ Swiss Steak

2 pounds boneless beef round steak
¼ cup all-purpose flour
1 teaspoon salt
¼ teaspoon pepper
1 cup thinly sliced celery
1 medium onion, thinly sliced and
    separated into rings
1 medium green pepper, thinly sliced
1 can (10¾ ounces) condensed tomato soup
⅔ cup water
1 tablespoon Worcestershire sauce

Makes 6 to 8 servings

1. Trim round steak; pound well. Cut into 6 to 8 pieces. Mix flour, salt and pepper. Coat beef with flour mixture. Place meat and any remaining flour mixture in rectangular baking dish, 12 × 8 inches or 10-inch square casserole.

2. Combine celery, onion and green pepper in small bowl. Microwave at HIGH (100%) until vegetables are tender, 3 to 5 minutes. Mix with remaining ingredients. Pour over beef.

3. Microwave, covered, at HIGH (100%) 5 minutes. Reduce power to MEDIUM (50%). Microwave until beef is tender, 40 to 50 minutes, rearranging pieces after half the cooking time.

Short Ribs in Beer

3 pounds beef short ribs, cut into 3-inch
    pieces
1 can (12 ounces) beer
2 stalks celery, thinly sliced
1 medium onion, thinly sliced and
    separated into rings
1 medium bay leaf
½ teaspoon salt
¼ teaspoon garlic salt
⅛ teaspoon pepper

Makes 3 to 4 servings

1. Place all ingredients in 5-quart casserole. Microwave, covered, at HIGH (100%) 5 minutes.

2. Reduce power to MEDIUM (50%). Microwave 25 minutes. Stir. Microwave, covered, at MEDIUM (50%) until beef is tender, 25 to 35 minutes. Let stand 10 minutes.

Directions for Pot Roast are in Learn While You Cook, page 27.

Beef Ragout

1 medium onion, thinly sliced and separated into rings
1 medium green pepper, thinly sliced
1 tablespoon olive oil
1½ pounds boneless beef chuck steak, cut into ½-inch cubes
1 can (17 ounces) stewed tomatoes
1 can (10¾ ounces) condensed beef broth
1 can (6 ounces) tomato paste
1 large potato, cut into ½-inch cubes
2 tablespoons all-purpose flour

Makes 6 to 8 servings

1. Combine onions, green pepper and olive oil in 3-quart casserole. Microwave at HIGH (100%) until green pepper is tender, 2 to 5 minutes.

2. Stir in remaining ingredients; cover. Microwave at HIGH (100%) 10 minutes. Reduce power to MEDIUM (50%). Microwave until beef and potatoes are tender, 50 minutes to 1 hour, stirring after half the cooking time. If using oven other than Sharp Carousel, stir 2 or 3 times during cooking. Let stand 5 to 10 minutes. Serve over rice, noodles or potatoes, if desired.

Sweet and Sour Beef Stew

1½ pounds boneless beef chuck steak, cut into ¾-inch cubes
2 tablespoons all-purpose flour
1 teaspoon salt
3 medium carrots, thinly sliced
1 medium onion, thinly sliced and separated into rings
1 can (8 ounces) tomato sauce
¼ cup packed brown sugar
¼ cup vinegar
¼ cup water
1 tablespoon Worcestershire sauce

Makes 6 to 8 servings

1. Stir beef, flour and salt in 2-quart casserole until beef is coated. Add remaining ingredients.

2. Microwave, covered, at HIGH (100%) 5 minutes. Reduce power to MEDIUM (50%). Microwave until beef is tender, 50 minutes to 1 hour, stirring 2 or 3 times during cooking. Let stand 5 to 10 minutes. Serve over rice or noodles, if desired.

Beef Stew ▼

1½ pounds boneless lean beef chuck steak, cut into ½-inch cubes
¼ cup all-purpose flour
2 teaspoons salt
¼ teaspoon pepper
2½ cups hot water
3 medium potatoes, cut into ½-inch cubes
2 medium carrots, thinly sliced
1 stalk celery, cut into ¼-inch slices
¼ cup catsup
1 teaspoon brown bouquet sauce
1 clove garlic, minced
2 tablespoons all-purpose flour
½ cup cold water
1 package (10 ounces) frozen green peas, thawed and drained

Makes 4 to 6 servings

1. Stir beef, ¼ cup flour, the salt and pepper in 3-quart casserole until beef is coated. Add 2½ cups water, the potatoes, carrots, celery, catsup, bouquet sauce and garlic.

2. Microwave, covered, at HIGH (100%) 5 minutes. Reduce power to MEDIUM (50%). Microwave until beef is tender, 40 minutes to 1 hour, stirring once or twice during cooking.

3. Mix 2 tablespoons flour and ½ cup cold water until smooth. Stir flour mixture and peas into stew; cover. Microwave at MEDIUM (50%) until mixture thickens slightly and peas are tender, 10 to 15 minutes. Serve with rice or noodles, if desired.

Beef with Peppers ▾ and Tomatoes

¼ cup soy sauce
¼ cup water
2 tablespoons sherry
½ teaspoon garlic powder
2 pounds beef flank steak, cut across grain into thin strips
2 medium green peppers, thinly sliced
2 tablespoons cornstarch
½ cup cold water
1 tomato, cut into 16 wedges

Makes 6 to 8 servings

1. Mix soy sauce, water, sherry, garlic powder and beef strips in plastic bag or medium bowl; close tightly or cover. Refrigerate 8 hours or overnight.

2. Combine green peppers, beef and marinade in 2-quart casserole; cover. Microwave at MEDIUM (50%) until beef is tender, 20 to 25 minutes, stirring after half the cooking time. Drain, reserving meat juices. Set beef mixture aside, covered.

3. Mix cornstarch and cold water in 2-cup measure or small bowl. Stir in reserved meat juices. Microwave at HIGH (100%) until sauce thickens, 2 to 4 minutes, stirring after half the cooking time. Stir sauce and tomatoes into beef and green pepper mixture; cover. Microwave at HIGH (100%) until tomatoes are heated through, 1 to 3 minutes.

Goulash

1½ pounds boneless beef chuck steak, cut into ¾-inch cubes
2 tablespoons all-purpose flour
1 teaspoon salt
¼ teaspoon pepper
¼ teaspoon garlic powder
1 can (8 ounces) tomato sauce
1 medium onion, chopped
½ cup water
1 tablespoon sugar
1 tablespoon paprika
2 tablespoons vinegar
2 tablespoons Worcestershire sauce
1 bay leaf

Makes 6 to 8 servings

1. Shake beef, flour, salt, pepper and garlic in plastic bag until beef is coated. Mix beef and remaining ingredients in 2-quart casserole.

2. Microwave, covered, at HIGH (100%) 5 minutes. Reduce power to MEDIUM (50%). Microwave until beef is tender and sauce is thickened, 50 minutes to 1 hour, stirring once or twice during cooking. Let stand 5 to 10 minutes. Serve over noodles, if desired.

Beef Supreme ▲

1½ pounds boneless beef chuck steak,
    cut into ½-inch cubes
¼ cup all-purpose flour
¾ teaspoon salt
¼ teaspoon pepper
1 medium onion, chopped
2 tablespoons margarine or butter
1 can (10¾ ounces) condensed cream
    of celery soup
1 can (10¾ ounces) condensed cream
    of mushroom soup
3 medium potatoes, cut into ½-inch cubes
3 medium carrots, thinly sliced
1 tablespoon Worcestershire sauce

Makes 6 to 8 servings

1. Shake beef, flour, salt and pepper in plastic bag until beef is coated. Set aside.

2. Place onion and margarine in 3-quart casserole. Microwave at HIGH (100%) until onions are tender, 3 to 4 minutes.

3. Stir beef and remaining ingredients into onions; cover. Microwave at HIGH (100%) 5 minutes. Reduce power to MEDIUM (50%). Microwave until beef and potatoes are tender, 45 minutes to 1 hour, stirring after half the cooking time. If using oven other than Sharp Carousel, stir 2 or 3 times during cooking. Let stand 5 to 10 minutes. Serve with rice, noodles or potatoes, if desired.

Beef Stroganoff

1½ cups fresh sliced mushrooms
1 medium onion, chopped
1 clove garlic, minced
2 tablespoons margarine or butter
1 pound boneless beef sirloin steak,
    ½ inch thick, cut across grain into
    thin strips
3 tablespoons all-purpose flour
½ teaspoon salt
¼ teaspoon pepper
1 cup hot water
1 tablespoon sherry
1 tablespoon catsup
2 teaspoons instant beef bouillon
½ teaspoon Worcestershire sauce
1 cup dairy sour cream

Makes 4 to 6 servings

1. Combine mushrooms, onion, garlic and margarine in 2-quart casserole; cover. Microwave at HIGH (100%) until mushrooms and onions are tender, 2 to 4 minutes.

2. Shake beef, flour, salt and pepper in plastic bag until beef is coated. Stir beef and remaining ingredients except sour cream into vegetable mixture.

3. Microwave, covered, at HIGH (100%) 5 minutes. Reduce power to MEDIUM-HIGH (70%). Microwave until beef is tender, 20 to 30 minutes, stirring after half the cooking time. Let stand 5 to 10 minutes. Stir in sour cream until blended.

◄ Basic Meat Loaf

- 1 slice bread, torn into small pieces
- 1 small onion, chopped
- ¼ cup chopped celery
- 1 egg, slightly beaten
- 1 clove garlic, minced
- ½ teaspoon salt
- ⅛ teaspoon pepper
- 1½ pounds lean ground beef
- ¼ cup catsup

Makes 4 servings

1. Mix bread, onion, celery, egg, garlic, salt and pepper. Crumble ground beef into mixture; blend thoroughly. Press into loaf dish, 9 × 5 inches.

2. Microwave at HIGH (100%) until internal temperature reaches 150°, 13 to 15 minutes. If using oven other than Sharp Carousel, rotate meat loaf once or twice during cooking. Spread with catsup.

3. Microwave at MEDIUM (50%) until catsup is heated, 2 to 3 minutes. Let stand 3 to 5 minutes.

Dressed-Up Meat Loaf

- 1½ pounds lean ground beef
- ½ cup soft bread crumbs
- ½ cup red wine
- 1 egg, beaten
- 2 tablespoons chopped onion
- 2 tablespoons chopped green pepper
- 1 teaspoon instant beef bouillon
- 1 teaspoon brown bouquet sauce
- ½ teaspoon salt
- ½ teaspoon dry mustard
- ¼ teaspoon pepper

Makes 4 servings

1. Thoroughly blend all ingredients. Press into loaf dish, 9 × 5 inches or 9-inch round baking dish with inverted custard cup in center.

2. Microwave at HIGH (100%) until internal temperature reaches 150°, 11 to 15 minutes. If using oven other than Sharp Carousel, rotate meat loaf once or twice during cooking. Let stand 3 to 5 minutes.

Directions for individual loaves and ring meat loaf are in Learn While You Cook, page 26.

Directions for hamburgers are in Learn While You Cook, page 25.

Texas Meatballs and Rice

- 1 pound ground beef
- 1 egg, slightly beaten
- 1½ teaspoons chili powder
- 1 teaspoon salt
- ¼ teaspoon pepper
- 1 can (16 ounces) stewed tomatoes
- 1 large onion, thinly sliced and separated into rings
- 1 large green pepper, chopped
- ¾ cup uncooked instant rice

Makes 4 servings

1. Mix ground beef, egg, chili powder, salt and pepper. Shape into 1½- to 2-inch balls. Place in 2-quart casserole. Microwave at HIGH (100%) until meatballs are set and lose pink color, 4 to 7 minutes, rearranging meatballs after half the cooking time. Drain.

2. Stir in remaining ingredients; cover. Microwave at HIGH (100%) until mixture is bubbly and onions are tender, 4 to 7 minutes. If using oven other than Sharp Carousel, stir after half the cooking time. Let stand until rice is tender, 2 to 3 minutes.

Texas Meatballs and Rice

- 1 pound ground beef
- 1 egg, slightly beaten
- 1½ teaspoons chili powder
- 1 teaspoon salt
- ¼ teaspoon pepper
- 1 can (16 ounces) stewed tomatoes
- 1 large onion, thinly sliced and separated into rings
- 1 large green pepper, chopped
- ¾ cup uncooked instant rice

Makes 4 servings

1. Mix ground beef, egg, chili powder, salt and pepper. Shape into 1½- to 2-inch balls. Place in 2-quart casserole. Microwave at HIGH (100%) until meatballs are set and lose pink color, 4 to 7 minutes, rearranging meatballs after half the cooking time. Drain.

2. Stir in remaining ingredients; cover. Microwave at HIGH (100%) until mixture is bubbly and onions are tender, 4 to 7 minutes. If using oven other than Sharp Carousel, stir after half the cooking time. Let stand until rice is tender, 2 to 3 minutes.

◄ Swedish Meatballs

1 pound ground beef
½ pound lean ground pork
½ cup dry bread crumbs
1 medium onion, chopped
⅓ cup milk
1 egg, beaten
1½ teaspoons salt
¾ teaspoon ground allspice
¼ teaspoon ground nutmeg
¼ teaspoon pepper
2 tablespoons all-purpose flour
½ cup water
1 teaspoon instant beef bouillon
½ teaspoon brown bouquet sauce
1 cup half-and-half

Makes 4 to 6 servings

1. Mix ground beef, ground pork, bread crumbs, onion, milk, egg, salt, allspice, nutmeg and pepper. Shape into 1- to 1½-inch balls. Place in single layer in rectangular baking dish, 12 × 8 inches or 10-inch square casserole. Microwave at HIGH (100%) until meatballs are set and lose pink color, 9 to 11 minutes, rearranging after half the time.

2. Remove meatballs, reserving meat juices. Stir flour into meat juices. Stir in water, instant bouillon and bouquet sauce. Microwave at HIGH (100%) until slightly thickened, 3 to 4 minutes, stirring once or twice during cooking. Gradually blend in half-and-half. Reduce power to MEDIUM-HIGH (70%). Microwave until thickened and smooth, 4 to 6 minutes, stirring once or twice during cooking.

3. Stir meatballs in sauce until coated. Microwave at MEDIUM-HIGH (70%) until heated through, 1½ to 2 minutes.

Lasagna ▲

1 pound ground beef
½ pound bulk hot or regular pork sausage
1 can (16 ounces) whole tomatoes
1 can (6 ounces) tomato paste
½ teaspoon salt
¼ teaspoon pepper
1 clove garlic, minced
1 carton (8 ounces) ricotta or creamed
    cottage cheese (about 1 cup)
1 egg, beaten
¼ cup grated Parmesan cheese
1 tablespoon dried parsley flakes
½ teaspoon dried oregano leaves
¼ teaspoon dried basil leaves
7 to 9 cooked lasagna noodles
1 cup shredded mozzarella cheese
    (about 4 ounces)

Makes 6 servings

1. Mix ground beef and sausage in 2-quart casserole. Microwave at HIGH (100%) until meat loses pink color, 5 to 9 minutes, stirring once to break up meat during cooking. Drain. Stir in tomatoes, tomato paste, salt, pepper and garlic. Microwave at HIGH (100%) until sauce thickens, 7 to 11 minutes, stirring occasionally.

2. While sauce is cooking, mix ricotta cheese, egg, Parmesan cheese, parsley, oregano and basil.

3. Layer one-third each of the noodles, meat sauce, ricotta cheese mixture and mozzarella in square baking dish, 8 × 8 inches. Repeat twice, ending with mozzarella. Microwave at MEDIUM-HIGH (70%) until sauce bubbles, 12 to 18 minutes. If using oven other than Sharp Carousel, rotate dish quarter turn every 3 to 4 minutes.

Sicilian Supper ▲

1 pound ground beef
½ cup chopped onion
½ cup chopped green pepper
1 package (8 ounces) cream cheese,
   cubed and softened
1 cup cooked egg noodles
1 can (6 ounces) tomato paste
½ cup water
½ cup milk
¼ teaspoon garlic salt
¼ teaspoon pepper
¼ cup grated Parmesan cheese

Makes 4 servings

1. Mix ground beef, onion and green pepper in 2-quart casserole. Microwave at HIGH (100%) until beef loses pink color, 5 to 9 minutes, stirring once to break up beef. Drain.

2. Stir in remaining ingredients except Parmesan. Microwave at HIGH (100%) 2 minutes. Reduce power to MEDIUM-HIGH (70%). Sprinkle with Parmesan. Microwave until heated through, 5 to 7 minutes. If using oven other than Sharp Carousel, rotate dish quarter turn every 2 minutes.

Italian Spaghetti Sauce

1 pound ground beef
1 medium onion, chopped
1 can (16 ounces) whole tomatoes
1 can (16 ounces) tomato sauce
1 can (6 ounces) tomato paste
½ cup water
1 teaspoon sugar
1 teaspoon dried parsley flakes
1 teaspoon salt
1 bay leaf
½ teaspoon dried oregano leaves
½ teaspoon dried basil leaves
¼ teaspoon pepper
   Cooked spaghetti

Makes 6 to 8 servings

1. Mix ground beef and onion in 3-quart casserole. Microwave at HIGH (100%) until beef loses pink color, 5 to 9 minutes, stirring once to break up beef. Drain. Stir in remaining ingredients; cover.

2. Microwave at HIGH (100%) 10 minutes. Stir. Reduce power to MEDIUM-HIGH (70%). Microwave, uncovered, until sauce thickens and flavors are blended, 15 to 20 minutes, stirring 2 or 3 times during cooking. Serve over spaghetti.

Oriental Hamburger ▾ Casserole

1 pound ground beef
1 medium onion, chopped
1 can (10½ ounces) condensed cream
  of mushroom soup
1 can (10½ ounces) condensed cream
  of chicken soup
1 can (8½ ounces) water chestnuts,
  drained and sliced
1 cup water
1 cup uncooked instant rice
1 tablespoon soy sauce
¼ teaspoon pepper
1 cup chow mein noodles

Makes 4 servings

1. Mix ground beef and onion in 2-quart casserole. Microwave at HIGH (100%) until beef loses pink color, 5 to 9 minutes, stirring once to break up beef. Drain.

2. Stir in remaining ingredients except chow mein noodles; cover. Microwave at HIGH (100%) until bubbly, 6 to 8 minutes, stirring once or twice during cooking time.

3. Sprinkle with chow mein noodles. Microwave, uncovered, at HIGH (100%) until noodles are heated through, 1 to 2 minutes.

Enchilada Casserole

1 pound ground beef
¼ cup chopped onion
1 clove garlic, minced
1 can (8 ounces) tomato sauce
½ cup water
1½ to 2½ teaspoons chili powder
½ teaspoon salt
½ teaspoon pepper
4 round corn tortillas
2 cups shredded sharp Cheddar cheese
  (about 8 ounces)

Makes 4 to 6 servings

1. Mix ground beef, onion and garlic in 2-quart casserole. Microwave at HIGH (100%) until beef loses pink color, 5 to 9 minutes, stirring once to break up beef. Drain.

2. Stir in tomato sauce, water, chili powder, salt and pepper. Microwave at HIGH (100%) until sauce is slightly thickened, 6 to 10 minutes, stirring after half the cooking time. If using oven other than Sharp Carousel, rotate casserole once or twice during cooking.

3. Alternately layer tortillas, meat sauce and cheese in 1½-quart round casserole, ending with layer of cheese. Microwave at HIGH (100%) until cheese is melted and bubbly, 1 to 3 minutes. Let stand 2 to 3 minutes.

◄ South of the Border Eggplant

1 pound ground beef
4 slices bacon, cut into ½-inch pieces
½ cup chopped onion
½ cup chopped green pepper
1 clove garlic, minced
1 medium eggplant, cut into ½-inch cubes
   (6 to 8 cups)
1 can (16 ounces) tomato sauce
¼ teaspoon pepper
1 cup shredded mozzarella cheese
   (about 4 ounces)

Makes 4 to 6 servings

1. Place ground beef in medium bowl. Microwave at HIGH (100%) until beef loses pink color, 5 to 9 minutes, stirring to break up beef after half the cooking time. Drain and set aside.

2. Mix bacon, onion, green pepper and garlic in rectangular baking dish, 12 × 8 inches or 10-inch square casserole. Microwave at HIGH (100%) until green pepper is tender and bacon is crisp, 4 to 8 minutes.

3. Stir in ground beef, eggplant, tomato sauce and pepper. Cover with plastic wrap. Microwave at HIGH (100%) until eggplant is tender, 12 to 16 minutes, stirring once or twice during cooking. Sprinkle with cheese. Microwave at HIGH (100%) until cheese melts, 1 to 2½ minutes.

Stuffed Green Peppers

3 medium green peppers
1 pound lean ground beef
1 can (8 ounces) tomato sauce
½ cup uncooked instant rice
1 egg, slightly beaten
½ teaspoon dried oregano leaves
½ teaspoon salt
¼ teaspoon pepper
⅛ teaspoon garlic powder
¼ cup catsup or tomato sauce

Makes 6 servings

1. Cut green peppers in half lengthwise. Remove seeds and membranes. Set aside.

2. Mix ground beef, tomato sauce, rice, egg, oregano, salt, pepper and garlic powder. Spoon into pepper halves. Place on roasting rack. Cover loosely with waxed paper.

3. Microwave at HIGH (100%) until green peppers are tender, 12 to 16 minutes. If using oven other than Sharp Carousel, rearrange peppers after half the cooking time. Top each green pepper with catsup during last 2 minutes of cooking.

Fiesta Tamale Pie

1 package (8½ ounces) corn muffin mix
1 egg
⅓ cup milk
1 pound ground beef
¼ pound bulk pork sausage
¼ cup chopped onion
1 clove garlic, minced
1 can (16 ounces) stewed tomatoes, drained
1 can (12 ounces) whole kernel corn, drained
1 can (6 ounces) tomato paste
1½ teaspoons chili powder
1 teaspoon salt
¼ cup pitted ripe olives, sliced
½ cup shredded Cheddar cheese (about 2 ounces)
Dash of paprika

Makes 4 to 6 servings

1. Mix corn muffin mix, egg and milk until just moistened. Set aside.

2. Mix ground beef, sausage, onion and garlic in square baking dish, 8 × 8 inches. Microwave at HIGH (100%) until meat loses pink color, 5 to 9 minutes, stirring once to break up beef. Drain. Stir in tomatoes, corn, tomato paste, chili powder and salt. Microwave at HIGH (100%) until mixture thickens, 4 to 8 minutes. Stir in olives.

3. Spread corn muffin mixture over beef mixture. Microwave at MEDIUM-HIGH (70%) 5 minutes. Increase power to HIGH (100%). Microwave until center is set, 4 to 8 minutes, sprinkling with cheese and paprika during last 2 minutes of cooking. If using oven other than Sharp Carousel, rotate baking dish quarter turn every 2 minutes.

◄ Roast Loin of Pork with Apricot Glaze

1 cup coarsely chopped dried apricots
¾ cup orange juice
½ cup apricot nectar
  Juice and peel of ½ medium lemon, seeds removed
1 tablespoon honey
¼ teaspoon ground cinnamon
3½ pound boneless pork loin roast

Makes 4 to 6 servings

1. Mix all ingredients except pork roast in medium bowl or 4-cup measure. Microwave at HIGH (100%) until apricots are tender, 8 to 10 minutes, stirring 2 or 3 times during cooking. Remove lemon peel. Set glaze aside.

2. Place pork roast on roasting rack. Cover with half of the glaze. Place thin strips of aluminum foil over top of each end of roast. Microwave at HIGH (100%) 5 minutes. Reduce power to MEDIUM-HIGH (70%). Microwave until internal temperature reaches 175°, 25 to 40 minutes, removing foil strips after first 15 minutes and basting 2 or 3 times with glaze during cooking. If using oven other than Sharp Carousel, rotate roasting rack half turn once during cooking.

3. Let stand loosely wrapped in aluminum foil until internal temperature reaches 185°, 10 to 15 minutes. Spoon any remaining glaze over roast.

Pork Chops and Sauerkraut

1 can (16 ounces) sauerkraut, undrained
1 small onion, thinly sliced and separated into rings
4 pork chops, about ½ inch thick
1 tablespoon water
¼ teaspoon brown bouquet sauce
½ teaspoon caraway seed
1 medium tart apple, cored and cut into thin rings

Makes 4 servings

1. Layer sauerkraut and onions in square baking dish, 8 × 8 inches. Top with pork chops. Mix water and bouquet sauce; brush over pork chops. Sprinkle with caraway. Cover with waxed paper.

2. Microwave at MEDIUM (50%) 10 minutes. Rearrange pork chops; top with apple. Cover. Microwave at MEDIUM (50%) until meat next to bone is no longer pink and apple rings are tender, 5 to 7 minutes. If using oven other than Sharp Carousel, rotate baking dish 2 or 3 times.

Applesauce-Barbecued ► Spareribs

- 1 medium onion, thinly sliced and separated into rings
- 1 tablespoon margarine or butter
- 1 cup applesauce
- ½ cup catsup
- 2 tablespoons lemon juice
- 1 tablespoon Worcestershire sauce
- ½ teaspoon salt
- ⅛ teaspoon pepper
- 2½ pounds fresh pork spareribs, cut into 2- or 3-rib pieces

Makes 3 to 4 servings

1. Mix onion and margarine in a small bowl. Microwave at HIGH (100%) until tender, 3 to 5 minutes. Stir in remaining ingredients except spareribs. Microwave at HIGH (100%) until hot and bubbly, 4 to 6 minutes, stirring 2 or 3 times during cooking. Set barbecue sauce aside.

2. Arrange spareribs in rectangular baking dish, 12 × 8 inches or 10-inch square casserole. Spread with ¾ cup of the barbecue sauce. Cover tightly with plastic wrap. Microwave at HIGH (100%) 5 minutes. Reduce power to MEDIUM (50%). Microwave 20 minutes. Rearrange and turn spareribs over. Cover.

3. Microwave at MEDIUM (50%) until fork-tender, 20 to 25 minutes. If using oven other than Sharp Carousel, rotate baking dish every 10 minutes during cooking. Drain. Spread remaining barbecue sauce over spareribs. Microwave, uncovered, at MEDIUM (50%) until barbecue sauce is hot and spareribs are glazed, 4 to 6 minutes.

Baked Pork Chops

- 4 pork loin or rib chops, ¾ inch thick
- 2 tablespoons Worcestershire sauce
- ¼ teaspoon dried thyme leaves
  Dash of pepper

Makes 4 servings

1. Arrange pork chops on roasting rack with meatiest portions to outside. Mix Worcestershire sauce, thyme and pepper. Brush half of the mixture over pork chops. Cover with waxed paper. Microwave at MEDIUM (50%) 8 minutes. Turn over and rearrange pork chops. Brush with remaining sauce.

2. Microwave, uncovered, at MEDIUM (50%) until meat next to bone is no longer pink, 4 to 10 minutes. If using oven other than Sharp Carousel, rotate rack 2 or 3 times during cooking.

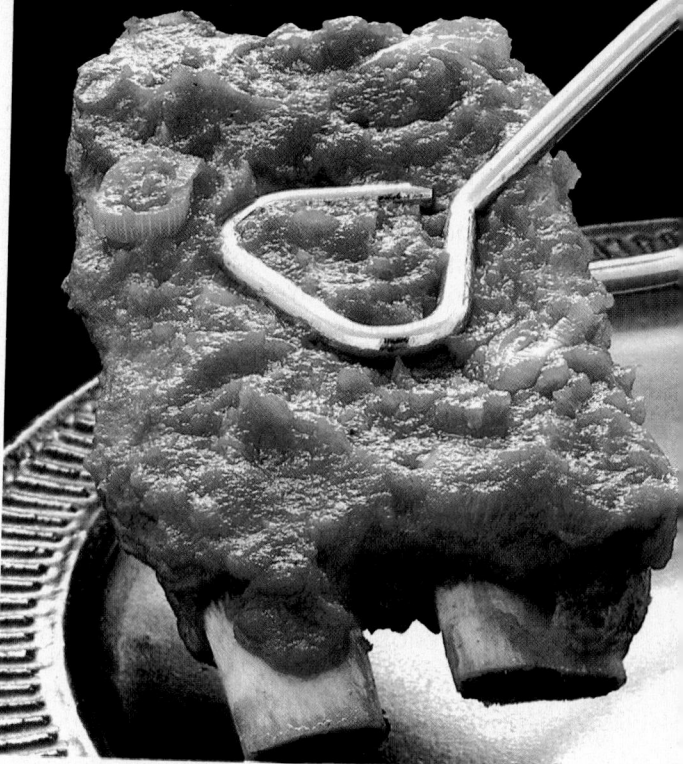

Almond-Stuffed Pork Chops

- ¼ cup chopped celery
- ¼ cup chopped onion
- ¼ cup chopped almonds
- 1 tablespoon margarine or butter
- 2 cups soft bread cubes
- 1 teaspoon instant chicken bouillon
- ½ teaspoon dried parsley flakes
- 2 tablespoons water
- ¼ teaspoon almond extract
- 4 pork loin or rib chops, about 1 inch thick (with pockets cut into chops on meat side)
- 1 tablespoon water
- ¼ teaspoon brown bouquet sauce

Makes 4 servings

1. Combine celery, onion, almonds and margarine in small bowl. Microwave at HIGH (100%) until celery is tender, 3 to 4 minutes, stirring after half the time. Stir in bread cubes, bouillon, parsley, 2 tablespoons water and the almond extract.

2. Divide stuffing mixture into four equal portions. Spoon into each pork chop pocket; place on roasting rack. Mix 1 tablespoon water and the bouquet sauce. Brush pork chops with half of the bouquet sauce mixture. Cover with waxed paper.

3. Microwave at MEDIUM (50%) 10 minutes. Turn over and rearrange pork chops. Brush with remaining bouquet sauce mixture. Microwave, uncovered, at MEDIUM (50%) until meat next to bone is no longer pink, 7 to 10 minutes.

Cinnamon Spareribs ▾

½ cup soy sauce
2 tablespoons packed brown sugar
½ teaspoon ground cinnamon
¼ teaspoon ground cloves
2½ pounds fresh pork spareribs, cut into
   2-rib pieces
1 tablespoon cornstarch
2 tablespoons water

Makes 2 to 4 servings

1. Mix soy sauce, brown sugar, cinnamon and cloves in small bowl or 1-cup measure. Microwave at HIGH (100%) until hot, 30 seconds to 1 minute, stirring 2 or 3 times during cooking. Arrange spareribs in rectangular baking dish, 12×8 inches or 10-inch square casserole. Pour soy sauce mixture over spareribs. Cover tightly with plastic wrap or glass cover.

2. Microwave at HIGH (100%) 5 minutes. Reduce power to MEDIUM (50%). Microwave 20 minutes. Rearrange and turn spareribs over. Cover. Microwave at MEDIUM (50%) until fork-tender, 20 to 25 minutes. If using oven other than Sharp Carousel, rotate baking dish every 10 minutes during cooking.

3. Drain liquid; reserve. Microwave spareribs, uncovered, at MEDIUM (50%) 4 minutes. Skim fat from reserved meat juices. Mix cornstarch and water. Stir into meat juices. Microwave at HIGH (100%) until thickened, 1½ to 2 minutes, stirring after half the cooking time. Serve over spareribs.

Sweet and Sour Pork

2 tablespoons packed brown sugar
2 tablespoons cornstarch
1 can (8 ounces) pineapple chunks
   (juice pack), drained (reserve juice)
¼ cup teriyaki sauce
3 tablespoons cider vinegar
1½ teaspoons catsup
1 pound boneless pork shoulder, cut into
   ¾-inch cubes
2 medium green peppers, cut into
   ¾-inch chunks

Makes 4 servings

1. Mix brown sugar and cornstarch in 2-quart casserole. Blend in pineapple juice, teriyaki sauce, vinegar and catsup. Stir in pork and pepper.

2. Cover. Microwave at HIGH (100%) 5 minutes. Stir in pineapple chunks. Cover. Microwave at MEDIUM (50%) until pork is cooked and sauce is thickened, 12 to 15 minutes, stirring once. Serve over rice, if desired.

Oriental Pork and Tomato Casserole

1 pound boneless pork loin, cut into
   thin strips
1 cup thinly sliced celery
1 medium onion, thinly sliced and
   separated into rings
1 clove garlic, minced
1 tablespoon cornstarch
2 tablespoons soy sauce
1 tablespoon water
1 tablespoon packed brown sugar
¼ teaspoon ground ginger
1 medium green pepper, thinly sliced
1 medium tomato, peeled and cut into
   wedges

Makes 4 servings

1. Combine pork, celery, onion and garlic in 2-quart casserole. Microwave at HIGH (100%) until pork loses pink color, 5 to 10 minutes, stirring twice during cooking. Drain.

2. Mix cornstarch, soy sauce and water. Stir soy sauce mixture, brown sugar, ginger and green pepper into pork. Microwave at HIGH (100%) until pepper is tender-crisp and sauce is thickened, 4 to 5 minutes, stirring after half the time.

3. Stir in tomato wedges. Microwave at HIGH (100%) until tomatoes are hot and green pepper is tender, 1½ to 2 minutes.

Glazed Baked Ham ►

3 pound canned ham
1 can (8 ounces) pineapple slices
 (juice pack), drained (reserve juice)
½ cup packed brown sugar
1 teaspoon dry mustard
16 whole cloves

Makes 6 to 8 servings

1. Place ham on roasting rack in rectangular baking dish, 12 × 8 inches or 10-inch square casserole. Cover loosely with plastic wrap. Microwave at MEDIUM-HIGH (70%) 15 minutes. Set aside.

2. Mix 3 tablespoons reserved pineapple juice, brown sugar and mustard in small bowl. Microwave at MEDIUM-HIGH (70%) until hot, 1 to 1½ minutes, stirring after half the cooking time. Place 4 cloves in each pineapple slice; arrange on top of ham. Pour half of the glaze over ham. Cover.

3. Microwave at MEDIUM-HIGH (70%) until internal temperature reaches 130°, 20 to 30 minutes, brushing with glaze 2 or 3 times. Cover with aluminum foil. Let stand 5 to 10 minutes.

Layered Dinner

1 can (16 ounces) French-style green
 beans, drained
1 can (10¾ ounces) condensed cream of
 celery soup
½ cup shredded Cheddar cheese
 (about 2 ounces)
½ cup seasoned croutons
¼ cup mayonnaise or salad dressing
1 teaspoon prepared mustard
3 cups diced fully cooked ham
¼ cup shredded Cheddar cheese
 (about 1 ounce)
1 can (3 ounces) French-fried onions

Makes 4 to 6 servings

1. Mix green beans, soup, ½ cup cheese, the croutons, mayonnaise and mustard.

2. Layer half each of the ham and green bean mixture in 1-quart casserole. Repeat once. Cover with waxed paper. Microwave at MEDIUM-HIGH (70%) until hot and bubbly, 13 to 15 minutes. If using oven other than Sharp Carousel, rotate casserole quarter turn every 5 minutes.

3. Sprinkle with ¼ cup cheese and the French-fried onions. Microwave, uncovered, at MEDIUM-HIGH (70%) until cheese is melted, 3 to 4 minutes.

Ham Loaf

¾ pound ground ham
½ pound ground veal
¼ pound ground pork
2 eggs, beaten
½ cup dry bread crumbs
½ cup pineapple juice
¼ cup chopped onion
1 teaspoon prepared mustard
⅛ teaspoon pepper
¼ cup packed brown sugar
2 tablespoons pineapple juice
2 teaspoons prepared mustard

Makes 4 to 6 servings

1. Mix ham, veal and pork in medium bowl. Mix eggs, bread crumbs, ½ cup pineapple juice, the onion, 1 teaspoon mustard and the pepper. Stir into meat mixture. Press into loaf dish, 9 × 5 inches.

2. Mix brown sugar, 2 tablespoons pineapple juice and 2 teaspoons mustard. Spread over ham loaf. Microwave at MEDIUM-HIGH (70%) until internal temperature reaches 160°, 15 to 25 minutes. If using oven other than Sharp Carousel, rotate dish quarter turn every 5 minutes. Let stand, covered, with aluminum foil 5 to 10 minutes.

◄ Ham-Broccoli Rolls

1 package (10 ounces) frozen broccoli spears
1 tablespoon margarine or butter
2 tablespoons all-purpose flour
2 teaspoons prepared horseradish
2 teaspoons prepared mustard
½ teaspoon Worcestershire sauce
½ teaspoon instant minced onion
   Pineapple juice
1 can (8 ounces) pineapple slices (juice pack), drained (reserve juice)
½ cup milk
1 egg, slightly beaten
4 1-ounce slices Swiss cheese (⅛ inch thick)
4 1-ounce slices boiled ham

Makes 4 servings

1. Place broccoli spears in 1-quart casserole. Microwave at HIGH (100%) until tender, 4 to 6 minutes; drain. Set aside.

2. Place margarine in a small bowl. Microwave at HIGH (100%) until hot and bubbly, 30 to 45 seconds. Stir in flour, horseradish, mustard, Worcestershire and instant onion. Add enough pineapple juice to reserved juice to measure 1 cup. Stir juice and milk into flour mixture. Blend in egg.

3. Microwave at MEDIUM-HIGH (70%) until thickened, 4 to 5 minutes, stirring after half the cooking time. If using oven other than Sharp Carousel, stir 2 or 3 times during cooking. Set sauce aside.

4. Divide broccoli spears into 4 equal portions. Place a cheese slice on top of each ham slice. Place broccoli spears on top of cheese. Spoon 1 tablespoon sauce over each. Roll ham and cheese around broccoli; place seam side down in loaf dish, 9 × 5 inches.

5. Pour ¼ cup sauce over ham-broccoli rolls. Top with pineapple slices. Microwave at MEDIUM-HIGH (70%) until cheese is melted and sauce bubbly, 4 to 6 minutes. If using oven other than Sharp Carousel, rotate loaf dish half turn every minute. Microwave remaining sauce at MEDIUM-HIGH (70%) until hot, 30 seconds to 1 minute. Stir. Serve over ham-broccoli rolls.

Directions for bacon are in Learn While You Cook, page 23.

Directions for Chili Cheese Dog are in Learn While You Cook, page 30.

Sausage Casserole ▲

1 pound bulk pork sausage
1 medium onion, chopped
¼ cup chopped green pepper
1 teaspoon brown bouquet sauce
1 pound head green cabbage, chopped
1 can (8 ounces) whole peeled tomatoes
1 tablespoon sugar
1 tablespoon all-purpose flour
¼ teaspoon dried oregano leaves
¼ teaspoon salt
¼ teaspoon pepper
⅛ teaspoon ground sage

Makes 4 to 6 servings

1. Crumble sausage into 2-quart casserole. Stir in onion and green pepper. Microwave at MEDI-UM-HIGH (70%) until sausage loses pink color, 7 to 10 minutes, stirring every 3 minutes. Drain off excess fat. Toss with bouquet sauce.

2. Stir in remaining ingredients. Microwave at MEDIUM-HIGH (70%) until cabbage is tender, 25 to 30 minutes.

Bratwurst in Beer

1 pound uncooked bratwurst
1 can (12 ounces) beer
1 can (16 ounces) sauerkraut, drained
4 to 6 hot dog buns

Makes 4 to 6 servings

1. Combine bratwurst and beer in 2-quart casserole; cover. Microwave at HIGH (100%) 5 minutes. Reduce power to MEDIUM-HIGH (70%). Microwave until internal temperature reaches 170°, 17 to 20 minutes, stirring once. If using oven other than Sharp Carousel, stir 2 or 3 times.

2. Add sauerkraut; cover and let stand 5 minutes. Serve on buns.

Polish Sausage and Macaroni

7 ounces elbow macaroni (about 2 cups), cooked and drained
1 jar (8 ounces) cheese spread
¼ cup half-and-half or milk
2 teaspoons onion powder
2 teaspoons prepared brown mustard
1 pound fully cooked Polish sausage, cut diagonally into ½-inch slices

Makes 4 to 6 servings

1. Combine macaroni and cheese spread in 2-quart casserole. Microwave at HIGH (100%) to soften cheese, 45 seconds to 1 minute. Stir to coat macaroni with cheese.

2. Mix in half-and-half, onion powder and mustard. Stir in sliced sausages. Microwave at MEDIUM-HIGH (70%) until hot, 7 to 10 minutes, stirring after half the cooking time. If using oven other than Sharp Carousel, stir 2 or 3 times.

Ring Bologna and Beans

¼ cup chopped onion
1 pound ring bologna, skin removed and cut into ½-inch slices
1 can (32 ounces) pork and beans
1 can (8 ounces) crushed pineapple (juice pack)
¼ cup chili sauce

Makes 4 to 6 servings

1. Place onion in 2-quart casserole. Microwave at HIGH (100%) until tender, 1½ to 2½ minutes. Stir in remaining ingredients; cover.

2. Microwave at MEDIUM-HIGH (70%) until hot, 8 to 12 minutes, stirring once during cooking. If using oven other than Sharp Carousel, stir twice during cooking. Let stand 2 minutes.

◄ Leg of Lamb with Sherry-Herb Sauce

4 to 5-pound leg of lamb
2 cloves garlic, cut into thin slices
1 teaspoon dried tarragon leaves
1 teaspoon dried rosemary leaves
1 teaspoon margarine or butter
2 tablespoons margarine or butter
1 tablespoon all-purpose flour
1½ cups half-and-half
1 tablespoon sherry
½ teaspoon salt
¼ teaspoon dried tarragon leaves
¼ teaspoon dried rosemary leaves

Makes 4 to 6 servings

1. Cut small slits in lamb roast. Place garlic slices in slits. Mix 1 teaspoon each tarragon, rosemary and margarine in small bowl. Microwave at HIGH (100%) until margarine is melted, 30 to 45 seconds. Spread over lamb roast. Place roast fat side down on roasting rack. Estimate total cooking time; divide in half.

2. Microwave at HIGH (100%) 5 minutes. Reduce power to MEDIUM (50%). Microwave remaining part of first half of cooking time. Turn roast over. Microwave until lamb reaches desired internal temperature. Let stand 10 minutes covered with aluminum foil. Remove garlic slices.

3. While lamb roast is standing, place 2 tablespoons margarine in small bowl. Microwave at HIGH (100%) until melted, 30 seconds to 1 minute. Blend in flour, half-and-half and sherry. Stir in salt and ¼ teaspoon each tarragon and rosemary. Microwave at MEDIUM-HIGH (70%) until thickened and hot, 3 to 4 minutes, stirring after half the cooking time. Pour over slices of roast.

Doneness	Time/Pound	Internal Temperature
Rare	8-11 min./lb.	120°
Medium	9-12¾ min./lb.	135°
Well Done	10-14 min./lb.	150°

Lamb Chops à l'Orange

4 lamb rib chops, about 1½ inches thick
¼ teaspoon garlic salt
½ cup orange marmalade
4 ¼-inch thick orange slices

Makes 4 servings

1. Sprinkle both sides of lamb chops lightly with garlic salt. Place in 10-inch square casserole with meatiest portions toward outside of casserole. Spoon one-fourth of the marmalade on each lamb chop; top each with 1 orange slice. Cover.

2. Microwave at MEDIUM-HIGH (70%) until lamb chops are desired doneness, 12 to 13 minutes. If using oven other than Sharp Carousel, rotate casserole and rearrange lamb chops 2 or 3 times during cooking.

Sweet and Sour Lamb Chops

1 can (8 ounces) pineapple chunks (juice pack), drained (reserve juice)
¼ cup packed brown sugar
¼ cup cider vinegar
2 tablespoons cornstarch
1 tablespoon soy sauce
2 carrots, thinly sliced
1 large green pepper, cut into 1-inch pieces
4 lamb rib chops, about 1½ inches thick

Makes 4 servings

1. Mix pineapple juice, brown sugar, vinegar, cornstarch and soy sauce in 4-cup measure. Stir in carrots, green pepper and pineapple. Microwave at HIGH (100%) until thickened, 3 to 7 minutes, stirring after half the cooking time. Set sauce aside.

2. Preheat 10-inch browning dish at HIGH (100%) 5 minutes. Place lamb chops on browning dish. Microwave at HIGH (100%) 1 minute; turn chops over. Microwave at HIGH (100%) 1 minute. Pour sauce over lamb chops; cover.

3. Microwave at MEDIUM-HIGH (70%) until lamb chops are desired doneness, 13 to 23 minutes. Rearrange lamb chops and stir sauce after half the cooking time.

Lamb Stew

2 pounds boneless lamb, cut into 1-inch cubes
2½ cups hot water
2 medium potatoes, cut into ½-inch cubes (about 2 cups)
2 medium carrots, thinly sliced
¼ cup all-purpose flour
1 clove garlic, minced
1 bay leaf
1 teaspoon dried thyme leaves
1 teaspoon salt
¼ teaspoon pepper
½ teaspoon brown bouquet sauce
1 package (10 ounces) frozen chopped broccoli

Makes 6 to 8 servings

1. Mix all ingredients except broccoli in a shallow 3-quart casserole; cover. Microwave at HIGH (100%) 10 minutes. Reduce power to MEDIUM-HIGH (70%). Microwave until lamb is tender, 30 to 35 minutes, stirring 2 or 3 times during cooking.

2. Add broccoli; cover. Microwave at MEDIUM-HIGH (70%) until stew is thickened and broccoli is tender, 15 to 20 minutes, stirring after half the cooking time. Let stand 5 minutes.

Lamb and Rice Casserole

1 medium green pepper, chopped
1 medium onion, chopped
1 tablespoon olive oil
1 clove garlic, minced
1 pound boneless lamb, cut into ¾-inch cubes
2 cups uncooked instant rice
1½ cups hot water
1 can (8 ounces) tomato sauce
1 teaspoon salt
½ teaspoon dried oregano leaves
½ teaspoon dried basil leaves
¼ teaspoon paprika
⅛ teaspoon pepper

Makes 4 servings

1. Combine green pepper, onion, oil and garlic in 2-quart casserole; cover. Microwave at HIGH (100%) until vegetables are tender, 3 to 6 minutes.

2. Stir in remaining ingredients; cover. Microwave at HIGH (100%) 5 minutes. Reduce power to MEDIUM-HIGH (70%). Microwave until lamb and rice are tender, 10 to 15 minutes, stirring once. Let stand 5 minutes.

Shepherd's Pie ▲

1½ pounds boneless lamb, cut
into ¾-inch cubes
2 medium tomatoes, chopped
1 medium onion, thinly sliced and
separated into rings
¼ cup all-purpose flour
2 teaspoons instant chicken bouillon
½ teaspoon salt
¼ teaspoon pepper
¾ cup water
6 servings instant mashed potatoes

Makes 4 to 6 servings

1. Place lamb, tomatoes and onion in 3-quart casserole. Mix flour, bouillon, salt, pepper and water; stir into lamb and vegetables. Cover.

2. Microwave at HIGH (100%) 5 minutes. Stir. Reduce power to MEDIUM-HIGH (70%). Microwave, covered, until lamb is tender, 25 to 30 minutes, stirring after half the cooking time. If using oven other than Sharp Carousel, stir 3 to 4 times during cooking.

3. Let stand, covered, while preparing potatoes according to package directions. Spoon mounds of hot mashed potatoes over lamb mixture. Microwave at HIGH (100%) 1 minute to set potatoes.

Veal Italienne

1 teaspoon vegetable oil
4 veal rib chops, about 1 inch thick
1 can (8 ounces) tomato sauce
2 tablespoons red wine
1 teaspoon dried oregano leaves
1 teaspoon dried chopped chives
½ teaspoon sugar
¼ teaspoon pepper
2 tablespoons grated Parmesan cheese

Makes 4 servings

1. Preheat 10-inch browning dish at HIGH (100%) 5 minutes. Immediately add oil and veal chops. Microwave at HIGH (100%) 1 minute. Turn chops over, placing meatiest portion toward outside of dish. Microwave at HIGH (100%) 1 minute.

2. Mix remaining ingredients except Parmesan cheese; pour over veal chops. Microwave at MEDIUM-HIGH (70%) 10 minutes. Sprinkle veal chops with cheese. If using oven other than Sharp Carousel, rearrange veal chops. Microwave at MEDIUM-HIGH (70%) until veal chops are tender, 6 to 9 minutes.

Veal Continental ▼

- 1 cup thinly·sliced fresh mushrooms
- ½ cup chopped onion
- 2 tablespoons margarine or butter
- 1½ pounds boneless veal, cut into ¾- to 1-inch cubes
- 1 cup water
- 1 can (8 ounces) tomato sauce
- ¼ cup all-purpose flour
- 2 teaspoons instant beef bouillon
- 1 bay leaf
- ½ teaspoon salt
- ¼ teaspoon pepper
- 1 medium tomato, cut into 8 wedges

Makes 4 servings

1. Combine mushrooms, onion and margarine in 2-quart casserole. Microwave at HIGH (100%) until onion is tender, 5 to 7 minutes. Stir in remaining ingredients except tomato wedges. Cover. Microwave at HIGH (100%) 5 minutes. Reduce power to MEDIUM-HIGH (70%). Microwave until veal is tender, 20 to 25 minutes, stirring after half the cooking time.

2. Stir in tomato wedges; cover. Microwave at MEDIUM-HIGH (70%) until tomatoes are tender, 6 to 8 minutes, stirring after half the cooking time. Serve over noodles or rice, if desired.

Veal á la Madelon

- 2 slices bacon, chopped
- ½ cup all-purpose flour
- 1 cup water
- 2 pounds boneless veal, cut into 1-inch cubes
- 1 package (10 ounces) frozen pearl onions
- 8 ounces fresh mushrooms, sliced
- 2 medium carrots, thinly sliced
- 1 clove garlic, minced
- 1 tablespoon dried parsley flakes
- 1 teaspoon salt
- ½ teaspoon grated lemon peel
- ¼ teaspoon pepper
- ½ cup dairy sour cream
- ¼ cup whipping cream

Makes 4 to 6 servings

1. Place bacon in 3-quart casserole; cover. Microwave at HIGH (100%) until bacon is light brown, 3 to 4 minutes. Mix flour and water; stir flour mixture and remaining ingredients except sour cream and whipping cream into casserole; cover.

2. Microwave at MEDIUM-HIGH (70%) until veal and vegetables are tender and sauce is thickened, 35 to 40 minutes. Blend in sour cream and whipping cream. Serve over rice or noodles, if desired.

POULTRY

Make frequent use of your microwave oven to prepare fast, easy, flavorful poultry. Microwaved poultry stays tender and juicy. The white meat won't dry out before the dark meat is done, as can happen in conventional cooking.

A large holiday bird is best roasted conventionally while you use the microwave oven for side dishes, but small turkeys are so easy to microwave that many families serve them as often as chicken, and enjoy the leftovers in casseroles, salads and sandwiches.

Roast Turkey

12 pound ready-to-cook turkey, giblets removed

Makes 12 to 14 servings

1. Place turkey breast side down on roasting rack or on inverted saucer in rectangular baking dish, 12 × 8 inches or 10-inch square casserole. Calculate total cooking time allowing 9 to 12 minutes per pound. Divide total time in half.

2. Microwave at HIGH (100%) 10 minutes. Reduce power to MEDIUM-HIGH (70%). Microwave remainder of first half of the total time. Turn turkey breast side up; baste. Shield turkey with aluminum foil as needed.

3. Microwave last half of total time or until internal temperature reaches 170° after 1 minute when meat thermometer is inserted in meatiest part of breast and thigh on both sides of turkey. If using oven other than Sharp Carousel, rotate baking dish 3 to 4 times during cooking. Let stand tented with aluminum foil 20 minutes.

Microwaving Poultry: Preparation

Recipe Conversion

Your favorite glazes, crumb coatings or stuffings can be used for microwaved poultry without any changes in ingredients. Sauté vegetables and sausage for stuffings in the mixing bowl to save preparation and clean-up time.

Recipes for casseroles and saucy chicken pieces convert easily. Reduce liquid as directed in Recipe Conversion, page 42, unless it is needed to rehydrate pasta. Because microwaving extracts fat from uncooked poultry, skim fat before finishing sauces. To take full advantage of microwave speed, substitute quick-cooking for long-grain rice and use a broiler-fryer in chicken soups and stews. Stewing hens take almost as much time in the microwave as they do conventionally.

There's no need to wait for leftovers when you want to prepare a casserole using cooked chicken. 2½ to 3½ pounds of chicken pieces microwave in minutes, following directions on page 24, and yield 2 to 3 cups of cut-up meat.

Defrost frozen poultry completely before cooking. Microwave defrosting is faster and safer than defrosting at room temperature. While you may defrost larger turkeys, the best size for microwave roasted turkey is 12 pounds or less.

Browning occurs naturally on microwaved turkey. Smaller birds and poultry pieces develop a light golden color which is satisfying to many people. For deeper color, sprinkle with dry microwave browning agent; brush on or rub a liquid agent into well-dried skin. For flavor as well as eye appeal, brush pieces with melted butter and sprinkle with paprika, or rub skin with soy sauce before microwaving; glaze whole birds during the last few minutes of microwaving; cook pieces in a colorful sauce or crisp coating.

Microwaving Poultry: Turkey

Place turkey, breast side down in baking dish. Estimate the total cooking time following recipe on page 97; divide in half. Microwave at HIGH (100%) to start cooking quickly, then reduce power to MEDIUM-HIGH (70%) and microwave remainder of first half of cooking time.

Turn turkey breast side up. Baste with drippings or melted butter. Shield areas which may be cooking too fast, such as wing or leg tips. Microwave for second half of cooking time, or until leg moves freely and flesh feels soft when pressed.

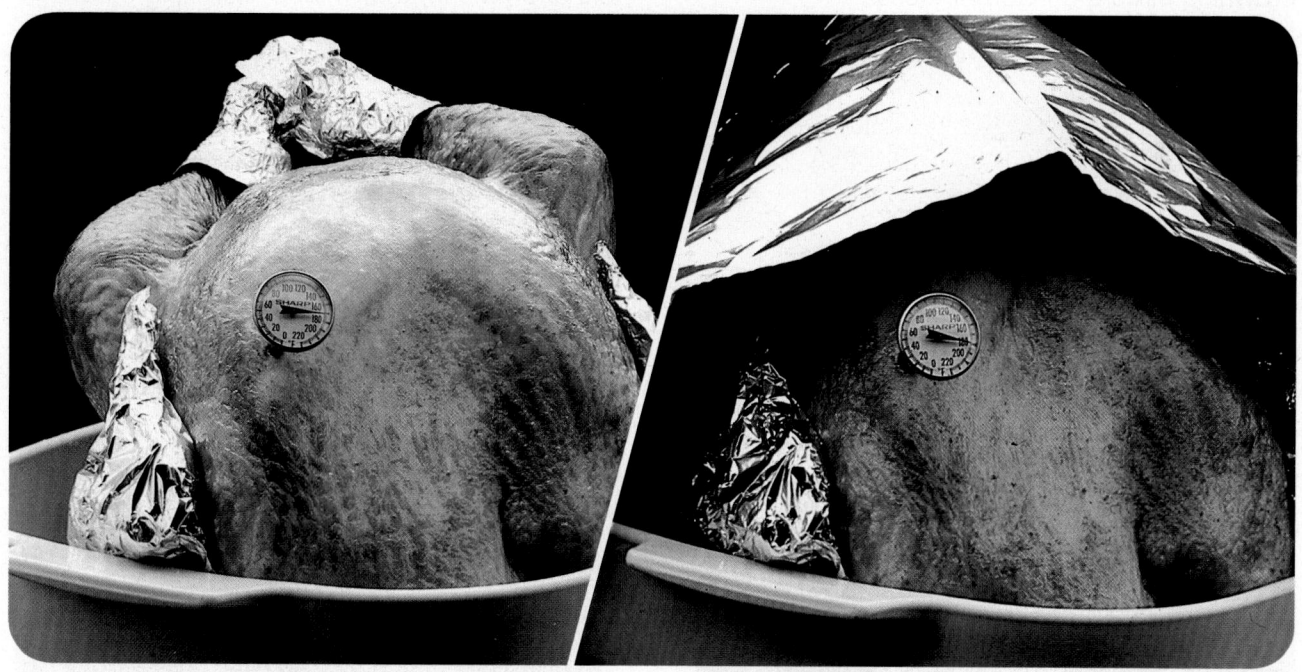

Insert a thermometer in the meatiest part of thigh and breast on both sides. After 1 minute, internal temperature should register 175°. If you microwave turkey with a temperature probe, hot fat may cause the probe to register done and shut off the oven before cooking is completed. Move probe to another place and continue cooking. Let turkey stand, tented with foil, 20 minutes. During standing, the internal temperature will equalize and rise to 185°.

Microwaving Poultry: Chicken, Ducks and Cornish Hens

Microwave other whole birds as you do turkey; however, chicken may be started breast side up and need not be turned over. When microwaving duck, drain fat several times during cooking. Use a browning mixture on Cornish hens.

Arrange poultry pieces on paper towel-lined carousel with meatiest portions to outside. Use baking dish for recipes with sauces. Cook uncovered or cover with waxed paper to prevent spatters and hold in heat without steaming meat.

Turn pieces over after half the cooking time. Do not turn over pieces with crumb coating or surface will become moist. If using oven other than Sharp Carousel, rearrange pieces so least cooked areas are toward outside of dish.

Test whole birds and parts for doneness by cutting meat near the bone. Juices should run clear and meat should no longer be pink.

Poultry Roasting Chart

Cut	Microwave Time: Start	Microwave Time: Finish	Internal Temp. at Removal	Internal Temp. after Standing
Chicken				
Whole	HIGH (100%) 3 min.	MED.-HIGH (70%) 9-13 min./lb.	175°	185°
Pieces		HIGH (100%) 6-9 min./lb.	175°	185°
Turkey				
Whole, up to 12 lbs.	HIGH (100%) 10 min.	MED.-HIGH (70%) 9-12 min./lb.	175°	185°
Breast	HIGH (100%) 5 min.	MED.-HIGH (70%) 8-12 min./lb.	175°	185°
Quarters or Halves	HIGH (100%) 10 min.	MED. (50%) 13-16 min./lb.	175°	185°
Legs or Thighs	HIGH (100%) 5 min.	MED. (50%) 12½-17½ min./lb.	175°	185°
Cornish Hen		HIGH (100%) 5½-9 min./lb.	175°	185°
Duck				
	HIGH (100%) 10 min.	MED. (50%) 7-10 min./lb.	175°	185°

Turkey Divan

- 2 tablespoons margarine or butter
- 2 tablespoons all-purpose flour
- 1/3 cup hot water
- 1 to 2 teaspoons instant chicken bouillon
- 1/4 cup whipping cream
- 2 tablespoons sherry
- 1/8 teaspoon nutmeg
- 1/4 cup grated Parmesan cheese
- 1 pound sliced cooked turkey or chicken
- 1 package (10 ounces) frozen broccoli spears, thawed
- 2 tablespoons grated Parmesan cheese
  Dash of paprika

Makes 4 servings

1. Place margarine in medium bowl. Microwave at HIGH (100%) until melted, 30 seconds to 1 minute. Blend in flour. Stir in water, bouillon, cream, sherry and nutmeg. Microwave at MEDIUM-HIGH (70%) until thickened, 4 to 7 minutes, stirring 2 or 3 times. Stir in 1/4 cup Parmesan. Set aside.

2. Place turkey slices in square baking dish, 8 × 8 inches. Arrange broccoli spears over top. Pour cream sauce over broccoli. Sprinkle with 2 tablespoons Parmesan cheese and the paprika. Microwave at MEDIUM-HIGH (70%) until heated through, 6 to 8 minutes. If using oven other than Sharp Carousel, rotate dish half turn every 2 minutes.

Turkey Tetrazzini ►

- 1/4 cup margarine or butter
- 1/4 cup all-purpose flour
- 1 teaspoon instant chicken bouillon
- 1/4 teaspoon salt
- 1/4 teaspoon pepper
- 1/2 cup hot water
- 1 1/2 cups whipping cream
- 3 cups spaghetti, cooked and drained
- 2 cups cut-up cooked turkey or chicken
- 1 can (4 ounces) sliced mushrooms, drained
- 1 tablespoon dried parsley flakes
- 2 tablespoons sherry
- 2 tablespoons grated Parmesan cheese
- 2 tablespoons shredded Cheddar cheese

Makes 4 servings

1. Place margarine in 2-quart casserole. Microwave at HIGH (100%) until melted, 30 seconds to 1 minute. Blend in flour, instant bouillon, salt and pepper. Gradually stir in water and cream. Microwave at MEDIUM-HIGH (70%) until thickened, 6 to 9 minutes, stirring once or twice during cooking.

2. Stir in spaghetti, turkey, mushrooms, parsley and sherry. Sprinkle with Parmesan and Cheddar. Microwave at MEDIUM-HIGH (70%) until heated, 8 to 10 minutes. If using oven other than Sharp Carousel, rotate half turn after half the time.

Chicken with Rye Stuffing

- 1 tablespoon margarine or butter
- 1 tablespoon brown bouquet sauce
- 3 tablespoons margarine or butter
- 1/2 cup chopped onion
- 1/2 cup chopped celery
- 3 cups cubed rye or pumpernickel bread
- 2 tablespoons water
- 1 teaspoon instant chicken bouillon
- 1/4 teaspoon pepper
- 1/4 teaspoon caraway seed
- 2 1/2 to 3-pound broiler-fryer chicken

Makes 4 servings

1. Combine 1 tablespoon margarine and the bouquet sauce in custard cup. Microwave at HIGH (100%) until margarine is melted, 30 seconds to 1 minute. Set aside. Combine 3 tablespoons margarine, the onion and celery in medium bowl. Microwave at HIGH (100%) until celery is tender, 3 to 6 minutes. If using oven other than Sharp Carousel, stir after half the time. Stir in bread cubes, water, bouillon, pepper and caraway.

2. Fill chicken cavity loosely with stuffing. Close body cavity with wooden skewers. Coat with bouquet sauce mixture. Place breast side up on roasting rack in rectangular baking dish, 12 × 8 inches, or 10-inch square casserole.

3. Microwave at HIGH (100%) 3 minutes. Reduce power to MEDIUM-HIGH (70%). Microwave until internal temperature reaches 170° and chicken next to bone is not pink, 24 to 29 minutes. If using oven other than Sharp Carousel, rotate once or twice during cooking. Let stand loosely covered with aluminum foil 5 to 10 minutes.

◄ Oven-Fried Chicken

1 cup seasoned dry bread crumbs, corn flake crumbs or packaged chicken coating mix
1 teaspoon paprika
2½ to 3-pound broiler-fryer chicken, cut up
⅓ cup milk

Makes 4 servings

1. Mix crumbs and paprika. Coat chicken pieces with milk, then crumb mixture. Place coated chicken pieces on paper towel-lined carousel with meatiest portions towards outside of carousel.

2. Microwave at MEDIUM-HIGH (70%) until chicken next to bone is not pink, 18 to 25 minutes. If using oven other than Sharp Carousel, place coated chicken pieces in rectangular baking dish, 12 × 8 inches or 10-inch square casserole with meatiest portions toward outside of dish. Rotate dish and rearrange chicken after half the time.

◄ Barbecued Chicken

2 tablespoons chopped onion
1 clove garlic, minced
1 teaspoon margarine or butter
1 can (8 ounces) tomato sauce
¼ cup cider vinegar
3 tablespoons packed brown sugar
1 tablespoon Worcestershire sauce
1 teaspoon salt
¼ teaspoon pepper
⅛ to ¼ teaspoon celery seed
3 drops liquid smoke
2½ to 3-pound broiler-fryer chicken, cut up

Makes 4 servings

1. Place onion, garlic and margarine in 2-cup measure. Microwave at HIGH (100%) until onion is tender, 1 to 3 minutes. Stir in remaining ingredients except chicken. Cover with waxed paper. Microwave at HIGH (100%) 3 minutes. Stir. Reduce power to MEDIUM (50%). Microwave, covered, 10 minutes, stirring twice during cooking. Set sauce aside.

2. Place chicken skin side down on roasting rack in rectangular baking dish, 12 × 8 inches or 10-inch square casserole. Brush with one-third of the sauce. Microwave at MEDIUM-HIGH (70%) until chicken next to bone is not pink, 20 to 25 minutes. After half the cooking time turn chicken, rearrange and brush with one-third of the sauce. Brush with remaining sauce before serving.

Chicken Fricassee ▲

- 1 medium onion, thinly sliced and separated into rings
- 1½ cups hot water
- 1½ teaspoons salt
- ¼ teaspoon pepper
- 1 bay leaf
- 2½ to 3-pound broiler-fryer chicken, cut up
- 3 tablespoons margarine or butter
- ¼ cup all-purpose flour
- 2 teaspoons dried parsley flakes
- 1 teaspoon paprika (optional)
- ½ cup milk

Makes 4 servings

1. Mix onion, water, salt, pepper and bay leaf in 3- to 5-quart casserole. Add chicken pieces; cover. Microwave at MEDIUM-HIGH (70%) until chicken next to bone is not pink, 24 to 29 minutes, rearranging after half the time. If using oven other than Sharp Carousel, rearrange chicken 2 or 3 times during cooking.

2. Remove chicken from liquid. Strain liquid, reserving 1½ cups. Place margarine in small bowl or 1-quart casserole. Microwave at HIGH (100%) until melted, 30 seconds to 1 minute. Stir in flour, parsley flakes and paprika. Blend in reserved liquid and milk until smooth. Microwave at HIGH (100%) until thickened, 5 to 6 minutes, stirring with a wire whisk once or twice during cooking.

3. Return chicken pieces to the casserole. Pour sauce over chicken. Microwave at MEDIUM-HIGH (70%) until hot, 3 to 5 minutes. Serve with mashed potatoes, if desired.

Coq Au Vin

- 3 slices bacon, chopped
- 1 medium onion, thinly sliced and separated into rings
- 1 stalk celery, thinly sliced
- 1 clove garlic, minced
- 3 tablespoons all-purpose flour
- 1 teaspoon salt
- ½ teaspoon pepper
- ¾ cup red wine
- ¼ cup water
- 1 tablespoon brandy (optional)
- 2½ to 3-pound broiler-fryer chicken, cut up
- 8 ounces fresh mushrooms, sliced
- 1 bay leaf

Makes 4 servings

1. Place bacon in 3- to 5-quart casserole. Microwave at HIGH (100%) until crisp, 3 to 4 minutes. Stir in onion, celery, garlic, flour, salt, pepper, wine, water and brandy. Add chicken pieces, mushrooms and bay leaf. Cover.

2. Microwave at HIGH (100%) 5 minutes. Reduce power to MEDIUM-HIGH (70%). Microwave until chicken next to bone is not pink and sauce is thickened, 24 to 29 minutes, stirring once or twice during cooking.

Directions for microwaving chicken are in Learn While You Cook, page 24.

Chicken and Shrimp in ▲ Red Wine Sauce

¼ cup margarine or butter
1 medium onion, chopped
2 cloves garlic, minced
2½ to 3-pound broiler-fryer chicken, cut up
1 can (8 ounces) tomato sauce
¾ cup rosé wine
¼ cup all-purpose flour
2 tablespoons snipped parsley
1 teaspoon salt
1 teaspoon dried basil leaves
½ teaspoon Italian seasoning
¼ teaspoon pepper
1 pound raw shrimp, shelled and deveined, fresh or frozen, thawed

Makes 4 to 6 servings

1. Combine margarine, onion and garlic in 3- to 5-quart casserole. Microwave at HIGH (100%) until onion is tender-crisp, 3 to 5 minutes. Stir in remaining ingredients except shrimp.

2. Microwave at MEDIUM-HIGH (70%) until chicken next to bone is not pink, 24 to 29 minutes, turning chicken pieces over after half the cooking time. If using oven other than Sharp Carousel, rearrange twice during the cooking time. Remove chicken pieces and place in serving dish. Cover; set aside.

3. Add shrimp to wine sauce. Microwave at HIGH (100%) until shrimp turns pink (do not overcook shrimp or it will become tough), 3 to 4 minutes, stirring after half the cooking time. Skim any fat from surface of sauce. Pour shrimp sauce over chicken pieces.

Chicken Curry

1 medium green pepper, chopped
1 medium onion, thinly sliced and separated into rings
1 clove garlic, minced
1 tablespoon margarine or butter
2 medium tomatoes, peeled and thinly sliced
1 medium apple, chopped
¼ cup all-purpose flour
1 tablespoon curry powder
1 tablespoon ground allspice
1 teaspoon ground ginger
1 teaspoon salt
¼ teaspoon pepper
2½ to 3-pound broiler-fryer chicken, cut up
1½ cups hot water
2 teaspoons instant chicken bouillon

Makes 4 to 6 servings

1. Place green pepper, onion, garlic and margarine in deep 3- to 5-quart casserole. Microwave at HIGH (100%) until onion and green pepper are tender, 3 to 5 minutes, stirring once during cooking. Stir in tomatoes and apple.

2. Mix flour, curry powder, allspice, ginger, salt and pepper. Add flour mixture to vegetables; toss to coat. Add remaining ingredients; cover. Microwave at MEDIUM-HIGH (70%) until chicken next to bone is not pink and sauce is thickened, 24 to 29 minutes, stirring twice during cooking.

Chicken Marengo ►

- ⅓ cup seasoned dry bread crumbs
- 1 package (1½ ounces) spaghetti sauce mix
- 2½ to 3-pound broiler-fryer chicken, cut up
- 1 cup thinly sliced fresh mushrooms
- ½ cup dry white wine
- ¼ teaspoon dried basil leaves
- 1 can (16 ounces) whole tomatoes

Makes 4 servings

1. Combine bread crumbs and spaghetti sauce mix in plastic bag. Shake chicken pieces in bag until coated. Place chicken pieces skin side up in rectangular baking dish, 12×8 inches or 10-inch square casserole with thickest portions to outside of dish. Sprinkle with any remaining crumb mixture. Cover with waxed paper.

2. Microwave at HIGH (100%) 10 minutes. Rearrange chicken. Add mushrooms, wine and basil. Break up tomatoes with spoon. Stir in tomatoes and juice from tomatoes. Cover with waxed paper. Microwave at MEDIUM-HIGH (70%) until chicken next to bone is not pink, 9 to 14 minutes.

Chicken Cacciatore

- 2 cups thinly sliced fresh mushrooms
- ½ cup chopped onion
- 1 clove garlic, minced
- 1 can (15 ounces) tomato sauce
- 1 can (6 ounces) tomato paste
- ½ cup water
- ½ cup red wine
- 1½ teaspoons dried oregano leaves
- 1½ teaspoons dried parsley flakes
- 1 teaspoon sugar
- ½ teaspoon salt
- ¼ teaspoon pepper
- ¼ teaspoon dried thyme leaves
- 2½ to 3-pound broiler-fryer chicken, cut up

Makes 4 servings

1. Combine mushrooms, onion and garlic in 3- to 5-quart casserole. Microwave at HIGH (100%) until tender, 4 to 6 minutes. If using oven other than Sharp Carousel, stir after half the cooking time. Stir in remaining ingredients except chicken. Add chicken pieces, stirring to coat.

2. Microwave at MEDIUM-HIGH (70%) until chicken next to bone is not pink, 24 to 29 minutes, rearranging after half the cooking time. If using oven other than Sharp Carousel, rearrange 2 or 3 times during cooking.

Chicken and Dumplings

2½ to 3-pound broiler-fryer chicken, cut up
3 medium carrots, thinly sliced
2 cups hot water
6 peppercorns
2 bay leaves
1½ teaspoons salt
¾ cup water
6 tablespoons all-purpose flour
½ teaspoon dried sage leaves
1 cup frozen peas, thawed
1 can (4 ounces) sliced mushrooms, drained
1 cup buttermilk baking mix
1 tablespoon dried parsley flakes
⅓ cup milk

Makes 4 to 6 servings

1. Place chicken, carrots, 2 cups water, the peppercorns, bay leaves and salt in 3- to 5-quart casserole; cover. Microwave at HIGH (100%) until chicken next to bone is not pink, 18 to 25 minutes, stirring after half the cooking time. Remove bones and skin from chicken; cut into small pieces. Return chicken pieces to casserole. Remove bay leaves and peppercorns. Skim excess fat from chicken broth.

2. Blend ¾ cup water, the flour and sage until smooth. Stir into chicken mixture. Cover. Microwave at HIGH (100%) until slightly thickened, 15 to 18 minutes, stirring after half the cooking time. If using oven other than Sharp Carousel, stir 2 or 3 times during cooking. Stir in peas and mushrooms.

3. Stir baking mix, parsley flakes and milk with fork just until moistened. Drop dough in 6 spoonfuls onto hot chicken mixture. Cover. Microwave at MEDIUM-HIGH (70%) until dumplings are set, 4 to 6 minutes. If using oven other than Sharp Carousel, rotate casserole half turn after half the cooking time.

Brunswick Stew ▲

1 package (10 ounces) frozen whole kernel corn
1 package (10 ounces) frozen lima beans
1 package (10 ounces) frozen okra
2½ to 3-pound broiler-fryer chicken, cut up
2 cups hot water
1 medium onion, thinly sliced and separated into rings
1 teaspoon salt
¼ teaspoon pepper
⅛ teaspoon garlic powder
1 bay leaf
2 medium tomatoes, each cut into 8 wedges
¼ cup all-purpose flour

Makes 4 to 6 servings

1. Place unopened packages of corn, lima beans and okra in oven. Microwave at HIGH (100%) until thawed, 6 to 8 minutes. If using oven other than Sharp Carousel, rotate after half the cooking time. Drain. Cut okra into ½-inch pieces. Set aside.

2. Combine chicken, water, onion, salt, pepper, garlic powder and bay leaf in 3- to 5-quart casserole; cover. Microwave at HIGH (100%) until chicken next to bone is not pink, 18 to 25 minutes. Remove bay leaf. Remove bones and skin from chicken; cut into 1-inch pieces. Add chicken pieces, tomatoes, flour, corn, lima beans and okra to chicken broth mixture.

3. Microwave, uncovered, at HIGH (100%) until stew is slightly thickened, 18 to 24 minutes, stirring after half the cooking time. If using oven other than Sharp Carousel, stir 2 or 3 times during cooking.

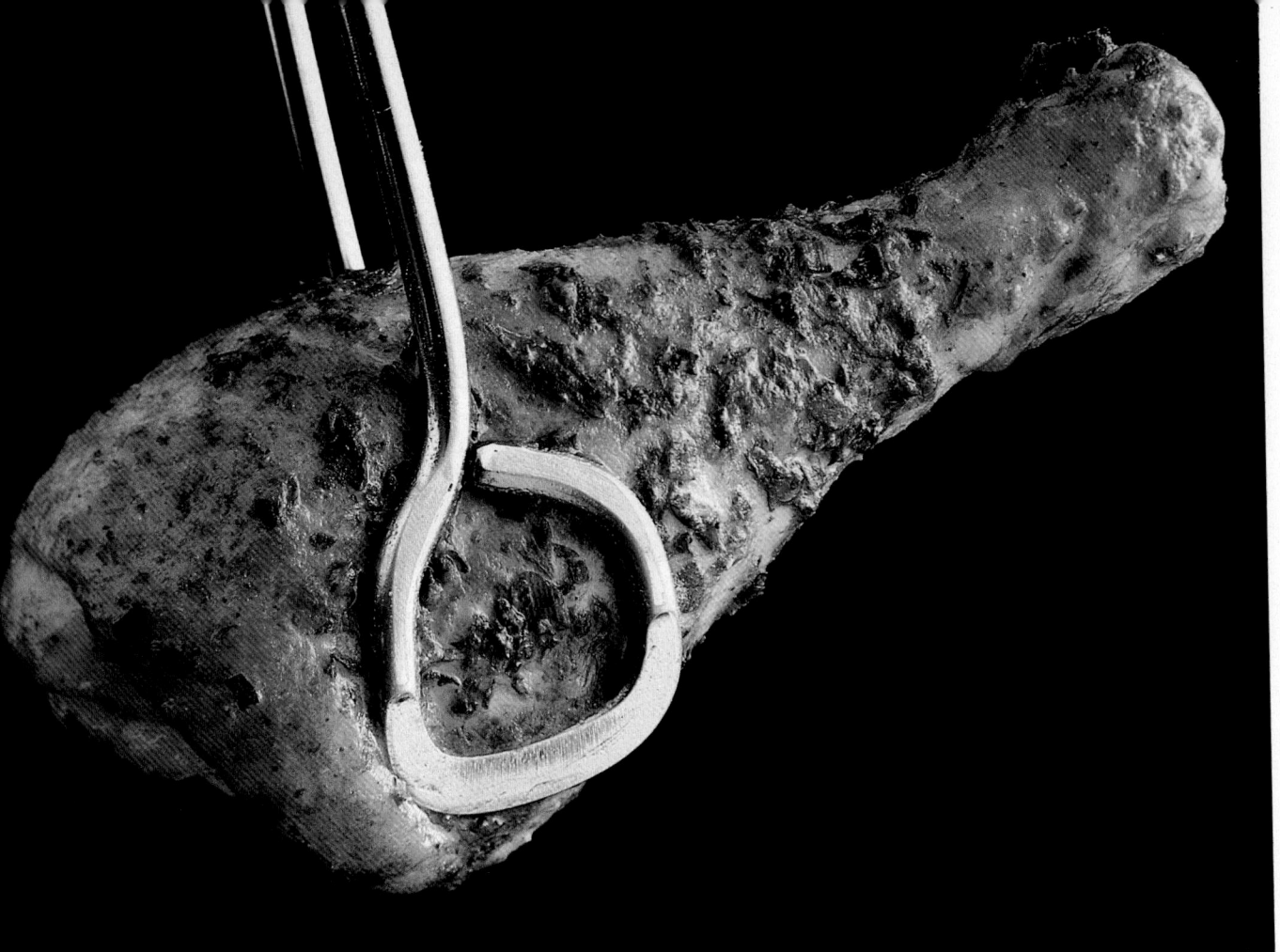

Herbed Drumsticks ▲

¼ cup margarine or butter
1 tablespoon dried parsley flakes
2 teaspoons chopped chives
1 teaspoon dried tarragon leaves
½ teaspoon salt
¼ teaspoon pepper
¼ teaspoon brown bouquet sauce
8 chicken drumsticks

Makes 4 servings

1. Place margarine in small bowl. Microwave at HIGH (100%) until melted, 45 seconds to 1 minute 30 seconds. Stir in remaining ingredients except chicken. Set aside.

2. Place chicken drumsticks in rectangular baking dish, 12 × 8 inches or 10-inch square casserole with meatiest portions to outside of dish. Brush with half of the margarine mixture. Microwave at MEDIUM-HIGH (70%) until chicken next to bone is not pink, 15 to 20 minutes, turning over and brushing with remaining margarine mixture after half the cooking time. If using oven other than Sharp Carousel, rearrange drumsticks after half the cooking time.

Teriyaki Chicken

½ cup packed brown sugar
½ cup soy sauce
½ cup sherry
1 teaspoon ground ginger
¼ teaspoon garlic powder
2½ to 3-pound broiler-fryer chicken, cut up

Makes 4 servings

1. Mix all ingredients except chicken in medium bowl. Microwave at HIGH (100%) until sugar dissolves, 1 to 1½ minutes. Place chicken in square baking dish, 8 × 8 inches or plastic bag. Pour marinade over chicken. Cover chicken only with plastic wrap or tightly close bag. Refrigerate 8 hours or overnight, turning chicken over occasionally.

2. Drain chicken; place in 10-inch square casserole. Cover with waxed paper. Microwave at MEDIUM-HIGH (70%) until chicken next to bone is not pink, 21 to 24 minutes, rearranging pieces after half the cooking time.

Chicken Breasts Parmesan

1 can (8 ounces) tomato sauce
1 teaspoon Italian seasoning
¼ teaspoon garlic salt
⅓ cup corn flake crumbs
¼ cup grated Parmesan cheese
1 teaspoon dried parsley flakes
2 large boneless chicken breasts (1½ to
    2 pounds), split and skin removed
1 egg, beaten
½ cup shredded mozzarella cheese
    (about 2 ounces)
   Grated Parmesan cheese

Makes 4 to 6 servings

1. Mix tomato sauce, Italian seasoning and garlic salt in 2-cup measure. Cover with waxed paper. Microwave at HIGH (100%) 2 minutes. Stir. Reduce power to MEDIUM (50%). Microwave 5 minutes; stirring once. Set sauce aside.

2. Mix corn flake crumbs, ¼ cup Parmesan cheese and the parsley flakes. Dip chicken breasts in beaten egg, then in crumb mixture. Place in rectangular baking dish, 12×8 inches or 10-inch square casserole. Cover with waxed paper. Microwave at MEDIUM-HIGH (70%) until chicken is tender, 9 to 14 minutes, rearranging after half the cooking time. (Do not turn over.)

3. Pour sauce over chicken. Sprinkle mozzarella over chicken breasts. Sprinkle with Parmesan. Microwave at MEDIUM-HIGH (70%) until mozzarella melts and sauce is hot, 2 to 5½ minutes.

Chicken à la King ▾

- 3 tablespoons margarine or butter
- 3 tablespoons all-purpose flour
- ¾ teaspoon salt
- ⅛ teaspoon pepper
- ¾ cup half-and-half
- ½ cup hot water
- 1 teaspoon instant chicken bouillon
- 2 cups cut-up cooked chicken
- 1 can (4 ounces) mushroom stems and pieces, drained
- 2 tablespoons finely chopped pimiento
- 4 baked puff pastry shells

Makes 4 servings

1. Place margarine in medium bowl. Microwave at HIGH (100%) until melted, 30 seconds to 1 minute. Blend in flour, salt and pepper. Gradually stir in half-and-half, water and instant bouillon. Microwave at MEDIUM-HIGH (70%) until thickened, 4 to 6½ minutes, stirring once. If using oven other than Sharp Carousel, stir 2 or 3 times.

2. Stir in chicken, mushrooms and pimiento. Microwave at MEDIUM-HIGH (70%) until chicken is heated through, 5 to 8 minutes, stirring once during cooking. Serve over pastry shells.

Oven Chicken Salad

- 1 cup thinly sliced celery
- 1 tablespoon chopped onion
- 2 cups cut-up cooked chicken
- ¾ cup sliced or slivered almonds
- ½ cup dairy sour cream
- ½ cup mayonnaise or salad dressing
- 1 tablespoon lemon juice
- ½ teaspoon salt
- ¼ teaspoon ground sage
- ⅛ teaspoon pepper
- ½ cup herb-flavored croutons
- ½ cup shredded sharp Cheddar cheese (about 2 ounces)

Makes 4 to 6 servings

1. Place celery and onion in 1½-quart casserole. Microwave at HIGH (100%) until vegetables are tender-crisp, 2 to 4 minutes. Stir in remaining ingredients except croutons and cheese. Microwave at MEDIUM-HIGH (70%) 5 minutes. If using oven other than Sharp Carousel, rotate casserole once during cooking time. Stir. Sprinkle with croutons and cheese.

2. Microwave at MEDIUM-HIGH (70%) until casserole is hot and cheese is melted, 2 to 5 minutes.

Chicken Livers and ▲ Mushrooms

3 slices bacon, chopped
½ medium onion, chopped
1 pound chicken livers
1 can (10¾ ounces) condensed cream of chicken soup
1 can (4 ounces) sliced mushrooms, drained
½ cup water
2 tablespoons snipped parsley
⅛ teaspoon pepper

Makes 4 servings

1. Place bacon and onion in 1½-quart casserole. Cover. Microwave at HIGH (100%) until bacon is crisp and onion is tender, 3 to 6 minutes. Stir in remaining ingredients.

2. Microwave at MEDIUM-HIGH (70%) until chicken livers are firm and tender and sauce is thickened, 17 to 22 minutes, stirring once or twice. Serve over rice or noodles, if desired.

Chicken Livers in Wine

¼ cup chopped onion
2 tablespoons margarine or butter
1½ pounds chicken livers
¾ cup dry white wine
3 tablespoons all-purpose flour
2 tablespoons snipped parsley
2 tablespoons catsup
½ teaspoon salt
⅛ teaspoon pepper

Makes 4 to 6 servings

1. Place onion and margarine in 1½-quart casserole. Microwave at HIGH (100%) until onion is tender, 2 to 4½ minutes.

2. Stir in remaining ingredients. Microwave at MEDIUM-HIGH (70%) until livers are firm and tender, 19 to 24 minutes, stirring 2 or 3 times during cooking. Serve over rice or noodles, if desired.

FISH & SEAFOOD

Microwaving is one of the easiest and most effective ways of preparing fish and seafood, which stay delicate and tender with quick, moist cooking. Overcooking dries out and toughens seafood, so you should check it after the minimum time. If thick pieces like fish steaks or lobster tails are done on the outside but still slightly translucent in the center, let them stand for a few minutes; internal heat will complete the cooking.

Shrimp Scampi

Makes 4 servings

½ cup margarine or butter
2 tablespoons dried parsley flakes
2 tablespoons lemon juice
1 large clove garlic, minced
½ teaspoon salt
1 pound jumbo raw shrimp, cleaned (page 117)
  Paprika (optional)

1. Place margarine in 2-quart casserole. Microwave at HIGH (100%) until melted, 1 to 2 minutes. Stir in parsley, lemon juice, garlic and salt. Add shrimp; toss to coat. Cover.

2. Microwave at HIGH (100%) until shrimp is pink, opaque and tender (do not overcook or shrimp will become tough), 3½ to 5½ minutes, stirring twice. Sprinkle with paprika.

Microwaving Fish and Seafood

Recipe Conversion

Reduce fat, liquid and seasonings as suggested in Recipe Conversion, page 42. If your recipe calls for poaching fish and then making a sauce with the broth, use only as much liquid as you will need for the sauce. When fish or seafood are cooked in a sauce, microwave the sauce first. Add fish or seafood toward the end of microwaving when they are combined with long-cooking ingredients.

Casseroles calling for cooked or canned ingredients will be done when heated through. When preparing uncooked fish or seafood, use a microwave recipe as a guide to time and check frequently to avoid overcooking. Loaves made with canned salmon or tuna usually need no change in ingredients.

Use HIGH (100%) unless the sauce is enriched with cream or eggs, which require a setting of MEDIUM-HIGH (70%) or lower. Stir seafood and casseroles when possible to speed cooking and help distribute heat.

Arrange fish fillets in baking dish with thickest parts to outside of dish. If fillets are very long, overlap thin areas in center of dish. After half the cooking time, reverse overlapped areas so parts which were on top are on the bottom.

Cover fish with waxed paper to hold in heat without producing excess steam. When poaching fillets or steaming seafood, cover tightly with plastic wrap or use a covered casserole.

Elevate fish on a roasting rack set in a baking dish when a dryer surface is desired. Do not overlap or cover crumb-coated fillets.

Test fish for doneness by flaking with a fork. Clams are cooked when the shells open partially. Oysters curl at the edges when done, and other seafood turns from translucent to opaque.

Do not overcook fish or seafood, which is delicate and may dry out or toughen. Check for doneness after the minimum time and let stand to complete cooking when the recipe directs it.

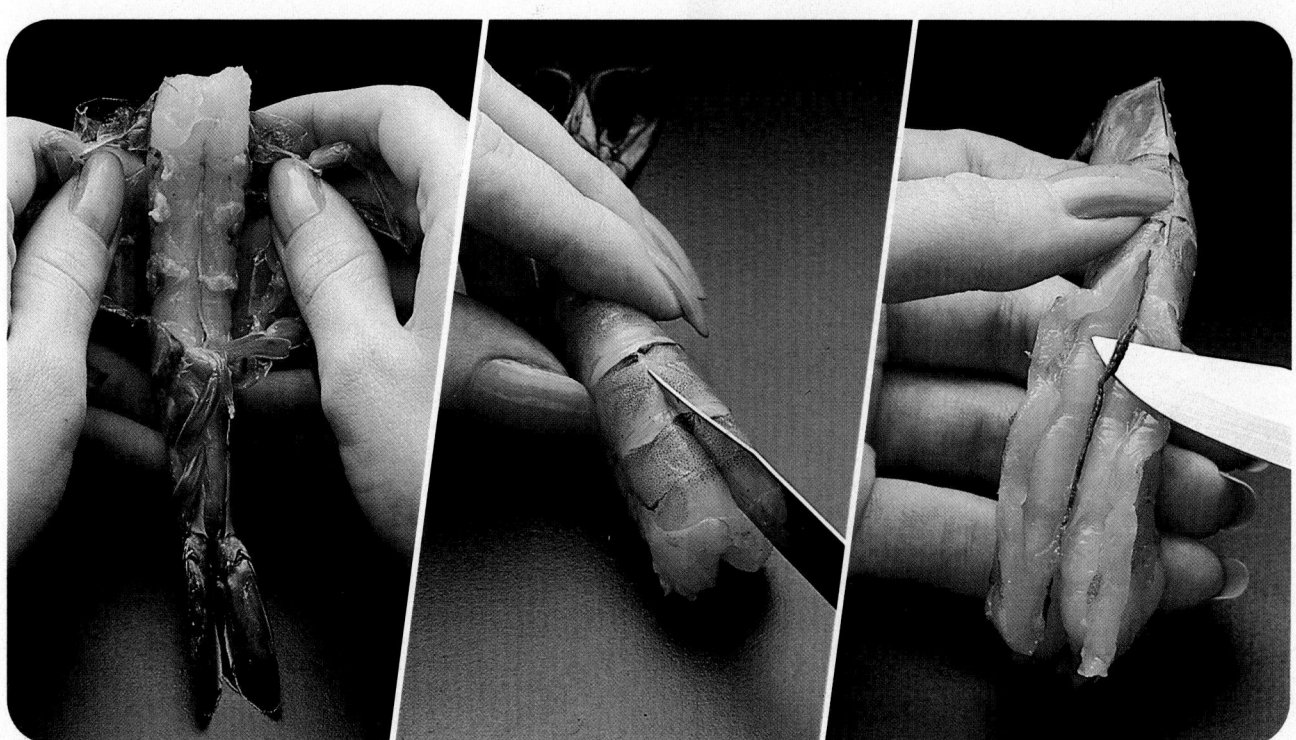

Clean shrimp by loosening shell from the underside and peeling off carefully, leaving tail intact. Make a cut down the back of the shrimp from the broad end to the tail, but do not cut all the way through. With the point of a knife or a wooden skewer, loosen and remove the vein.

◄ Baked Fish

1 package (2 ounces) seasoned coating
    mix for fish
12 ounces fish fillets, fresh or
    frozen, thawed

Makes 4 servings

1. Empty seasoned coating mix into plastic shaker bag. Shake 1 or 2 fillets at a time in bag until evenly coated. Place on roasting rack.

2. Microwave at HIGH (100%) until fish flakes easily in center with fork, 5 to 7 minutes. If using oven other than Sharp Carousel, rotate roasting rack half turn after half the cooking time.

◄ Poached Fish

12 ounces fish fillets, fresh or
    frozen, thawed
½ cup dry white wine
¼ teaspoon salt
⅛ teaspoon pepper

Makes 3 to 4 servings

1. Place fish fillets in square baking dish, 8 × 8 inches. Pour wine over fish fillets. Sprinkle with salt and pepper.

2. Cover with plastic wrap. Microwave at MEDIUM (50%) until fish flakes easily in center with fork, 10 to 15 minutes.

◄ Teriyaki Fish

½ cup water
¼ cup soy sauce
¼ cup dry sherry
2 tablespoons packed brown sugar
½ teaspoon ground ginger
⅛ teaspoon garlic powder
12 ounces fish fillets, fresh or
    frozen, thawed

Makes 4 servings

1. Combine all ingredients except fish in square baking dish, 8 × 8 inches. Stir until blended. Add fish, coating both sides. Cover; refrigerate 1 hour.

2. Place fish fillets on roasting rack. Microwave at HIGH (100%) until fish flakes easily in center with fork, 5 to 7 minutes. If using oven other than Sharp Carousel, rotate baking dish half turn after half the cooking time.

Fillet of Sole in Lemon Parsley Butter

½ cup margarine or butter
2 tablespoons all-purpose flour
2 tablespoons fresh lemon juice
1 tablespoon snipped parsley
¼ teaspoon salt
⅛ teaspoon pepper
⅛ teaspoon celery seed
1 pound sole or flounder fillets,
    fresh or frozen, thawed

Makes 4 servings

1. Place margarine in rectangular baking dish, 12 × 8 inches or 10-inch square casserole. Microwave at HIGH (100%) until melted, 45 seconds to 1 minute 30 seconds. Blend in remaining ingredients except fish fillets.

2. Coat both sides of fish fillets with butter sauce. Arrange in the baking dish. Cover with waxed paper. Microwave at HIGH (100%) until fish flakes easily in center with fork, 5 to 6 minutes.

Salmon-Stuffed Sole ▲

¼ cup chopped onion
¼ cup chopped celery
2 tablespoons margarine or butter
1 can (7¾ ounces) salmon, drained and
    bones removed
3 tablespoons dry bread crumbs
1 teaspoon grated lemon peel
⅛ teaspoon salt
⅛ teaspoon pepper
2 (8 ounces each) fresh sole fillets
⅛ teaspoon paprika
2 tablespoons margarine or butter
1½ tablespoons all-purpose flour
¼ teaspoon salt
⅛ teaspoon pepper
⅛ teaspoon paprika
¾ cup half-and-half
¼ cup white wine

Makes 4 servings

1. Place onion, celery and 2 tablespoons margarine in medium bowl. Microwave at HIGH (100%) until tender, 2 to 4 minutes. Stir in salmon, crumbs, lemon, ⅛ teaspoon salt and pepper.

2. Place 1 fillet on roasting rack. Top with stuffing and remaining fillet. Sprinkle with ⅛ teaspoon paprika. Cover with waxed paper. Microwave at HIGH (100%) until fish flakes easily, 5½ to 7½ minutes. If using oven other than Sharp Carousel, rotate dish after half the time. Let stand, covered.

3. Place 2 tablespoons margarine in medium bowl. Microwave at HIGH (100%) until melted, 30 seconds to 1 minute. Stir in flour, ¼ teaspoon salt, ⅛ teaspoon pepper and paprika. Blend in half-and-half and wine. Microwave at HIGH (100%) until thickened, 2½ to 5 minutes, stirring once.

Fillet of Flounder with Broccoli

1 package (10 ounces) frozen chopped
    broccoli
¼ cup margarine or butter
¼ cup all-purpose flour
1 teaspoon dried tarragon leaves
½ teaspoon salt
⅛ teaspoon pepper
¼ teaspoon paprika
1 cup milk
¼ cup dry white wine
1 tablespoon lemon juice
12 ounces flounder fillets, fresh or
    frozen, thawed

Makes 4 servings

1. Place frozen broccoli in 1-quart casserole; cover. Microwave at HIGH (100%) until broccoli is tender, 4 to 7 minutes. Drain. Set aside. Place margarine in medium bowl. Microwave at HIGH (100%) until melted, 30 seconds to 1 minute. Blend in flour, tarragon, salt, pepper and paprika. Gradually stir in milk, wine and lemon juice. Microwave at MEDIUM-HIGH (70%) until thickened, 5 to 7 minutes, stirring once or twice. Set sauce aside.

2. Place fish in rectangular baking dish, 12 × 8 inches or 10-inch square casserole. Cover with waxed paper. Microwave at HIGH (100%) until fish flakes easily in center with fork, 5 to 7 minutes. Drain and remove fish fillets.

3. Spread reserved broccoli in baking dish. Arrange fish fillets over top. Pour reserved sauce over fish and broccoli. Microwave at MEDIUM-HIGH (70%) until heated through, 2 to 4 minutes.

Creamed Flounder Tarragon

1 medium onion, chopped
2 tablespoons margarine or butter
1 cup dairy sour cream
1 can (4 ounces) sliced mushrooms, drained
¼ cup half-and-half
1 tablespoon all-purpose flour
½ teaspoon salt
½ teaspoon paprika
¼ teaspoon dried tarragon leaves
1 pound flounder fillets, fresh or frozen, thawed

Makes 4 servings

1. Combine onion and margarine in medium bowl. Microwave at HIGH (100%) until onion is tender, 4 to 6 minutes. Stir in remaining ingredients except fish fillets. Microwave at MEDIUM-HIGH (70%) until slightly thickened, 3 to 6 minutes, stirring once. Set mushroom mixture aside.

2. Place fish fillets in square baking dish, 8 × 8 inches. Cover with waxed paper. Microwave at MEDIUM-HIGH (70%) 3 minutes; drain and rearrange fillets. Spoon mushroom mixture over fish. Microwave at MEDIUM-HIGH (70%) until fish flakes easily in center with fork, 6 to 9 minutes.

Trout Almondine ▶

¼ cup margarine or butter
½ cup slivered almonds
2 teaspoons almond liqueur
2 packages (10 ounces each) frozen whole pan-dressed trout, thawed or 4 (5 ounces each) fresh pan-dressed trout

Makes 4 servings

1. Place margarine in 1-quart casserole or small bowl. Microwave at HIGH (100%) until melted, 45 seconds to 1 minute 30 seconds. Stir in almonds and liqueur. Microwave at HIGH (100%) until almonds are light brown, 3 to 3½ minutes, stirring after every minute with a slotted spoon. Remove almonds. Set almonds and margarine aside.

2. Arrange trout in rectangular baking dish, 12 × 8 inches or 10-inch square casserole. Pour reserved margarine over trout. Cover with waxed paper. Microwave at HIGH (100%) until fish flakes easily in center with a fork, 5 to 9 minutes, turning over after half the time. If using oven other than Sharp Carousel, turn and rearrange fish after half the time. Sprinkle with almonds.

Salmon Loaf

2 cans (15½ ounces each) salmon, drained (reserve liquid) and bones removed
  Milk
1 cup dry bread crumbs
2 eggs, beaten
2 tablespoons lemon juice
1 tablespoon instant minced onion
1 tablespoon dried parsley flakes
½ teaspoon salt
¼ teaspoon pepper

Makes 4 to 6 servings

1. Add enough milk to reserved salmon liquid to make 1 cup. Mix thoroughly with remaining ingredients. Pour into loaf dish, 9 × 5 inches.

2. Microwave at HIGH (100%) until center is set, 7 to 11 minutes. If using oven other than Sharp Carousel, rotate loaf dish half turn after half the cooking time. Let stand 5 minutes.

◄ Crab Newburg

2 tablespoons margarine or butter
2 tablespoons all-purpose flour
½ teaspoon salt
¼ teaspoon paprika
Dash of cayenne pepper
1 cup half-and-half
½ cup milk
¼ cup sherry
2 egg yolks, beaten
2 cans (7½ ounces each) crabmeat, drained and cartilage removed

Makes 4 servings

1. Place margarine in 1½-quart casserole. Microwave at HIGH (100%) until melted, 30 seconds to 1 minute. Stir in flour, salt, paprika and cayenne pepper. Blend in half-and-half, milk and sherry. Microwave at MEDIUM-HIGH (70%) until thickened, 4 to 7 minutes, stirring with wire whisk 2 or 3 times during cooking.

2. Stir small amount of hot mixture into egg yolks; return to mixture. Microwave at MEDIUM-HIGH (70%) until thickened, 1 to 3 minutes, stirring once or twice. Stir in crabmeat. Serve over toast points or patty shells, if desired.

Lobster Tails

4 (8 ounces each) frozen lobster tails
2 tablespoons margarine or butter

Makes 4 servings

1. Arrange frozen lobster tails around outer edges of rectangular baking dish, 12 × 8 inches or 10-inch square casserole. Microwave at HIGH (100%) until lobster tails are flexible, 5 minutes. Let stand, covered, 10 minutes.

2. Place margarine in small bowl. Microwave at HIGH (100%) until melted, 30 to 45 seconds. With a sharp knife split shells on the underside of each tail and brush with margarine. Cover. Microwave at HIGH (100%) until lobster flesh is opaque, 6 to 10 minutes. If using oven other than Sharp Carousel, rotate casserole every 2 to 3 minutes.

Directions for Tuna Casserole are in Learn While You Cook, page 28.

Shrimp de Jonghe ▲

½ cup margarine or butter, cut into 4 pieces
4 cloves garlic, sliced
½ cup sherry
1 tablespoon snipped parsley
1 teaspoon salt
1 teaspoon chopped chives
¼ teaspoon dried tarragon leaves
¼ teaspoon instant minced onion
Dash of ground nutmeg
Dash of dried thyme leaves
¾ cup dry bread crumbs
2 pounds raw shrimp, shelled and deveined

Makes 4 to 6 servings

1. Combine margarine and garlic in 1½-quart casserole. Microwave at HIGH (100%) until garlic is browned, 4 to 5 minutes. Remove and discard garlic. Stir in sherry, parsley, salt, chives, tarragon, instant onion, nutmeg and thyme. Remove ¼ cup of seasoned margarine; stir into bread crumbs.

2. Mix shrimp into remaining margarine in casserole until coated. Microwave at MEDIUM-HIGH (70%) 5 minutes. Stir. Sprinkle with bread crumbs. Microwave at MEDIUM-HIGH (70%) until shrimp is pink and opaque, 1 to 4 minutes. Let stand 2 minutes.

Shrimp Creole ▲

1 medium onion, chopped
¾ cup chopped green pepper
¼ cup chopped celery
3 tablespoons margarine or butter
1 can (16 ounces) whole tomatoes
1 can (6 ounces) tomato paste
1 cup water
2 tablespoons all-purpose flour
2 tablespoons dried parsley flakes
1½ teaspoons sugar
1 teaspoon salt
½ teaspoon chili powder
⅛ teaspoon pepper
⅛ teaspoon dried thyme leaves
⅛ teaspoon red pepper sauce
12 ounces raw shrimp, shelled and deveined

Makes 4 servings

1. Combine onion, green pepper, celery and margarine in 3-quart casserole. Microwave at HIGH (100%) until vegetables are tender, 3 to 6 minutes. Add tomatoes, tomato paste, water and flour, stirring to break up tomatoes. Mix in remaining ingredients except shrimp. Cover.

2. Microwave at HIGH (100%) until mixture is bubbly, 8 to 10 minutes, stirring twice during cooking. Stir in shrimp; cover. Microwave at HIGH (100%) until shrimp is opaque and tender (do not overcook or shrimp will become tough), 4 to 6 minutes, stirring once or twice during cooking. Let stand 2 minutes. Serve with rice, if desired.

Coquilles St. Jacques

1 tablespoon margarine or butter
1 tablespoon chopped onion
1 pound scallops
1 cup sliced fresh mushrooms
⅓ cup white wine
1½ teaspoons lemon juice
¼ teaspoon salt
    Dash of dried marjoram leaves
    Dash of paprika
3 tablespoons margarine or butter
2 tablespoons all-purpose flour
½ cup whipping cream
1 tablespoon snipped parsley

Makes 4 servings

1. Combine 1 tablespoon margarine and onion in 1½-quart casserole. Microwave at HIGH (100%) 1 minute. Stir in scallops, mushrooms, wine, lemon juice, salt, marjoram and paprika. Microwave, covered, at HIGH (100%) 3 minutes. Drain and reserve liquid.

2. Place 3 tablespoons margarine in small bowl. Microwave at HIGH (100%) until melted, 30 seconds to 1 minute. Blend in flour. Stir in ½ cup reserved scallop liquid, cream and parsley. Microwave at MEDIUM-HIGH (70%) until thickened, 3 to 5 minutes, stirring once. Stir sauce into scallops.

3. Spoon scallop mixture into 4 ramekins or small bowls. Microwave at MEDIUM-HIGH (70%) until heated through, 2 to 3½ minutes. If using oven other than Sharp Carousel, rearrange ramekins after 1 minute. (Do not overcook.)

Scalloped Oysters

- 2 tablespoons margarine or butter
- ½ cup dry bread crumbs
- ¼ teaspoon paprika
- ¼ cup chopped celery
- 1 tablespoon margarine or butter
- 1 pint shucked oysters, drained
- 1 can (10½ ounces) condensed cream of chicken soup
- ¼ cup dry bread crumbs
- 2 tablespoons half-and-half or milk
- 1 tablespoon dried parsley flakes
- ½ teaspoon salt
- ⅛ teaspoon pepper

Makes 4 servings

1. Place 2 tablespoons margarine in small bowl. Microwave at HIGH (100%) until melted, 30 seconds to 1 minute. Stir in ½ cup bread crumbs and the paprika. Set aside.

2. Place celery and 1 tablespoon margarine in 1-quart casserole. Microwave at HIGH (100%) until celery is tender, 2 to 4 minutes. Add oysters; cover. Microwave at HIGH (100%) until edges of oysters are curled, 3 to 4 minutes. Stir in soup, ¼ cup bread crumbs, the half-and-half, parsley, salt and pepper.

3. Microwave at HIGH (100%) until hot and bubbly, 5 to 7 minutes, stirring after half the cooking time. Sprinkle with buttered bread crumbs during last 2 minutes of cooking time.

Oyster Stew

- 2 tablespoons margarine or butter
- 1 can (8 ounces) oysters, drained (reserve liquid) or ½ pint shucked oysters, drained (reserve liquid)
  Milk
- ¼ teaspoon celery seed
  Dash of cayenne pepper
  Dash of paprika

Makes 2 to 4 servings

1. Place margarine in 1-quart casserole. Microwave at HIGH (100%) until melted, 30 to 45 seconds. Add oysters; cover. Microwave at HIGH (100%) until edges are curled, 2 to 4 minutes.

2. Add enough milk to oyster liquid to measure 1½ cups. Add milk mixture, celery seed and cayenne to oysters; cover. Microwave at MEDIUM-HIGH (70%) until mixture is hot, 4 to 6 minutes. Sprinkle with paprika. Serve with crackers, if desired.

Steamed Clams ▲

- 2 pounds shell clams (soft or longneck)
- ½ cup water

Makes 4 to 6 servings

1. Wash shell clams thoroughly, discarding any broken-shell or open clams. Set aside.

2. Pour water into 2-quart casserole; cover. Microwave at HIGH (100%) until water boils, 3 to 4 minutes. Add clams; cover. Microwave at HIGH (100%) until clams open, 4 to 6 minutes, stirring after half the cooking time.

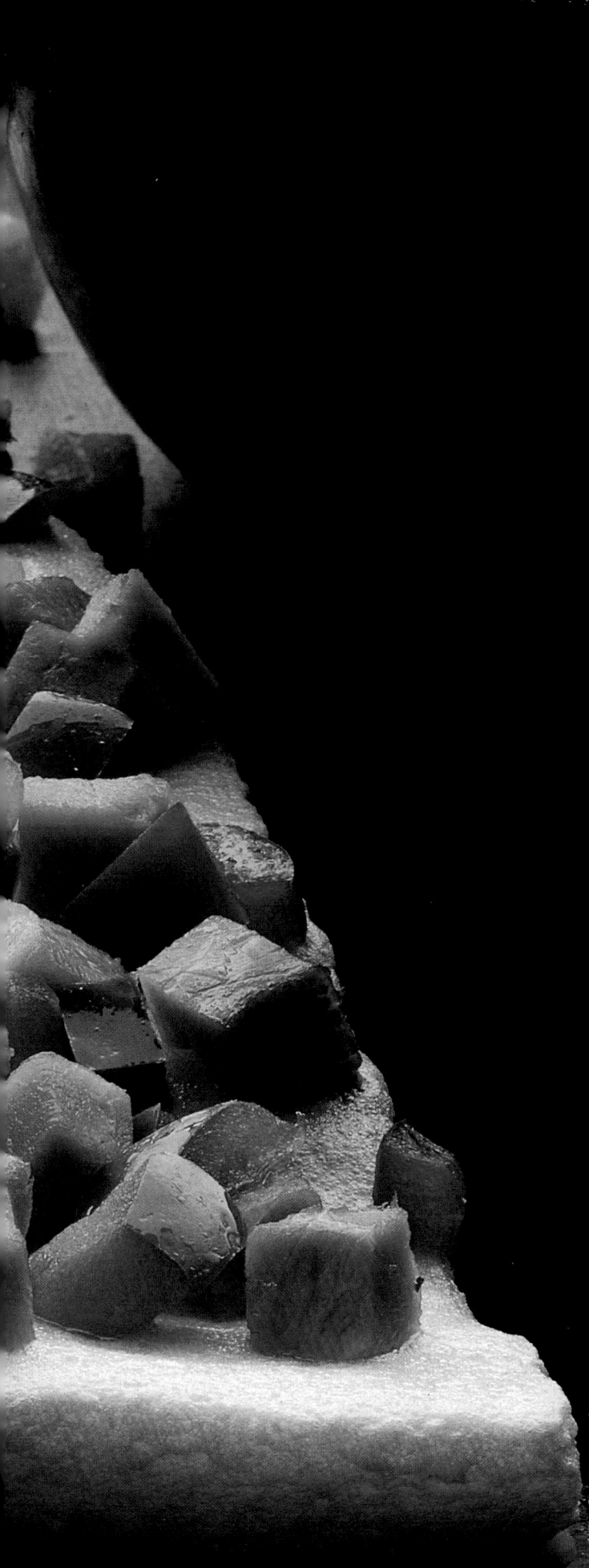

EGGS & CHEESE

Many of your favorite egg and cheese dishes will be faster and easier to make in the microwave oven. Macaroni and cheese is ready in minutes; fondues do not need constant stirring; poached eggs require no special expertise. You save energy with puffy omelets because there's no need to heat both a surface unit and the conventional oven. Scrambled eggs are fluffier, have more volume, and don't leave a hard-to-remove crust in the pan.

Puffy Omelet

 1 tablespoon margarine or butter
 4 eggs
 ¼ cup milk or half-and-half
 ¼ teaspoon baking powder
 ¼ teaspoon salt
   Dash of pepper

Makes 2 to 4 servings

1. Place margarine in 9-inch pie plate. Microwave at HIGH (100%) until melted, 30 to 45 seconds. Separate eggs, placing egg whites in large mixing bowl and egg yolks in medium bowl. Blend remaining ingredients into egg yolks. Beat whites with electric mixer until stiff but not dry.

2. Fold egg yolk mixture into beaten egg whites with rubber spatula. Pour into pie plate. Microwave at MEDIUM (50%) until center is set, 4 to 6 minutes. If using oven other than Sharp Carousel, rotate plate once or twice during cooking.

Cheese Omelet Variation: Sprinkle ½ cup shredded cheese over cooked omelet. Microwave at MEDIUM-HIGH (70%) until cheese melts, 30 seconds to 1 minute.

Western Omelet Variation: Combine ½ cup chopped onion, ½ cup chopped green pepper and 1 tablespoon olive oil in medium bowl or 4-cup measure. Microwave at HIGH (100%) until vegetables are tender, 2½ to 3 minutes. Stir in 1 cup diced fully cooked ham. Sprinkle over omelet during last minute of cooking time. If necessary, microwave an additional 30 seconds to 1 minute.

Microwaving Eggs and Cheese

Recipe Conversion

Scrambled eggs and puffy omelets convert easily to microwaving. Follow your conventional recipe for ingredients and a recipe from this book for microwave methods and times. Use your microwave oven to make fillings, too.

Quiches are also easy to microwave. Be sure to microwave the pastry shell first. Reduce liquid by about one-third. Heat and stir the egg mixture until slightly set before pouring it into the shell. This helps the filling cook smoothly and set quickly.

For rarebits and fondues, reduce liquid slightly and heat thoroughly before adding cheese. Constant stirring is not needed; just blend well with a wire whisk.

Do not microwave eggs in the shell. Steam builds up inside and pressure causes the egg to burst. Cut up conventionally hard-cooked eggs before reheating in the microwave oven.

Mix yolks and whites together, as you do in scrambled eggs or omelets to help them cook evenly. The vinegar and hot water used to poach eggs coagulates and sets the whites. Egg yolks contain more fat than whites, so they attract more microwave energy, and cook faster.

Use a lower power level to microwave cheese and eggs. Overcooking makes eggs tough and rubbery while cheese becomes stringy. Very fresh or soft natural cheese and process cheese are less apt to become stringy than hard cheese. Shred cheese to help it melt quickly.

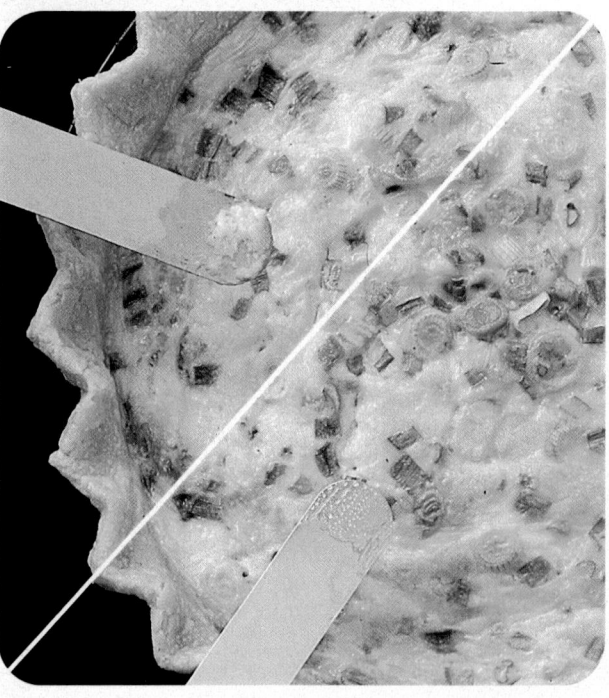

Standing time is important for many egg dishes, even when they can be stirred during cooking, because eggs are very delicate and can overcook from internal heat. Here, quiche is removed from oven when set but not dry, and firms up after standing 5 minutes.

Poached Eggs

½ cup hot tap water
1 teaspoon white vinegar
4 eggs

Makes 4 servings

1. Place 2 tablespoons water and ¼ teaspoon vinegar in each of four 6-ounce custard cups. Arrange in oven in a circle. Microwave at HIGH (100%) until water boils, 1 to 1½ minutes.

2. Break 1 egg into each custard cup. Cover each loosely with plastic wrap. Reduce power to MEDIUM-HIGH (70%). Microwave until egg whites are opaque and egg yolks are soft-set, 1½ to 2½ minutes.

Eggs Benedict

1 package (10 ounces) frozen asparagus spears
    Poached Eggs (above)
2 English muffins, split and toasted
4 slices (1 ounce each) fully cooked ham
¼ cup margarine or butter
¼ cup half-and-half
2 egg yolks, slightly beaten
1 tablespoon lemon juice
½ teaspoon dry mustard
¼ teaspoon salt
    Dash of cayenne pepper

Makes 4 servings

1. Place package of asparagus spears in oven. Microwave at HIGH (100%) 4 minutes, turning over after half the time. Drain and set aside.

2. Prepare Poached Eggs as directed above. Place toasted English muffin halves in square baking dish, 8 × 8 inches. Top each with a ham slice and one-fourth of the asparagus spears. With a slotted spoon remove eggs from custard cups, placing 1 on each muffin.

3. Place margarine in a 4-cup measure. Microwave at HIGH (100%) until melted, 45 seconds to 1 minute. Beat in half-and-half, egg yolks, lemon juice, mustard, salt, and cayenne pepper with a wire whisk. Microwave at MEDIUM-HIGH (70%) until fluffy and thickened, 2 to 3½ minutes, beating every 30 seconds to 1 minute.

4. Pour sauce evenly over egg-topped muffins. Microwave at MEDIUM-HIGH (70%) until thoroughly heated, 4 to 5 minutes. If using oven other than Sharp Carousel, rotate muffins 3 to 4 times during cooking.

Quiche Lorraine ▲

6 slices bacon (about ¼ pound)
3 eggs
1 cup half-and-half
¼ cup chopped green onion
1 tablespoon all-purpose flour
½ teaspoon salt
⅛ teaspoon pepper
⅛ teaspoon cayenne pepper
    Baked Pie Shell (page 180)
1 cup shredded Swiss cheese (about 4 ounces)

Makes 4 to 6 servings

1. Place bacon on roasting rack; cover with paper toweling. Microwave at HIGH (100%) until crisp, 5 to 6 minutes. Crumble and set aside.

2. Combine eggs, half-and-half, green onion, flour, salt, pepper and cayenne pepper in medium bowl. Beat with a wire whisk or electric mixer until well blended. Microwave at MEDIUM (50%) until thoroughly heated and slightly thickened, 4 to 6 minutes, stirring every 1 to 2 minutes.

3. Place crumbled bacon evenly in pastry shell. Sprinkle with cheese. Pour hot egg mixture over cheese. Place quiche on inverted saucer in oven. Microwave at MEDIUM (50%) until center is set but not dry, 16 to 25 minutes. If using oven other than Sharp Carousel, rotate quiche every 2 to 3 minutes. Let stand 5 minutes to complete cooking.

◄ Sausage Sour Cream Puff

½ pound bulk pork sausage
4 eggs, separated
¼ cup dairy sour cream
2 tablespoons milk
½ teaspoon salt
¼ teaspoon pepper

Makes 2 to 4 servings

1. Crumble sausage into 1-quart casserole. Microwave at HIGH (100%) until sausage is set and no longer pink, 4 to 6 minutes, stirring once or twice to break up. Drain on paper toweling. Set sausage aside.

2. Beat egg whites until stiff peaks form. Set aside. Blend egg yolks, sour cream, milk, salt and pepper. Fold egg yolk mixture into beaten egg whites. Spread sausage in round baking dish, 9 × 1½ inches. Slowly pour egg mixture over sausage.

3. Microwave at MEDIUM (50%) until set, 5 to 8 minutes, lifting edges with spatula after 3 minutes. If using oven other than Sharp Carousel, rotate baking dish twice during cooking.

Ham Quiche Ring

3 eggs
1 cup half-and-half
1 tablespoon all-purpose flour
½ teaspoon salt
¼ teaspoon ground nutmeg
⅛ teaspoon pepper
⅛ teaspoon cayenne pepper
4 ounces fully cooked ham, cut into thin strips
1 cup shredded Swiss cheese
  (about 4 ounces)

Makes 2 to 3 servings

1. Mix eggs, half-and-half, flour, salt, nutmeg, pepper and cayenne pepper in medium bowl. Microwave at MEDIUM (50%) until thoroughly heated and slightly set, 4 to 6 minutes, stirring every 1 to 2 minutes.

2. Place ham evenly on bottom of glass ring mold. Pour egg mixture over ham; sprinkle with cheese. Microwave at MEDIUM (50%) until set, 10 to 15 minutes. If using oven other than Sharp Carousel, rotate 2 or 3 times during cooking. Let stand 5 minutes covered with aluminum foil. (Do not unmold.) Cut into serving pieces.

Directions for scrambled eggs are in Learn While You Cook, page 22.

Cheese Fondue ▲

 1 clove garlic, cut in half
 4 cups shredded Swiss cheese
     (about 16 ounces)
 ¼ cup all-purpose flour
 ¼ teaspoon salt
 ¼ teaspoon ground nutmeg
 ⅛ teaspoon pepper
1½ cups white wine
     French bread, cut into 1-inch cubes

Makes 4 to 6 servings

1. Rub inside of 2-quart casserole with garlic. Discard garlic. Combine cheese, flour, salt, nutmeg and pepper in plastic bag. Shake to coat cheese. Set aside.

2. Pour wine into 2-quart casserole. Microwave at MEDIUM-HIGH (70%) until wine is very hot but not boiling, 2 to 4 minutes. Add all ingredients from plastic bag. Blend with wire whisk.

3. Microwave at MEDIUM-HIGH (70%) until bubbly, 4 to 9 minutes. Stir with wire whisk until smooth. Serve with bread cubes.

Macaroni and Cheese

 3 tablespoons margarine or butter
 2 tablespoons all-purpose flour
 1 teaspoon salt
 ½ teaspoon dry mustard
 ¼ teaspoon pepper
 4 drops red pepper sauce
1½ cups milk
 2 cups shredded Cheddar cheese or 1 cup
     each shredded Cheddar and
     Swiss cheese (about 8 ounces)
 7 ounces elbow macaroni, cooked
     and drained
 3 tablespoons margarine or butter
 ½ cup seasoned dry bread crumbs

Makes 4 to 6 servings

1. Place 3 tablespoons margarine in 1½-quart casserole. Microwave at HIGH (100%) until melted, 30 seconds to 1 minute. Blend in flour, salt, mustard, pepper and pepper sauce. Stir in milk.

2. Microwave at HIGH (100%) until thickened, 4 to 6 minutes, blending with wire whisk once or twice during cooking. Stir in cheese. Microwave at HIGH (100%) to soften cheese, 30 seconds to 1 minute 30 seconds. Stir in macaroni.

3. Place 3 tablespoons margarine in small bowl. Microwave at HIGH (100%) until melted, 30 seconds to 1 minute. Stir in bread crumbs; sprinkle over casserole. Microwave at MEDIUM-HIGH (70%) until heated through, 5 to 7 minutes. If using oven other than Sharp Carousel, rotate casserole once during last cooking time.

SOUPS & BEVERAGES

With your microwave oven, you can prepare and serve a soup or beverage in the same oven-to-table container. Make a full recipe or a single serving. Cooking times are shorter when you microwave, especially for soups which require several hours of conventional simmering to develop flavor; you save both cooking and clean-up time, and the results are delicious.

Autumn Soup

1 pound lean ground beef
1 cup chopped onion
1 cup chopped celery
4 cups hot water
2 cups ½-inch potato cubes
1 cup thinly sliced carrots
1 teaspoon salt
½ teaspoon dried basil leaves
¼ teaspoon pepper
1 bay leaf
3 tomatoes, cut into eighths and sliced in half

Makes 8 servings

1. Mix ground beef, onion and celery in 5-quart casserole. Microwave at HIGH (100%) until ground beef loses its pink color, 5 to 7 minutes, stirring after half the cooking time.

2. Add hot water, potatoes, carrots, salt, basil, pepper and bay leaf; cover. Microwave at HIGH (100%) until potatoes are tender, 18 to 20 minutes.

3. Add tomatoes. Microwave at HIGH (100%) until tomatoes are tender, 8 to 10 minutes.

Microwaving Soups and Beverages

Recipe Conversion

When converting soup recipes, reduce the amount of liquid by one-fourth, since there will be less evaporation. Exceptions are soups made with dried beans, peas or lentils, which absorb moisture as they cook.

Reduce salt and other seasonings by one-half. Add more to taste after microwaving.

Type of liquid and main bulky ingredient determines the power level. When making soup with less tender meat, start it at HIGH (100%), then reduce the power to MEDIUM (50%). Vegetable soup and soup with tender meat, like a broiler-fryer chicken, can be microwaved at HIGH (100%).

Microwaving time is based on quantity; more food takes more time. Your best guide is a microwave recipe for a similar type and quantity of soup.

Cut dense vegetables like carrots and potatoes in thin slices or small cubes for fast, uniform cooking. Cut less tender meat, like stewing beef, into ¾-inch cubes so energy can penetrate from all sides.

HIGH (100%) is used for liquids like water, broth, or tomato juice. Milk-based soups and beverages which are stirred during cooking can also be microwaved at HIGH (100%), but should be placed in a deep container to prevent boiling over.

MEDIUM-HIGH (70%) and MEDIUM (50%) are needed for cream, which curdles at high temperatures, and soups which require simmering to develop flavor or tenderize ingredients like stewing beef, uncooked macaroni, dried beans or peas.

Egg Drop Soup ▲

  1 can (10¾ ounces) condensed chicken broth
1¼ cups water
  2 tablespoons chopped green onion
  1 tablespoon soy sauce
  2 eggs, beaten

Makes 4 servings

1. Mix broth, water, onions and soy sauce in 1½-quart casserole; cover. Microwave at HIGH (100%) until mixture boils, 8 to 10 minutes.

2. Pour eggs into mixture, stirring gently until eggs form strings. Serve with fried noodles, if desired.

> Directions for cream soup are in Learn While You Cook, page 19.

Quick Corn Chowder

  3 slices bacon, chopped
 ¼ cup finely chopped onion
  2 tablespoons all-purpose flour
  1 package (10 ounces) frozen whole kernel corn
1½ cups milk
1½ teaspoons snipped parsley
 ½ teaspoon salt
 ¼ teaspoon pepper

Makes 4 servings

1. Combine bacon and onion in 2-quart casserole. Microwave at HIGH (100%) until bacon is crisp and onion is tender, 4 to 6 minutes, stirring after half the cooking time.

2. Blend in flour. Stir in corn, milk, parsley, salt and pepper. Microwave at HIGH (100%) until slightly thickened and corn is tender, 7 to 12 minutes, stirring after half the cooking time. If using oven other than Sharp Carousel, stir 2 or 3 times during cooking time.

◄ Onion Soup

¼ cup margarine or butter
2 medium onions, thinly sliced
4 cups hot water
1 package (1⅜ ounces) onion soup mix
2 teaspoons instant beef bouillon
1 teaspoon Worcestershire sauce
4 ½-inch slices toasted French bread
¼ cup grated Parmesan cheese

Makes 4 servings

1. Combine margarine and onion in 2-quart casserole. Microwave at HIGH (100%) until onions are tender-crisp, 4 to 6 minutes.

2. Add water, onion soup mix, instant bouillon and Worcestershire sauce; cover. Microwave at HIGH (100%) 5 minutes. Reduce power to MEDIUM (50%). Microwave until onions are tender and flavors are blended, 15 to 20 minutes.

3. Ladle soup into 4 individual serving bowls. Place toast on top. Sprinkle each with 1 tablespoon Parmesan cheese. Microwave at HIGH (100%) until cheese softens, 5 to 7 minutes.

New England Clam Chowder

3 slices bacon, chopped
2 cans (6½ ounces each) minced clams, drained (reserve ⅓ cup liquid)
1½ cups ½-inch potato cubes
½ cup chopped onion
3 tablespoons all-purpose flour
1½ cups milk
1 teaspoon salt
⅛ teaspoon pepper
1 cup half-and-half

Makes 4 servings

1. Place bacon in 2-quart casserole. Microwave at HIGH (100%) until bacon is crisp, 3 to 4 minutes. Add reserved clam juice, potatoes and onion. Cover. Microwave at HIGH (100%) until potatoes are tender, 8 to 10 minutes, stirring after half the cooking time.

2. Blend in flour. Stir in milk, salt and pepper. Microwave at HIGH (100%) until thickened, 5 to 7 minutes, stirring after half the cooking time. If using oven other than Sharp Carousel, stir 2 or 3 times during cooking.

3. Blend in half-and-half; stir in clams. Microwave at MEDIUM-HIGH (70%) until thickened and heated through, 4 to 5 minutes.

Split Pea Soup

6 cups water
1 pound dried green split peas (about 2½ cups)
3 medium carrots, coarsely grated
1 medium onion, thinly sliced
1½ teaspoons salt
¼ teaspoon pepper

Makes 8 servings

1. Combine all ingredients in 3-quart casserole; cover. Microwave at HIGH (100%) 10 minutes.

2. Reduce power to MEDIUM (50%). Microwave until vegetables are tender and soup is thickened, 1 hour to 1 hour 10 minutes, stirring 2 or 3 times during cooking.

Vegetable Soup

3 slices bacon, chopped
1 cup chopped celery
¼ cup chopped onion
2 cups ½-inch potato cubes
1 cup thinly sliced carrots
¼ cup water
3 tablespoons all-purpose flour
3 cups vegetable juice cocktail
2 cups water
1 package (10 ounces) frozen green peas
1 teaspoon salt
¼ teaspoon pepper

Makes 8 servings

1. Combine bacon, celery and onion in 5-quart casserole. Microwave at HIGH (100%) until bacon is crisp and vegetables tender, 4 to 6 minutes.

2. Add potatoes, carrots and ¼ cup water; cover. Microwave at HIGH (100%) until potatoes are tender, 12 to 15 minutes, stirring after half the cooking time.

3. Blend in flour. Stir in vegetable juice, 2 cups water, the green peas, salt and pepper. Cover. Microwave at HIGH (100%) until soup is slightly thickened and peas are heated through, 8 to 10 minutes. If using oven other than Sharp Carousel, stir after half the cooking time.

Canadian Cheese Soup ▲

1 cup water
1 large potato, shredded
1 medium onion, chopped
1 medium carrot, grated
1 stalk celery, finely chopped
1 cup chicken consommé or broth*
½ cup half-and-half
1½ cups shredded sharp Cheddar cheese
(about 6 ounces)

Makes 4 servings

1. Combine water, potato, onion, carrot and celery in 2-quart casserole; cover. Microwave at HIGH (100%) until potatoes are tender, 12 to 17 minutes, stirring after half the cooking time.

2. Stir in consommé and half-and-half; cover. Microwave at MEDIUM-HIGH (70%) until heated through, 6 to 8 minutes. Mix in cheese, stirring until melted.

*Or use 2 teaspoons instant chicken bouillon dissolved in 1 cup hot water.

Hot Buttered Rum

⅔ cup apple cider
1 tablespoon packed brown sugar
1 1-inch stick cinnamon
1½ ounces rum
1 teaspoon butter
Dash of ground nutmeg

Makes 1 serving

1. Stir cider and brown sugar in large mug or cup. Add cinnamon stick.

2. Microwave at HIGH (100%) until cider boils, 2 to 2½ minutes. Stir in rum. Top with butter and ground nutmeg.

Irish Coffee ►

¾ to 1 cup strong black coffee
1½ ounces Irish whiskey
 1 teaspoon sugar
 1 tablespoon whipped cream

Makes 1 serving

1. Mix coffee, whiskey and sugar in large mug or cup.

2. Microwave at HIGH (100%) until hot, 1½ to 2 minutes. Top with whipped cream.

Hot Cocoa for One

2 tablespoons sugar
2 teaspoons cocoa
2 tablespoons cold water
¾ cup milk

Makes 1 serving

1. Mix sugar, cocoa and cold water in large mug or cup. Microwave at HIGH (100%) until thickened, 30 seconds to 1 minute.

2. Blend in milk. Microwave at HIGH (100%) until hot, 2 to 3 minutes, stirring once or twice.

Hot Cocoa for Four

¼ cup sugar
¼ cup cold water
3 tablespoons cocoa
3 cups milk

Makes 4 servings

1. Mix sugar, cold water and cocoa in medium mixing bowl. Microwave at HIGH (100%) until thickened, 1½ to 2 minutes, stirring after half the cooking time.

2. Blend in milk. Microwave at HIGH (100%) until hot, 4 to 6 minutes, stirring once or twice.

Directions for coffee are in Learn While You Cook, page 19.

SAUCES & GRAVIES

The art of making sauces and gravies becomes a simple matter with a microwave oven. You don't have to worry about scorching, sticking or over-cooking. Occasional, rather than constant, stirring prevents lumping.

Hollandaise Sauce

Makes ⅔ cup

3 egg yolks
2 tablespoons lemon juice
¼ teaspoon salt
  Dash of cayenne pepper (optional)
½ cup margarine or butter

1. Blend egg yolks, lemon juice, salt and cayenne pepper in small bowl. Set aside. Place margarine in another small bowl. Microwave at HIGH (100%) just until melted, 15 seconds to 1 minute, stirring once or twice.

2. Blend egg yolk mixture into margarine with wire whisk. Microwave at MEDIUM (50%) until thickened, 45 seconds to 1 minute 45 seconds, blending with wire whisk every 30 seconds. Check sauce often when it begins to thicken. Blend with wire whisk before serving.

Microwaving Sauces and Gravies

Recipe Conversion

Most sauces can be converted to microwaving without a change in ingredients, using the methods given here for combining the liquid and thickening. If your recipe calls for long, slow simmering to reduce the sauce, add a little more flour, since the liquid will not evaporate in the short microwaving time. After the sauce has thickened, reduce the power to MEDIUM (50%) and microwave 20 to 30 minutes to develop flavor.

Microwave sauces made with cream at MEDIUM-HIGH (70%) and stir frequently. Double boiler sauces can be cooked at MEDIUM (50%). Use recipe on opposite page as a guide when converting Béarnaise and other sauces of the Hollandaise type.

Cooking time will depend on the amount and temperature of the ingredients used. The cook-and-look method works well. Once the ingredients are heated, stir the sauce every minute and check the consistency.

Wire whisk is the preferred utensil for blending ingredients and smoothing sauces rapidly and easily. A quart measure makes a convenient utensil for about 1 cup of liquid. A 2-quart bowl prevents boiling over of larger amounts.

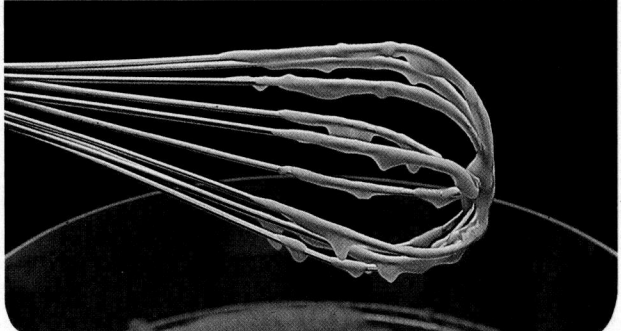

Flour-based sauces are made by stirring flour into melted fat and adding cooking liquid. For brown sauces, microwave the flour and fat a few minutes to develop color. Then blend in liquid, using a wire whisk; microwave until thickened, stirring occasionally. Power level depends on type of liquid used.

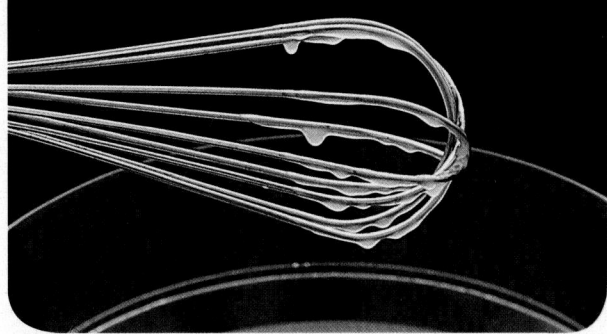

Cornstarch is usually dissolved in cold water before it is combined with hot liquid. In sweet sauces, dry cornstarch and sugar are blended together before liquid is added. Microwave until the sauce is thickened and translucent, stirring halfway through and at the end of cooking.

Mornay Sauce ▲

2 tablespoons margarine or butter
2 tablespoons all-purpose flour
1 cup chicken stock or broth
¼ cup half-and-half
¼ cup grated Romano cheese
¼ cup shredded Swiss cheese
   (about 1 ounce)
1 tablespoon dried parsley flakes

Makes 1½ cups

1. Place margarine in 2-cup measure. Microwave at HIGH (100%) until melted, 30 seconds to 1 minute. Stir in flour. Blend in chicken stock or broth and half-and-half.

2. Microwave at MEDIUM-HIGH (70%) until thickened and smooth, 4 to 7 minutes, stirring 2 or 3 times. Stir in Romano and Swiss cheese and parsley. Microwave at MEDIUM-HIGH (70%) 1 minute. Stir until cheese melts. Serve with fish.

Medium White Sauce ▲

2 tablespoons margarine or butter
2 tablespoons all-purpose flour
½ teaspoon salt
1 cup milk

Makes 1 cup

1. Place margarine in 1-quart casserole. Microwave at HIGH (100%) until melted, 30 seconds to 1 minute. Stir in flour and salt. Blend in milk.

2. Microwave at HIGH (100%) until thickened, 3 to 6 minutes, stirring once or twice during cooking.

Cheese Sauce Variation: Stir ¾ cup shredded Cheddar cheese and a dash of cayenne pepper into cooked white sauce. Microwave at HIGH (100%) to melt cheese, 30 seconds to 1 minute.

Mushroom Sauce

1 tablespoon margarine or butter
8 ounces fresh mushrooms, sliced
3 tablespoons margarine or butter
3 tablespoons all-purpose flour
½ teaspoon salt
1 cup milk

Makes 1½ cups

1. Combine 1 tablespoon margarine and the mushrooms in medium bowl. Microwave at HIGH (100%) until mushrooms are tender, 2 to 5 minutes, stirring once or twice. Set aside.

2. Place 3 tablespoons margarine in 1-quart casserole. Microwave at HIGH (100%) until melted, 30 seconds to 1 minute. Stir in flour and salt. Blend in milk. Microwave at HIGH (100%) until very thick, 3 to 6 minutes, stirring once or twice. Stir in mushrooms and liquid from mushrooms. Serve over vegetables or meat.

Barbecue Sauce

1 medium onion, chopped
1 clove garlic, minced
1 tablespoon vegetable oil
1 cup catsup
¼ cup packed brown sugar
2 tablespoons cider vinegar
¼ teaspoon dry mustard
¼ teaspoon salt
4 to 6 drops red pepper sauce

Makes 1⅔ cups

1. Combine onion, garlic and oil in 2-quart casserole. Microwave at HIGH (100%) until onion is tender, 2½ to 4½ minutes, stirring once.

2. Stir in remaining ingredients. Microwave at HIGH (100%) until hot, 2 to 3 minutes. Reduce power to MEDIUM-HIGH (70%). Microwave until flavors blend, 5 minutes. Serve over meat.

Orange Glaze

½ cup orange marmalade
¼ cup honey

Makes ½ cup

1. Combine marmalade and honey in small bowl.

2. Microwave at HIGH (100%) 1 minute. Use as a glaze on poultry.

Brown Gravy ▲

2 tablespoons fat
1 cup cooking liquid or beef broth
1 tablespoon all-purpose flour
Salt and pepper

Makes 1 cup

1. After roasting meat, remove from baking dish; cover to keep warm and set aside. Pour cooking liquid from meat into bowl, leaving particles in baking dish. Allow fat to rise to the top. Return 2 tablespoons fat to the baking dish. Skim off any remaining fat and discard. Pour cooking liquid into 1-cup measure. If necessary add beef broth to measure 1 cup. Set aside.

2. Blend flour into fat in baking dish. Microwave at HIGH (100%) until lightly browned, 3 to 7 minutes. Gradually stir in reserved cooking liquid. Microwave at HIGH (100%) until slightly thickened and smooth, 3 to 6 minutes, stirring several times during cooking. Sprinkle with salt and pepper to taste. Stir in a few drops brown bouquet sauce, if desired.

VEGETABLES

Because vegetables are microwaved quickly in a minimum of liquid, they retain more of the vitamins and minerals which are water soluble or destroyed by prolonged heat. Best of all, they keep their fresh color, texture and flavor. Frozen vegetables can be microwaved in a paper carton. The ice crystals provide enough moisture and the wax won't melt because paraffin is transparent to microwaves.

Plastic pouches serve as utensils too. Before cooking, slit or prick the pouch so excess steam can escape. Flexing the pouch part way through cooking helps equalize heat.

Fresh, frozen or canned vegetables can also be prepared in oven-proof serving dishes. Drain all but 2 tablespoons of liquid from canned vegetables to shorten microwaving time.

Broccoli-Mushroom Scallop

1½ pounds fresh broccoli, cut into
    2-inch pieces
¼ cup water
1 cup sliced fresh mushrooms
2 tablespoons margarine or butter
2 tablespoons all-purpose flour
½ teaspoon onion powder
¼ teaspoon salt
⅛ teaspoon pepper
¾ cup milk
½ cup shredded sharp Cheddar cheese
    (about 2 ounces)

Makes 4 servings

1. Place broccoli and water in 2-quart casserole; cover. Microwave at HIGH (100%) until broccoli is fork-tender, 8 to 10 minutes, stirring after half the cooking time. Drain and set aside.

2. Place mushrooms and margarine in 4-cup measure or medium bowl. Microwave at HIGH (100%) until margarine is melted and mushrooms are tender, 1½ to 2½ minutes, stirring once. Stir in flour, onion powder, salt and pepper. Blend in milk. Microwave at MEDIUM-HIGH (70%) until thickened, 3 to 5 minutes, stirring every minute.

3. Pour sauce over broccoli. Sprinkle with cheese. Microwave at MEDIUM-HIGH (70%) until heated and cheese is melted, 2 to 5 minutes.

Variation: Substitute 1 package (10 ounces) frozen cut broccoli for the fresh broccoli. Microwave at HIGH (100%) until fork-tender, 5 to 7 minutes, stirring after half the cooking time. Continue as directed.

Microwaving Vegetables

Recipe Conversion

When converting vegetable recipes, observe the microwave techniques given here. Reduce the liquid from your conventional recipe to the amount needed for microwaving. Consult the vegetable cooking chart, page 148 as a guide to time; remember that time depends on amount as well as type of vegetable.

With vegetable combinations, add quick-cooking ingredients toward the end of microwaving. Pre-cook the fillings for stuffed vegetables, then microwave the stuffed vegetable for the same amount of time as a whole one. Partially cook large, dense vegetables, like squash, before stuffing.

Casseroles made with pre-cooked vegetables need only be microwaved until heated through. Follow the directions in Recipe Conversion, page 42, for reducing the amount of fat and liquid or adding toppings.

Use a minimum of water. Some vegetables cook in their own natural moisture. Two tablespoons to ¼ cup of liquid is usually sufficient for others. Salt after cooking or dissolve salt in water before adding vegetables. Salting vegetables directly dries them out.

Cover dish tightly to hold in steam. Vegetables with skins like squash or potatoes should be pricked with a fork to allow excess steam to escape. Wrap large vegetables without skins in plastic or microwave in a covered casserole.

More Time   Less Time

Quantity and size affect cooking time. Two servings take less time than four; small pieces cook faster than large ones. For fast, even microwaving, cut vegetables in small, uniform pieces and stir once during cooking.

Arrange halved or whole vegetables, like green peppers or potatoes, in a ring, leaving center open and space between, when possible. Place tender ends of asparagus or broccoli toward center of dish, so stalks will receive more energy. If using oven other than Sharp Carousel, rotate dish or rearrange food several times.

Standing time is important, especially with large, whole vegetables. It allows the center of the vegetable to tenderize without overcooking the outside. During standing, keep the food covered to hold in heat. Long standing times can be used to microwave other foods.

Blanch 2 cups fresh vegetables for the freezer in a covered dish, using 1 cup water. Microwave at HIGH (100%) for about the same time recommended for cooking the frozen vegetable in the chart on page 148, or until vegetables become hot and begin to change color. Then immerse vege-

tables in ice water to stop cooking and cool quickly. Spread on paper toweling and blot up excess moisture. Package in freezer boxes or heavy plastic bags. Seal tightly, label and freeze. To loose-pack, spread vegetables on cookie sheet and freeze before sealing pieces in large packages.

Vegetable Chart

Vegetable	Amount	Cooking Procedure	Microwave Time at HIGH (100%)	Standing Time, covered
Artichokes				
Fresh	2 medium	Trim and rinse. Wrap in plastic wrap. Arrange in oven with spaces between.	5½-8½ min.	3 min.
Asparagus				
Fresh	1 lb.	12×8-in. dish. ¼ cup water. Re-arrange after 4 min.	6½-9½ min.	3 min.
Frozen	10-oz. pkg.	1-qt. casserole. 2 tbsp. water. Separate after 3 min.	5-7 min.	3 min.
	10-oz. pouch	Slit pouch with knife.	4-6½ min.	
Beans				
Fresh, Green and Wax	1 lb.	1½-in. pieces. 1½-qt. casserole. ¼ cup water. Stir after 4 min.	7-13½ min.	3 min.
Frozen, Green	9-oz. pkg.	1-qt. casserole. 2 tbsp. water. Stir after 3 min.	4-7 min.	3 min.
	10-oz. pouch	Slit pouch with knife.	5-6 min.	3 min.
Frozen, Lima	10-oz. pkg.	1-qt. casserole. 2 tbsp. water. Stir after 2 min.	4-7 min.	3 min.
	10-oz. pouch	Slit pouch with knife.	4½-6 min.	
Beets				
Fresh, whole	5 medium	Wash; cut off tops. 1½-qt. casserole. ½ cup water. ½ tsp. salt. Turn, rotate every 7 min.	17-19 min.	3-5 min.
Broccoli				
Fresh, spears	1½ lbs.	12×8-in. dish. ½ cup water. Rotate ½ turn after 5 min.	8-12 min.	2-3 min.
Fresh, pieces	1 lb.	1-in. pieces. 2-qt. casserole. ½ cup water. Stir after 4 min.	8-10 min.	3-5 min.
Frozen, spears, cuts, chopped	10-oz. pkg.	1-qt. casserole. 2 tbsp. water. Stir after 2 min.	5-7 min.	3 min.
	10-oz. pouch	Slit pouch with knife.	5½-7½ min.	2 min.
Brussels Sprouts				
Fresh	4 cups	1½-qt. casserole. ¼ cup water. Stir after 3 min.	4-8 min.	3 min.
Frozen	10-oz. pkg.	1-qt. casserole. 2 tbsp. water. Stir after 3 min.	5-7 min.	3 min.
	10-oz. pouch	Slit pouch with knife.	5-7 min.	3 min.
Cabbage				
Shredded	1 lb.	1½-qt. casserole. 2 tbsp. water. Stir after 5 min.	7½-13½ min.	3 min.
Wedges	1 lb.	12×8-in. dish. ¼ cup water. Re-arrange, rotate dish after 6 min.	12½-15½ min.	2-3 min.
Carrots				
Fresh, slices	2 cups	1-qt. casserole. 2 tbsp. water. Stir after 3 min.	4½-6½ min.	3 min.
Frozen, slices	2 cups	1-qt. casserole. 2 tbsp. water. Stir after 3 min.	4-7 min.	3 min.
	10-oz. pouch	Slit pouch with knife.	5-6 min.	
Cauliflower				
Fresh, flowerets	2 cups	1-qt. casserole. 2 tbsp. water. Stir after 3 min.	5-7 min.	3 min.
Fresh, whole	1 lb.	Wrap in plastic wrap. Turn over after 3 min.	5½-7½ min.	3 min.
Frozen, flowerets	10-oz. pkg.	1-qt. casserole. 2 tbsp. water. Stir after 3 min.	5-7 min.	3 min.

Vegetable	Amount	Cooking Procedure	Microwave Time at HIGH (100%)	Standing Time, covered
Corn				
Fresh, on cob	2 ears	12 × 8-in. dish. ¼ cup water. Turn over, rearrange after 3 and 6 min.	7-10 min.	5 min.
	4 ears		12-16 min.	5 min.
Frozen, on cob	2 ears	12 × 8-in. dish. 2 tbsp. water. Turn over, rearrange after 3 and 6 min.	5½-7½ min.	3 min.
	4 ears		10½-12½ min.	3 min.
Frozen, whole kernel	10-oz. pkg.	1-qt. casserole. 2 tbsp. water. Stir after 2 min.	4-6 min.	3 min.
	10-oz. pouch	Slit pouch with knife.	4½-5 min.	
Okra				
Fresh, whole	¾ lb.	1-qt. casserole. ¼ cup water. ¼ tsp. salt. Stir after 3 min.	6½-10 min.	3-5 min.
Frozen, whole or slices	10-oz. pkg.	1-qt. casserole. 2 tbsp. water. Stir after 2 and 4 min.	5-7 min.	
Peas, Black-eyed				
Frozen	10-oz. pkg.	1-qt. casserole. ¼ cup water. Stir at 2 min. intervals.	8-9 min.	2 min.
Peas, Green				
Fresh	2 cups	1-qt. casserole. ¼ cup water. Stir after 3 min.	5-8 min.	3 min.
Frozen	10-oz. pkg.	1-qt. casserole. 2 tbsp. water. Stir after 2 min.	4-6 min.	3 min.
	10-oz. pouch	Slit pouch with knife.	5-6 min.	
Potatoes				
Baked	2 medium	Prick; place on paper towels. Turn over, rearrange after 4 or 5 min. Let stand wrapped in foil.	5-7½ min.	5-10 min.
	4 medium		10½-12½ min.	5-10 min.
Boiled	4 medium	Peel and quarter potatoes. 1½-qt. casserole. ¼ cup water. ½ tsp. salt. Rearrange after 5 min.	9-12 min.	3 min.
Spinach				
Fresh	1 lb.	3-qt. casserole. 2 tbsp. water. Stir after 3 min.	5-8 min.	3 min.
Frozen, leaf or chopped	10-oz. pkg.	1-qt. casserole. 2 tbsp. water. Stir after 4 min.	7-9 min.	2-5 min.
	10-oz. pouch	Slit pouch with knife.	5-6½ min.	
Squash				
Fresh, Acorn	1 whole	Halve; wrap each with plastic wrap. Rotate, rearrange after 5 or 6 min.	8½-11½ min.	5-10 min.
	2 whole		13-16 min.	5-10 min.
Fresh, Zucchini, slices	2 cups	2-qt. casserole. 2 tbsp. margarine. Stir after 2 min.	2½-6½ min.	3 min.
Frozen, mashed	12-oz. pkg.	1-qt. casserole. Break apart after 2 min., then stir at 2 min. intervals.	5½-8 min.	
Sweet Potatoes				
Baked	2 whole	Prick; place on paper towels. Turn over, rearrange after 4 min.	5-9 min.	3 min.
	4 whole		8-13 min.	3 min.
Tomatoes				
Fresh	2 medium	Halve tomatoes. Round dish.	1-3 min.	2 min.
	4 medium		2½-4½ min.	2 min.

Canned Vegetables (15 to 16 ounces): Drain all but 2 tablespoons liquid. Microwave in 1-qt. casserole at HIGH (100%) 2 to 4 minutes, or until thoroughly heated, stirring after half the time.

149

◄ Artichokes with Mustard Sauce

4 medium artichokes
¼ cup water
½ cup prepared brown mustard
¼ cup mayonnaise or salad dressing
1 tablespoon horseradish sauce (optional)

Makes 4 servings

1. Slice 1 inch from top of artichokes; trim stem even with base. Cut off sharp tips of outer leaves. Rinse artichokes under cold water. Arrange in upright position in square baking dish, 8 × 8 inches. Pour ¼ cup water into baking dish. Cover with plastic wrap.

2. Microwave at HIGH (100%) until lower leaves can be pulled off with a slight tug and base is fork-tender, 10 to 16½ minutes. If using oven other than Sharp Carousel, rotate baking dish and re-arrange artichokes 2 to 3 times during cooking. Mix remaining ingredients. Serve with artichokes.

Scalloped Asparagus

2 packages (10 ounces each) frozen cut
    asparagus
2 tablespoons water
2 tablespoons margarine or butter
¼ cup slivered almonds
1 tablespoon margarine or butter
1 tablespoon all-purpose flour
¼ teaspoon salt
½ cup milk
½ cup shredded sharp Cheddar cheese
    (about 2 ounces)

Makes 4 to 6 servings

1. Place asparagus and water in 1½-quart casserole; cover. Microwave at HIGH (100%) until heated through, 8 to 10 minutes, stirring to break apart after half the time. Drain and set aside.

2. Place 2 tablespoons margarine in small bowl. Microwave at HIGH (100%) until melted, 30 seconds to 1 minute. Mix in almonds until coated. Microwave at HIGH (100%) until light brown, 2 to 3 minutes. Set aside.

3. Place 1 tablespoon margarine in small bowl or 2-cup measure. Microwave at HIGH (100%) until melted, 30 seconds to 1 minute. Stir in flour and salt. Blend in milk. Reduce power to MEDIUM-HIGH (70%). Microwave until thickened, 2 to 3½ minutes, stirring every 30 seconds to 1 minute. Stir in cheese until melted. Pour over asparagus. Sprinkle with almonds. Microwave at MEDIUM-HIGH (70%) until heated through, 2 to 3 minutes.

Sunshine Brussels Sprouts ▲

2 packages (10 ounces each) frozen
    Brussels sprouts
2 tablespoons water
¼ cup chopped onion
1 tablespoon margarine or butter
¼ cup half-and-half
2 egg yolks, slightly beaten
1 tablespoon fresh lemon juice
⅛ teaspoon salt
    Dash of pepper

Makes 4 to 6 servings

1. Place Brussels sprouts and water in 2-quart casserole; cover. Microwave at HIGH (100%) until tender, 8 to 10 minutes, stirring after half the cooking time. Drain and set aside.

2. Place onion and margarine in 2-cup measure. Microwave at HIGH (100%) until onion is tender, 1 to 2 minutes. Blend in remaining ingredients. Reduce power to MEDIUM-HIGH (70%). Microwave until thickened, 30 seconds to 2 minutes, stirring every 30 seconds. Pour over Brussels sprouts. Microwave at HIGH (100%) until heated through, 1 minute.

Broccoli in Lemon Sauce

2 packages (10 ounces each) frozen broccoli
    spears
2 tablespoons water
2 tablespoons margarine or butter
1 tablespoon all-purpose flour
½ cup milk
2 teaspoons grated lemon rind
⅛ teaspoon salt

Makes 4 to 6 servings

1. Place broccoli and water in 2-quart casserole; cover. Microwave at HIGH (100%) until heated through, 8 to 12 minutes, stirring to break apart after half the time. Drain and set aside.

2. Place margarine in small bowl or 2-cup measure. Microwave at HIGH (100%) until melted, 30 seconds to 1 minute. Stir in flour. Blend in remaining ingredients. Reduce power to MEDIUM-HIGH (70%). Microwave until thickened, 2½ to 3 minutes, stirring every 30 seconds to 1 minute. Pour over broccoli. Microwave at MEDIUM-HIGH (70%) until heated through, 2 to 3 minutes.

Directions for broccoli spears are in Learn While You Cook, page 29.

◄ Glazed Carrots

4 large carrots (1 pound)
3 tablespoons packed brown sugar
2 tablespoons margarine or butter
1 tablespoon water
½ teaspoon salt
⅛ teaspoon ground cinnamon

Makes 4 to 6 servings

1. Cut carrots into long thin strips. Set aside. Combine brown sugar, margarine, water, salt and cinnamon in 1½-quart casserole.

2. Microwave at HIGH (100%) until margarine is melted, 45 seconds to 1 minute 30 seconds. Stir to blend. Stir in carrots until coated. Cover. Microwave at HIGH (100%) until carrots are tender, 5 to 8 minutes, stirring once.

Fresh Cauliflower Au Gratin

1 medium head cauliflower (about 1 pound),
    separated into flowerets
2 tablespoons water
1 tablespoon margarine or butter
1 tablespoon all-purpose flour
½ cup milk
1 teaspoon prepared mustard (optional)
¼ teaspoon salt
½ cup shredded Cheddar cheese
    (about 2 ounces)
⅛ teaspoon paprika

Makes 4 servings

1. Place cauliflowerets and water in 1-quart casserole; cover. Microwave at HIGH (100%) until tender, 8½ to 10½ minutes, stirring after half the cooking time. Drain and set aside.

2. Place margarine in 2-cup measure. Microwave at HIGH (100%) until melted, 30 seconds to 1 minute. Stir in flour. Blend in milk, mustard and salt. Reduce power to MEDIUM-HIGH (70%). Microwave until thickened, 2 to 5 minutes, stirring every minute. Stir in cheese until melted. Pour over cauliflowerets; sprinkle with paprika.

Orange Carrots

4 large carrots (1 pound), cut in thin slices
¼ cup margarine or butter
1 tablespoon grated orange rind
1 teaspoon sugar

Makes 4 to 6 servings

1. Combine all ingredients in 1-quart casserole.

2. Cover. Microwave at HIGH (100%) until carrots are tender, 4 to 6 minutes, stirring after half the cooking time.

Cauliflower Scramble

2 packages (10 ounces each) cauliflower
   in cheese sauce
1 medium zucchini, thinly sliced
¼ cup chopped onion
2 tablespoons margarine or butter
2 medium tomatoes, each cut into 8 wedges
½ teaspoon salt
¼ teaspoon dried thyme leaves

Makes 4 to 6 servings

1. Remove cauliflower pouches from boxes. Place both pouches in oven. Microwave at HIGH (100%) until thawed but not hot, 4 to 6 minutes. If using oven other than Sharp Carousel, rearrange pouches once. Set aside.

2. Combine zucchini, onion and margarine in 2-quart casserole. Microwave at HIGH (100%) until vegetables are tender-crisp, 2½ to 4 minutes. Stir in cauliflower, tomatoes, salt and thyme. Microwave, covered, at HIGH (100%) until heated through, 4½ to 6½ minutes. Stir before serving.

Green Beans Almondine ▲

1½ pounds fresh green beans
½ cup hot water
1 teaspoon salt
⅓ cup slivered almonds
3 tablespoons margarine or butter
¼ teaspoon ground nutmeg (optional)
¼ teaspoon pepper

Makes 4 to 6 servings

1. Wash beans and break off ends. Break beans into 1- to 1½-inch pieces. Place beans in 2-quart casserole. Stir water and salt until salt is dissolved. Stir into beans. Cover.

2. Microwave at HIGH (100%) until beans are tender-crisp, 9 to 13 minutes, stirring once. Let stand 2 to 3 minutes. Drain.

3. Mix in almonds, margarine, nutmeg and pepper until margarine is melted. Microwave at HIGH (100%) until heated through, 1 minute.

Sautéed Green Beans

1½ pounds fresh green beans
¼ cup margarine or butter
½ teaspoon salt
¼ teaspoon dried savory leaves
⅛ teaspoon dried oregano leaves
⅛ teaspoon pepper

Makes 4 to 6 servings

1. Wash beans and break off ends. Break beans into 1- to 1½-inch pieces. Place in 2-quart casserole. Place margarine in small bowl or 2-cup measure. Microwave at HIGH (100%) until melted, 1 to 1½ minutes. Blend in remaining ingredients.

2. Pour seasoned margarine mixture over beans. Toss to coat. Cover. Microwave at HIGH (100%) until beans are tender-crisp, 9 to 13 minutes, stirring once. Cover; let stand 2 to 3 minutes.

German Potato Salad ▶

- 6 slices bacon, chopped
- ½ cup chopped green onion
- ¼ cup white vinegar
- 2 tablespoons sugar
- 1 teaspoon salt
- 6 medium potatoes (about 2½ pounds), peeled and cut into ¼-inch slices
- ¼ cup water

Makes 4 to 6 servings

1. Place bacon and green onion in small bowl or 1-quart casserole; cover. Microwave at HIGH (100%) until bacon is light brown, 5 to 7 minutes. Stir in vinegar, sugar and salt. Set aside.

2. Place potato slices and water in 2-quart casserole; cover. Microwave at HIGH (100%) until potatoes are fork-tender, 10 to 15 minutes, stirring after half the cooking time. Drain. Pour bacon and vinegar mixture over potato slices. Toss to coat.

Stuffed Baked Potatoes

- 4 baking potatoes (about 6 to 8 ounces each)
- ½ cup half-and-half
- ¼ cup shredded Cheddar cheese (about 1 ounce)
- 2 tablespoons margarine or butter
- 2 teaspoons dried parsley flakes
- ¾ teaspoon salt
- ¼ teaspoon pepper
- ¼ teaspoon dry mustard
- ¼ cup shredded Cheddar cheese (about 1 ounce)
- ⅛ teaspoon paprika

Makes 4 servings

1. Bake potatoes as directed in chart on page 29. Cut thin slice from the top of each potato. Scoop out inside with a spoon, leaving a thin shell. Add remaining ingredients except ¼ cup cheese and paprika to potatoes. Mash until no lumps remain.

2. Spoon one-fourth of the potato mixture into each shell. Place stuffed potatoes in square baking dish, 8 × 8 inches. Sprinkle with remaining ¼ cup cheese and the paprika. Microwave at MEDIUM-HIGH (70%) until cheese is melted and potatoes are heated through, 3 to 4 minutes.

Directions for baked potatoes are in Learn While You Cook, page 29.

Parsley Potatoes

- 6 medium red potatoes (about 2½ pounds), peeled and quartered
- ¼ cup water
- ¼ cup margarine or butter
- 1 tablespoon dried parsley flakes
- ½ teaspoon salt
- ⅛ teaspoon pepper

Makes 4 to 6 servings

1. Place potatoes and water in 2-quart casserole; cover. Microwave at HIGH (100%) until fork-tender, 12 to 15 minutes, stirring after half the time. Let stand 5 minutes. Drain and set aside.

2. Place margarine in 2-cup measure. Microwave at HIGH (100%) 1 to 1½ minutes. Stir in remaining ingredients. Pour over potatoes. Toss to coat.

Sweet Potato Casserole ▲

- 4 medium sweet potatoes or yams (about 2 pounds)
- ¼ cup packed brown sugar
- ¼ cup margarine or butter
- ½ teaspoon salt
- 1 can (8 ounces) crushed pineapple
- 1 tablespoon packed brown sugar
- 1 tablespoon margarine or butter
- 1 teaspoon water
- ½ teaspoon ground cinnamon
- ¼ teaspoon ground nutmeg
- 1½ cups miniature marshmallows
- ¼ cup chopped pecans

Makes 4 to 6 servings

1. Wash sweet potatoes. Prick each 2 or 3 times with fork to allow steam to escape. Arrange in oven at least 1 inch apart. Microwave at HIGH (100%) until fork-tender, 8 to 10 minutes. Cover and let stand 5 minutes.

2. Peel and slice potatoes. Place in 2-quart casserole. Add ¼ cup brown sugar, ¼ cup margarine and the salt. Mash until no lumps remain. Mix in pineapple. Microwave at HIGH (100%) 2 minutes. Stir and set aside.

3. Place 1 tablespoon brown sugar, 1 tablespoon margarine, the water, cinnamon and nutmeg in medium bowl. Microwave at HIGH (100%) until margarine is melted, 1 to 1½ minutes, stirring after half the time. Add marshmallows; toss to coat. Top sweet potato mixture with marshmallows. Microwave at HIGH (100%) until marshmallows are melted and potatoes are heated through, 2 to 4 minutes. Sprinkle with pecans.

Acorn Squash with ► Cranberry Filling

- 2 large acorn squash (about 2 pounds each)
- 1 can (16 ounces) whole cranberry sauce
- 1 tablespoon honey
- ¼ teaspoon ground allspice

Makes 4 servings

1. Prick squash several times with fork to allow steam to escape. Place in oven. Microwave at HIGH (100%) until soft when pricked with fork, 10 to 12 minutes. If using oven other than Sharp Carousel, turn squash over and rotate after half the cooking time. Let stand 5 minutes. Cut in half and remove seeds. Place cut side up in 10-inch square casserole. Set aside.

2. Combine cranberry sauce, honey and allspice in small bowl. Microwave at HIGH (100%) until hot and bubbly, 3 to 4 minutes, stirring after half the cooking time. Spoon into squash halves. Microwave at HIGH (100%) until heated through, 2 to 3 minutes. If using oven other than Sharp Carousel, rotate after half the cooking time.

Squash Parmesan

- 3 small yellow summer squash (about 1 pound), thinly sliced
- ¼ cup chopped onion
- 2 tablespoons water
- 2 tablespoons grated Parmesan cheese

Makes 4 servings

1. Place squash, onion and water in 1-quart casserole; cover. Microwave at HIGH (100%) until vegetables are tender, 7 to 9 minutes.

2. Sprinkle with Parmesan cheese. Microwave at HIGH (100%) until cheese melts, 1 to 2 minutes.

Zesty Squash ▲

- ¼ cup margarine or butter
- 1 clove garlic, minced
- 1 teaspoon dried oregano leaves
- ½ teaspoon dried basil leaves
- ½ teaspoon salt
- ⅛ teaspoon pepper
- 2 medium zucchini, thinly sliced
- 1 medium yellow summer squash, thinly sliced
- 1 large tomato, cut into 8 wedges

Makes 4 servings

1. Place margarine and garlic in 2-quart casserole. Microwave at HIGH (100%) until margarine is melted, 1 to 1½ minutes. Mix in oregano, basil, salt and pepper. Add remaining ingredients except tomato. Toss to coat. Cover.

2. Microwave at HIGH (100%) until squash is tender, 8 to 10 minutes, stirring after half the cooking time. Stir in tomato. Cover; let stand 2 minutes.

Wilted Spinach Salad

- 1 pound fresh spinach
- 6 slices bacon, chopped
- 3 tablespoons chopped onion
- ⅓ cup vinegar
- ⅓ cup water
- 2 tablespoons sugar
- ¼ teaspoon pepper

Makes 4 servings

1. Wash spinach. Remove thick stems and bruised leaves. Drain well and set aside in salad bowl.

2. Place bacon pieces in 1-quart casserole. Microwave at HIGH (100%) until bacon is crisp, 6 to 8 minutes, stirring after half the cooking time. Remove bacon and set aside on paper toweling.

3. Add onion to bacon fat. Microwave at HIGH (100%) until tender, 1½ to 2½ minutes. Add vinegar, water, sugar and pepper. Microwave at HIGH (100%) until boiling, 3 to 6 minutes. Immediately pour over spinach. Add bacon and toss well. Serve immediately.

Creamed Spinach ►

2 packages (10 ounces each) frozen
    chopped spinach
½ cup chopped onion
2 tablespoons margarine or butter
1 package (6 ounces) cream cheese
½ teaspoon salt
¼ teaspoon pepper
¼ teaspoon ground nutmeg
⅓ cup milk

Makes 4 to 6 servings

1. Place unopened packages of spinach in oven. Microwave at HIGH (100%) until completely thawed, 6 to 9 minutes. If using oven other than Sharp Carousel, rearrange packages once. Drain thoroughly and set aside.

2. Place onion and margarine in 1-quart casserole. Microwave at HIGH (100%) until onion is tender, 3 to 4 minutes. Add cream cheese. Microwave at MEDIUM (50%) until softened, 1 to 1½ minutes. Stir in salt, pepper and nutmeg until smooth. Blend in milk. Mix in spinach.

3. Microwave at MEDIUM-HIGH (70%) until heated through, 4 to 6 minutes, stirring once. Stir before serving.

Ratatouille

1 medium eggplant (1 to 1½ pounds),
    peeled and cut into ½-inch cubes
1 medium onion, thinly sliced and separated
    into rings
1 green pepper, thinly sliced
1 large clove garlic, minced
¼ cup olive oil
1 medium zucchini (½ to ¾ pound),
    thinly sliced
1½ teaspoons dried basil leaves
1½ teaspoons dried marjoram leaves
1 teaspoon salt
¼ teaspoon pepper
1 large tomato, chopped

Makes 6 to 8 servings

1. Mix eggplant, onion, green pepper, garlic and olive oil in 3-quart casserole. Microwave, covered, at HIGH (100%) until onion and green pepper are tender, 8 to 10 minutes, stirring once or twice during cooking time.

2. Add zucchini, basil, marjoram, salt and pepper. Microwave, covered, at HIGH (100%) until eggplant and zucchini are tender, 5 to 7 minutes. Gently stir in tomato. Let stand 5 minutes.

Italian Zucchini ▲

4 medium zucchini (about 1½ pounds),
    thinly sliced
1 tablespoon margarine or butter
1 tablespoon olive oil
2 teaspoons snipped parsley
½ teaspoon dried basil leaves
½ teaspoon dried oregano leaves
½ teaspoon salt

Makes 4 to 6 servings

1. Place zucchini in 1½-quart casserole; cover. Microwave at HIGH (100%) until tender-crisp, 4 to 6 minutes. Drain.

2. Stir in remaining ingredients. Microwave at HIGH (100%) until vegetables are tender, 2 to 4 minutes, stirring after half the cooking time.

CEREALS & GRAINS

Cereal may be microwaved and served in individual bowls. It won't crust on the utensil, so there is no loss in cooking and clean-up is easy.

Raw or converted long grain rice takes time to rehydrate. Microwaving time is a little shorter than conventional, but the greatest advantage is the ease with which you can prepare fluffy rice without sticking or scorching.

There is little advantage in microwaving pasta because of the large amount of water needed. You'll save most time if you microwave the sauce while cooking pasta conventionally.

Cooked rice and pasta reheat easily in the microwave oven without loss of flavor or texture. No extra water is needed to prevent sticking or drying, so there's no danger of overcooking rice and pasta or thinning sauces.

Fried Rice

2 tablespoons chopped onion
1 tablespoon margarine or butter
2 teaspoons instant chicken bouillon
1⅔ cups hot water
2 cups uncooked instant rice
2 tablespoons finely chopped green onion
2 eggs, beaten
1 tablespoon plus 2 teaspoons soy sauce

Makes 4 to 6 servings

1. Combine onion and margarine in 2-quart casserole. Microwave at HIGH (100%) until onion is tender, 1 to 3 minutes. Set aside.

2. Stir bouillon into hot water until dissolved. Add bouillon mixture, rice and green onion to casserole; cover. Microwave at HIGH (100%) until mixture boils, 4 to 8 minutes. Let stand, covered, until liquid is absorbed, 5 to 6 minutes.

3. Stir in eggs and soy sauce. Microwave, uncovered, at HIGH (100%) until eggs are set, 2 to 4½ minutes, stirring several times during cooking. Fluff with fork before serving.

Microwaving Cereals and Grains

Recipe Conversion

The easiest and fastest way to convert a main dish or casserole calling for uncooked rice, meat and vegetables is to substitute quick-cooking rice for uncooked long grain rice.

Meats and vegetables microwave so rapidly that they will be overcooked in the time it takes to tenderize raw rice. To obtain the same number of servings, substitute twice the amount of quick-cooking rice and use the quantity of liquid recommended on the package.

If you prefer to use raw or converted long grain rice, microwave it until almost tender, using the recipes in this book as a guide. Add the meat toward the end of cooking.

Casseroles made with pre-cooked ingredients need only be microwaved until heated through. Reduce liquid as directed in Recipe Conversion, page 42.

Select a large bowl or casserole when microwaving cereals, which boil over easily. Stir cereal once during cooking and again before serving.

Microwave long grain rice at HIGH (100%) 5 minutes, then reduce power to MEDIUM (50%) to give the rice time to absorb liquid and to tenderize. Fluff rice with fork before serving.

Cereal Cooking Chart

Power Level: HIGH (100%)

Cereal	Amount	Salt (tsp.)	Water (cups)	Time (min.)
Quick Oatmeal				
1 serving	⅓ cup	¼	¾	2-2½
4 servings	1⅓ cups	¾	3	6-7
Old-Fashioned Oatmeal				
1 serving	⅓ cup	¼	¾	4-6
4 servings	1⅓ cups	1	2½	8-9
Instant Cream of Wheat				
1 serving	2½ tbsp.	⅛	¾	1½-2½
4 servings	⅔ cup	½	2¾	4½-6
Regular Cream of Wheat				
1 serving	2½ tbsp.	⅛	1	4-6
4 servings	⅔ cup	½	3½	9-12

Rice Pilaf ▲

¼ cup chopped onion
¼ cup chopped celery
¼ cup chopped green pepper
2 tablespoons margarine or butter
1 cup hot water
1 can (4 ounces) sliced mushrooms, drained
⅓ cup uncooked long grain rice
1 tablespoon instant chicken bouillon

Makes 2 to 3 servings

1. Combine onion, celery, green pepper and margarine in 1-quart casserole. Microwave at HIGH (100%) until vegetables are tender-crisp, 3 to 5 minutes. Stir in remaining ingredients; cover.

2. Microwave at HIGH (100%) 5 minutes. Reduce power to MEDIUM (50%). Microwave until liquid is absorbed, 10 to 12 minutes. Let stand, covered, 5 minutes. Fluff with fork before serving.

Instant Rice

1¼ cups uncooked instant rice
1¼ cups hot water
1 teaspoon salt
1 teaspoon margarine or butter (optional)

Makes 3 to 4 servings

1. Combine all ingredients in 2-quart casserole.

2. Cover. Microwave at HIGH (100%) until water boils, 4 to 8 minutes. Let stand, covered, 5 minutes. Fluff with fork before serving.

Long Grain Rice

1 cup uncooked long grain rice
2 cups hot water
1 tablespoon margarine or butter (optional)
1 teaspoon salt

Makes 4 servings

1. Combine all ingredients in 2-quart casserole.

2. Cover. Microwave at HIGH (100%) 5 minutes. Reduce power to MEDIUM (50%). Microwave until liquid is absorbed and rice is tender, 10 to 13 minutes. Fluff with fork before serving.

Brown Rice

1 cup parboiled long grain brown rice
2¾ cups hot water
1 tablespoon margarine or butter (optional)
1 teaspoon salt

Makes 4 servings

1. Combine all ingredients in 3-quart casserole.

2. Cover. Microwave at HIGH (100%) 5 minutes. Reduce power to MEDIUM (50%). Microwave until liquid is absorbed and rice is tender, 25 to 35 minutes. Fluff with fork before serving.

Stuffing ►

- 8 ounces fresh mushrooms, sliced
- ½ cup chopped onion
- ½ cup chopped celery
- ½ cup margarine or butter
- 1 egg
- 1 package (8 ounces) seasoned stuffing mix (about 4 cups)
- 1 cup hot water
- 2 teaspoons instant chicken bouillon
- 1 teaspoon ground sage

Makes 6 to 8 servings

1. Combine mushrooms, onion, celery and margarine in 1½-quart casserole. Microwave at HIGH (100%) until vegetables are tender, 5 to 8 minutes.

2. Stir in remaining ingredients. Microwave at HIGH (100%) until heated through, 4 to 7 minutes, stirring once during cooking.

Cream of Wheat

- 1¾ cups hot water
- ¼ teaspoon salt
- ⅓ cup uncooked regular cream of wheat

Makes 2 servings

1. Combine hot water and salt in 2-quart casserole. Stir in cream of wheat.

2. Microwave at HIGH (100%) 3 minutes. Stir. Microwave at HIGH (100%) until desired thickness, 2½ to 4½ minutes. Stir before serving.

Regular Oatmeal

- 1⅓ cups hot water
- ½ teaspoon salt
- ⅔ cup regular oats

Makes 2 servings

1. Combine hot water and salt in 1½-quart casserole. Microwave at HIGH (100%) until boiling, 2 to 3½ minutes. Stir in oats.

2. Microwave at HIGH (100%) until desired thickness, 1 to 3 minutes. Stir before serving.

Variation: Substitute ⅔ cup quick-cooking oats for the regular oats.

BREADS

Most quick and yeast breads can be baked in your microwave oven, except those which require a firm crust, like French bread, hard rolls or popovers. The carousel simplifies microwaving; in other ovens, breads must be rotated frequently to help them rise and bake evenly.*

Warming pre-baked breads by microwave is quick, convenient and easy. Day old or slightly dry breads may be refreshened. Always place breads on paper toweling or napkin to absorb moisture which collects under the bread. Use MEDIUM-HIGH (70%) and reheat briefly; over-heating toughens bread. A single roll may take as little as 15 to 25 seconds.

For 8 ounces of rolls, microwave about 1 minute 15 seconds. Instructions for thawing and warming frozen convenience baked goods are on page 40.

*To thaw frozen bread dough, follow directions in the recipe on page 171.

Bran Muffins

Makes 18 to 24 muffins

2¼ cups whole bran cereal
¼ cup packed dark brown sugar
1 cup buttermilk
⅓ cup dark molasses
1¼ cups all-purpose flour
1 teaspoon baking powder
1 teaspoon baking soda
½ teaspoon salt
½ cup dark raisins
½ cup vegetable oil
1 egg, slightly beaten

1. Mix bran cereal, brown sugar, buttermilk and molasses in medium bowl. Let stand until all liquid is absorbed. Combine flour, baking powder, baking soda and salt. Stir raisins, oil and egg into bran mixture. Stir in flour until evenly moist.

2. Spoon batter into 18 to 24 paper-lined muffin cups, 2½ × 1¼ inches, filling each half full. Microwave 6 muffins at HIGH (100%) until wooden pick inserted in center comes out clean, 2 to 3 minutes. Repeat with remaining muffins. If using oven other than Sharp Carousel, rearrange muffins once or twice during cooking.

Microwaving Breads

Recipe Conversion

A slight increase in shortening may be needed to adapt yeast doughs for microwaving. Allow at least ¼ cup shortening for 2½ to 3 cups of flour. Add coatings or toppings for eye appeal; use a microwave recipe as a guide to baking techniques, power level and time.

Changes in quick bread doughs depend upon the recipe. Decrease liquid by 1 to 2 tablespoons in dense batters and by one-third in moist batters. Increase shortening by 1 to 2 tablespoons. Chop nuts and fruits finely.

Quick breads rise higher in a microwave oven, so fill dishes no more than one-third to half full. If your recipe calls for more than 1¼ to 1⅓ cups of flour, bake extra batter as cupcakes.

For coffee cakes, decrease baking powder by one-fourth. Use a microwave layer cake recipe as a guide to baking. Cakes with a heavy topping on the batter or in the bottom of the dish should be elevated on an inverted saucer during cooking.

Use naturally colorful ingredients or toppings, since microwaved breads will not brown. Yeast bread loaves may be greased or brushed lightly with milk, then coated with wheat germ, cornmeal or oatmeal. Coat heavily, as surface will expand during rising and baking.

Ring shapes are ideal for yeast and quick breads, because energy penetrates evenly. Elevate loaves on an inverted saucer. If using oven other than Sharp Carousel, rotate baked goods every 1 to 3 minutes, depending on the density of the dough.

Test yeast breads for doneness by touching lightly in several places. Surface should spring back. It will not appear brown, but should not look doughy. Overbaking toughens bread; let stand 2 to 3 minutes to complete cooking.

Line microwave muffin cups, custard cups, coffee cups or plastic coffee cup holders with paper baking cups to absorb excess moisture when microwaving muffins. If you have no cups, 3 paper baking cups are strong enough to support muffins.

Fill cups with batter no more than half full, since quick breads rise higher when microwaved. Arrange cups in ring and microwave 6 at a time. Remove muffins from dishes immediately after baking so bottoms will not become soggy from trapped steam. Cool on wire rack.

Shield ends of quick bread loaves with 2-inch wide strips of foil. Cover 1 inch of batter and mold remaining foil around handles of dish. Elevate loaf on inverted saucer in oven.

Look through bottom of loaf dish to test for doneness. No unbaked batter should appear. A wooden pick, inserted in center of loaf, should come out clean. Cool directly on countertop 5 to 10 minutes before removing from dish.

Whole Wheat Bread ▲

Wheat germ
1 package active dry yeast
2 tablespoons warm water (105 to 115°)
1 cup milk
¼ cup sugar
2 tablespoons shortening
1 teaspoon salt
1½ cups all-purpose flour
1½ cups whole wheat flour

Makes 1 loaf

1. Lightly grease loaf dish, 9 × 5 inches; coat with wheat germ. Dissolve yeast in 2 tablespoons warm water in small bowl. Set aside. Combine milk, sugar, shortening and salt in large bowl. Microwave at HIGH (100%) until shortening melts and sugar dissolves, 2 to 4 minutes, stirring 2 to 3 times during cooking. Let cool until warm (105 to 115°). Stir in dissolved yeast.

2. Combine flours; stir into milk and yeast mixture. Turn dough onto well-floured surface. Knead until smooth and elastic and dough no longer sticks to board. Place in greased bowl; turn greased side up. Cover; let rise in warm place until double in size. (Dough is ready if an indentation remains when touched.)

3. Punch down dough. Shape and place in loaf dish. Turn loaf to coat all sides with wheat germ. Cover; let rise in warm place until double. Remove cover. Place on inverted saucer in oven. Microwave at MEDIUM (50%) until loaf is no longer doughy and springs back when touched lightly, 10 to 15 minutes. If using oven other than Sharp Carousel, rotate loaf every 2 minutes. Let stand 3 minutes. Remove from loaf dish; cool on wire rack.

White Bread Variation: Increase all-purpose flour to 3 cups and omit the whole wheat flour.

Cornmeal-Molasses Bread

Cornmeal
3 tablespoons shortening
¾ cup boiling water
½ cup cornmeal
¼ cup dark molasses
2 teaspoons salt
1 package active dry yeast
¼ cup warm water (105 to 115°)
1 egg, beaten
3 cups all-purpose flour
Milk

Makes 1 loaf

1. Lightly grease 10-inch baking ring; coat with cornmeal. Place shortening in large bowl. Pour ¾ cup boiling water over shortening; stir until shortening melts. Add the ½ cup cornmeal, molasses and salt. Let stand until warm (105 to 115°). Dissolve yeast in ¼ cup warm water.

2. Stir dissolved yeast and egg into warm cornmeal mixture. Mix in flour all at once. Turn dough onto well-floured surface. Knead until smooth and elastic. Shape dough into roll, 15 inches long. Brush lightly with milk. Sprinkle with cornmeal. Place in baking ring. Pinch edges to seal. Let rise in warm place until double in size. (Dough is ready if an indentation remains when touched.)

3. Microwave at MEDIUM (50%) until loaf is no longer doughy and springs back when touched lightly, 8 to 13 minutes. If using oven other than Sharp Carousel, rotate every 2 minutes. Let stand 2 minutes. Remove from ring; cool on wire rack.

Carrot Bread

½ cup whole wheat flour
½ cup all-purpose flour
½ cup granulated sugar
¼ cup packed brown sugar
1 teaspoon baking soda
1 teaspoon baking powder
1 teaspoon ground cinnamon
¾ teaspoon salt
½ cup vegetable oil
2 eggs
1 teaspoon vanilla
2 cups grated carrot
⅓ cup raisins (optional)

Makes 1 loaf

1. Lightly grease bottom of loaf dish, 9 × 5 inches. Combine flours, sugars, baking soda, baking powder, cinnamon and salt in medium mixing bowl. Add remaining ingredients except carrots and raisins. Beat at low speed until just blended. Stir in carrots and raisins. Pour into loaf dish.

2. Place loaf dish on inverted saucer or roasting rack in oven. Microwave at MEDIUM-HIGH (70%) 6 minutes. Cover ends of loaf dish with 2-inch strips of aluminum foil and mold to fit around handles. Microwave at MEDIUM-HIGH (70%) until no uncooked batter can be seen through bottom of dish and wooden pick inserted in center comes out clean, 3 to 8 minutes. If using oven other than Sharp Carousel, rotate dish quarter turn every 2 to 3 minutes. Cool on countertop 5 minutes. Remove from dish.
Store in refrigerator.

◄ Banana Bread

1¾ cups all-purpose flour
1½ teaspoons baking powder
½ teaspoon baking soda
½ teaspoon salt
1 cup mashed ripe banana
1 tablespoon lemon juice
¾ cup sugar
⅓ cup margarine or butter
2 eggs
⅓ cup milk
½ cup coarsely chopped walnuts

Makes 1 loaf

1. Lightly grease bottom only of loaf dish, 9 × 5 inches. Combine in medium mixing bowl flour, baking powder, baking soda and salt. Set aside. Mix mashed banana and lemon juice. Set aside.

2. Beat sugar and margarine in a large bowl until light and fluffy. Add eggs, one at a time, beating well after each. Alternately stir in milk and dry ingredients. Fold in walnuts and banana mixture. Pour batter into loaf dish. Cover ends of loaf with 2-inch strips of aluminum foil and mold to fit around handles. Place loaf dish on inverted saucer in oven.

3. Microwave at MEDIUM-HIGH (70%) 8 to 10 minutes. If using oven other than Sharp Carousel, rotate loaf dish quarter turn 2 or 3 times. Increase power to HIGH (100%). Microwave until no un-cooked batter can be seen through bottom of dish and wooden pick inserted in center comes out clean, 1 to 2 minutes. Cool on countertop 10 min-utes. Remove from loaf dish.

Corn Bread from a Mix

1 package (8½ ounces) corn bread mix

Makes 6 to 8 servings

1. Prepare corn bread according to package directions. Spread batter in round baking dish, 9 × 1½ inches. Place in oven on inverted saucer.

2. Microwave at MEDIUM-HIGH (70%) until loaf springs back when touched lightly in center, 4 to 5½ minutes. If using oven other than Sharp Carousel, rotate dish half turn every 2 minutes.

Directions for Muffins from a Mix are in Learn While You Cook, page 32.

Cinnamon Nut Rolls ▲

Margarine or butter
1 loaf (16 ounces) frozen bread dough
1½ cups water
2 tablespoons powdered sugar
1½ teaspoons ground cinnamon
1 tablespoon margarine or butter
¼ cup packed brown sugar
½ to ¾ teaspoon ground cinnamon
¼ cup margarine or butter
¼ cup packed brown sugar
⅓ cup chopped pecans

Makes 14 rolls

1. Grease loaf dish, 9×5 inches with margarine. Grease frozen loaf on all sides with margarine; place in loaf dish. Pour 1½ cups water into rectangular baking dish, 12×8 inches or 10-inch square casserole. Microwave at HIGH (100%) until water boils, 1½ to 2½ minutes. Place loaf dish in baking dish; cover with waxed paper. Microwave at MEDIUM (50%) 2 minutes. If using oven other than Sharp Carousel, rotate baking dish quarter turn every 30 seconds.

2. Turn loaf over. Re-cover. Microwave at MEDIUM (50%) until dough is thawed and slightly warm, 2 to 4 minutes. If using oven other than Sharp Carousel, rotate baking dish quarter turn every 30 seconds. Let stand 10 minutes. Blot any excess margarine from dough. Let stand, covered with waxed paper, in warm place until double in size, 30 minutes to 1 hour. (Dough is ready if an indentation remains when touched.)

3. Mix powdered sugar and 1½ teaspoons cinnamon; sprinkle over 17-inch sheet of waxed paper. Turn dough onto waxed paper. Roll into rectangle, 14×9 inches. Place 1 tablespoon margarine in small bowl. Microwave at HIGH (100%) until melted, 30 to 45 seconds. Brush dough with margarine. Mix ¼ cup brown sugar and ½ to ¾ teaspoon cinnamon. Sprinkle evenly over dough. Roll up tightly, beginning at 14-inch side. Pinch edge of dough into roll to seal. Cut into fourteen 1-inch slices.

4. Place ¼ cup margarine in round baking dish, 9×1½ inches. Microwave at HIGH (100%) until melted, 45 seconds to 1 minute 30 seconds. Sprinkle ¼ cup brown sugar evenly over margarine in baking dish. (Do not stir.) Sprinkle pecans over brown sugar. Place 11 rolls around outer edge of baking dish and 3 in center. Cover with waxed paper. Let stand in warm place until light and double in size, 30 minutes to 1 hour. (Dough is ready if an indentation remains when touched.)

5. Microwave at MEDIUM-HIGH (70%) until rolls spring back when touched lightly, 4 to 7 minutes. If using oven other than Sharp Carousel, rotate dish once or twice. Immediately invert baking dish on heatproof serving plate. Let baking dish remain several minutes so brown sugar mixture drizzles over rolls.

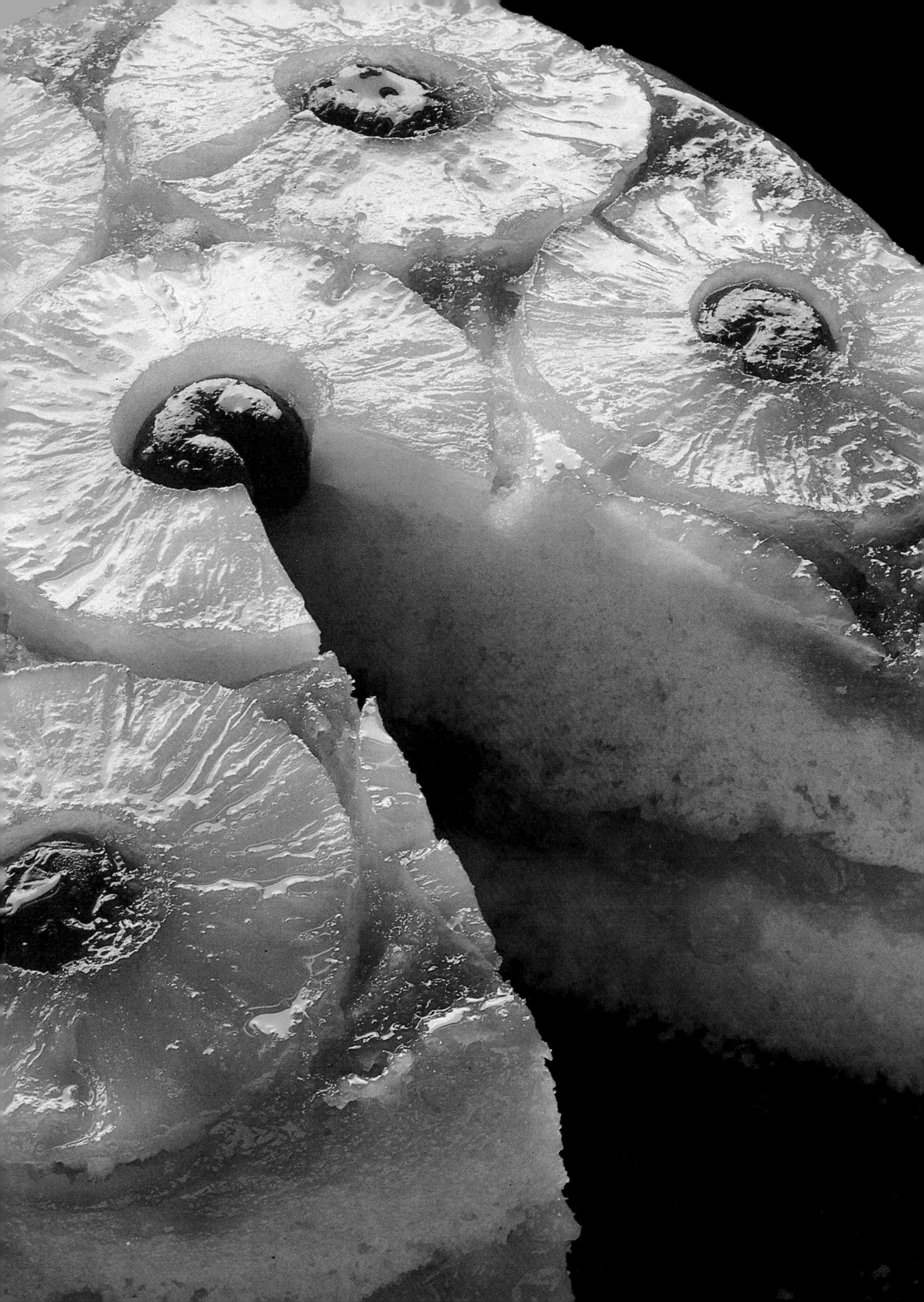

DESSERTS

There's always time to make dessert with a microwave oven. Fruit desserts have a remarkably fresh flavor and texture. Microwaved cakes are higher and more tender than conventionally baked; since cakes are usually frosted, browning is unimportant. Microwaved pie crusts are exceptionally tender and flaky, while delicate custards and puddings are easy to prepare.

Two-Layer Pineapple Upside-Down Cake

1 can (15½ ounces) crushed pineapple (juice pack), drained (reserve juice)
1 tablespoon cornstarch
2 tablespoons packed brown sugar
1 tablespoon honey
½ teaspoon lemon juice
2 tablespoons margarine or butter
¼ cup packed brown sugar
1 can (8 ounces) pineapple slices (juice pack), drained (reserve juice)
7 maraschino cherries, drained
1 package (18½ ounces) yellow cake mix

Makes two 9-inch layers

1. Blend juice from crushed pineapple and cornstarch in small bowl. Stir in crushed pineapple, 2 tablespoons brown sugar, the honey and lemon juice. Microwave at HIGH (100%) until thickened, 4 to 5 minutes, stirring after half the time.

Set aside. Place margarine in round baking dish, 9 × 1½ inches. Microwave at HIGH (100%) until melted, 30 to 45 seconds. Stir in ¼ cup brown sugar; spread evenly in dish. Arrange pineapple slices and cherries over brown sugar. Set aside.

2. Line round baking dish, 9 × 1½ inches, with waxed paper. Add enough additional water to juice reserved from pineapple slices to equal amount of water needed for preparing cake mix. Prepare cake mix according to package directions using pineapple juice-water mixture. Pour half of the batter into paper-lined baking dish and half over pineapple slices.

3. Microwave first layer (paper-lined baking dish) at MEDIUM-HIGH (70%) 5 minutes. Increase power to HIGH (100%). Microwave until wooden pick inserted in center comes out clean, 1 to 4 minutes. Invert onto serving plate; spread with crushed pineapple mixture. Microwave pineapple layer at MEDIUM-HIGH (70%) 4 minutes. Increase power to HIGH (100%). Microwave until wooden pick inserted in center comes out clean, 5 to 8 minutes. Cool 2 minutes. Invert second layer on top of first.

Microwaving Desserts

Recipe Conversion

Rich cakes using whole eggs adapt well to microwaving. Add an extra egg to a 1- or 2-egg cake. If your recipe already calls for 3 eggs, reduce liquid by about one-third. Less reduction of liquid is needed if you bake your layer cake recipe in a ring-shaped dish. Use a microwave recipe as a guide to time and power levels. To convert single crust pies, prepare and microwave the pie shell first. Then add filling and microwave again. Timing for fruit pies depends on the type of fruit. Check for doneness after about 10 minutes. Filling should be hot and starting to cook in center. It will complete cooking as it cools. Double crust pies cannot be microwaved because the bottom crust will not cook properly.

Your microwave oven simplifies the preparation of puddings and custards as well as precooked fillings for cream, chiffon and marshmallow pies. HIGH (100%) softens gelatin in 1 to 2 minutes or melts marshmallows in 2 to 4 minutes. Use a microwave recipe as a guide to method and time for custards and creams.

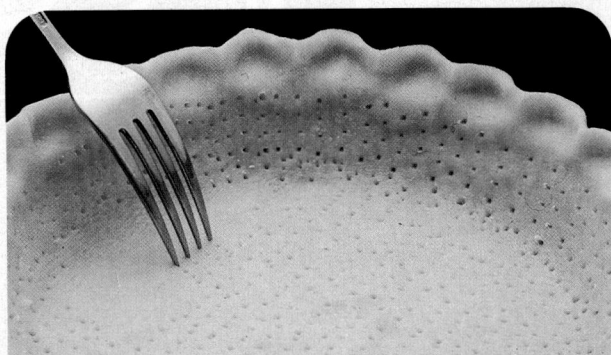

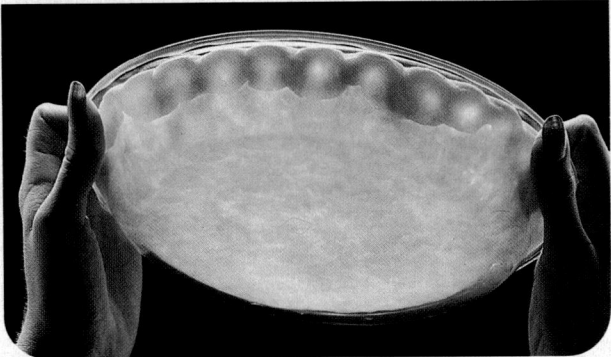

Add a few drops food coloring to pastry dough, as crust will not brown. Prick pie shell generously to prevent shrinking, and microwave before filling. Check for doneness through bottom of dish; crust should be dry and flaky.

Carousel promotes even microwaving of cakes, pie shells and baked custards. If using oven other than Sharp Carousel, rotate or rearrange dishes several times during cooking.

Prepare dish for ring cake by greasing well, then sprinkle with graham cracker crumbs. Line bottoms of layer cake dishes with waxed paper for easy removal. No special preparation is needed if cake is to be served from the dish.

Fill dishes no more than half full, because micro-waved cakes rise higher than conventionally baked. If you have extra batter from a cake mix, use it to bake cupcakes.

Shield corners of square cakes with triangles of foil to prevent overbaking. Elevate cake on inverted saucer or trivet in oven. Rectangular cakes do not microwave evenly.

Check for doneness through bottom of clear dish; 2 to 3 inches in center of round or square cake will finish cooking as cake cools. No unbaked batter should appear on bottom of tube cake.

Cool cakes directly on countertop. Heat trapped between dish and countertop helps complete cooking on bottom of cake. A few moist spots on surface of cake will dry as cake cools.

Cheesecake ▾

Graham Cracker Crust (page 180)
2 packages (8 ounces each) cream cheese, softened
½ cup sugar
2 eggs, separated
1 tablespoon lemon juice
1 teaspoon grated lemon peel
½ cup dairy sour cream
1 tablespoon sugar
½ teaspoon vanilla

Makes 9-inch cake

1. Prepare crust. Set aside. Beat cream cheese and ½ cup sugar in large mixing bowl until light and fluffy. Beat in egg yolks, lemon juice and peel until smooth.

2. Beat egg whites in small mixing bowl until stiff peaks form. Fold beaten egg whites into cream cheese mixture. Spread evenly in prepared crust.

3. Microwave at MEDIUM (50%) until center is set, 10 to 15 minutes. If using oven other than Sharp Carousel, rotate several times during cooking. Refrigerate several hours before serving. Mix sour cream, 1 tablespoon sugar and the vanilla. Carefully spread over cheesecake before serving.

Applesauce Cake

1 cup packed brown sugar
½ cup margarine or butter
1 egg
1 cup unsweetened applesauce
1¼ cups all-purpose flour
1 teaspoon ground cinnamon
½ teaspoon baking soda
½ teaspoon salt
½ teaspoon ground cloves
½ teaspoon ground nutmeg
½ teaspoon ground allspice
½ cup raisins

Makes one ring cake

1. Lightly grease 8- to 10-cup baking ring. Beat brown sugar and margarine until smooth. Beat in egg. Stir in applesauce. Mix in flour, cinnamon, baking soda, salt, cloves, nutmeg and allspice. Stir in raisins.

2. Pour batter into baking ring. Microwave at MEDIUM-HIGH (70%) 4 minutes. Increase power to HIGH (100%). Microwave until wooden pick inserted in center comes out clean, 4 to 7 minutes. Cool 5 minutes. Invert onto serving plate.

Fruitcake ▲

½ cup diced candied green cherries
½ cup diced candied red cherries
½ cup chopped citron
½ cup golden raisins
½ cup chopped dates
¼ cup currants
⅓ cup brandy
½ cup packed dark brown sugar
½ cup margarine or butter
1 teaspoon vanilla
3 eggs
2 tablespoons molasses
¾ cup all-purpose flour
½ teaspoon salt
½ teaspoon baking powder
½ teaspoon ground nutmeg
½ teaspoon ground allspice
1 cup coarsely chopped walnuts

Makes one fruitcake

1. Lightly grease 8- to 10-cup baking ring. Mix green and red cherries, citron, raisins, dates, currants and brandy. Set aside. Beat brown sugar, margarine and vanilla until fluffy; add eggs and molasses. Beat in remaining ingredients except nuts until well blended. Stir in fruit and brandy mixture and nuts. Pour into baking ring.

2. Microwave at MEDIUM-HIGH (70%) until wooden pick inserted in center comes out clean, 10 to 16 minutes. If using oven other than Sharp Carousel, rotate 2 or 3 times. Let stand 5 minutes; remove from baking ring. Cool. Wrap in cheesecloth which has been dampened with wine or brandy, if desired. Store tightly covered.

Sour Cream Brunch Cake

⅔ cup sugar
⅓ cup margarine or butter, softened
⅔ cup dairy sour ceam
2 eggs
1⅓ cups all-purpose flour
½ teaspoon baking soda
½ teaspoon baking powder
½ teaspoon salt
¼ cup margarine or butter
⅓ cup packed brown sugar
¾ teaspoon ground cinnamon
½ cup chopped nuts

Makes 9-inch cake

1. Beat sugar and ⅓ cup margarine until light and fluffy. Beat in sour cream and eggs until smooth. Add flour, baking soda, baking powder and salt. Beat at medium speed of electric mixer 2 to 3 minutes. Set batter aside.

2. Place ¼ cup margarine in round baking dish, 9 × 1½ inches. Microwave at HIGH (100%) until melted, 45 seconds to 1 minute 15 seconds. Mix brown sugar and cinnamon; sprinkle over margarine. Sprinkle nuts over brown sugar. Gently spread batter in baking dish.

3. Microwave at MEDIUM-HIGH (70%) until wooden pick inserted in center comes out clean, 6 to 9 minutes. Let stand 3 minutes to cool. Invert onto serving plate.

Layer Cake from a Mix

1 package 2-layer-size cake mix

Makes two 9-inch layers

1. Line 2 round baking dishes, 9 × 1½ inches, with waxed paper. Prepare mix according to package directions. Divide batter between baking dishes.

2. Microwave 1 layer at MEDIUM-HIGH (70%) 5 minutes. Increase power to HIGH (100%). Microwave until top springs back when touched lightly in several places, 1 to 4 minutes. Cool directly on countertop 5 to 10 minutes; remove from baking dish. Repeat with remaining layer. Cool completely before frosting.

Snack Cake from a Mix

1 package (14½ to 15½ ounces) snack cake mix

Makes 8-inch cake

1. Prepare mix according to package directions in square baking dish, 8 × 8 inches or round baking dish, 9 × 1½ inches. Shield corners with aluminum foil. Place on inverted saucer in oven.

2. Microwave at HIGH (100%) until center is dry and springs back when touched lightly, 6 to 8 minutes. If using oven other than Sharp Carousel, rotate 2 to 3 times during cooking. Cool directly on countertop before serving.

Ring Cake from a Mix

Graham cracker crumbs
1 package marble supreme, lemon blueberry, chocolate macaroon or streusel swirl ring cake mix

Makes one ring cake

1. Grease 8- to 10-cup baking ring; sprinkle with graham cracker crumbs. Prepare cake mix according to package directions. Pour into ring.

2. Microwave at MEDIUM-HIGH (70%) 10 to 13 minutes. Increase power to HIGH (100%). Microwave until wooden pick inserted in center comes out clean, 1 to 2 minutes. If using oven other than Sharp Carousel, rotate 2 to 3 times during cooking. Cool 8 to 10 minutes; remove from pan.

Chocolate Frosting

6 tablespoons margarine or butter, softened
1 teaspoon vanilla
3½ cups powdered sugar
¼ cup cocoa
¼ cup milk

Fills and frosts two 9-inch layers

1. Beat margarine and vanilla until light and fluffy. Beat in powdered sugar and cocoa at high speed until smooth.

2. Place milk in 1-cup measure. Microwave at MEDIUM-HIGH (70%) until very warm, 30 to 45 seconds. Add milk to frosting, 1 tablespoon at a time; beat until desired consistency.

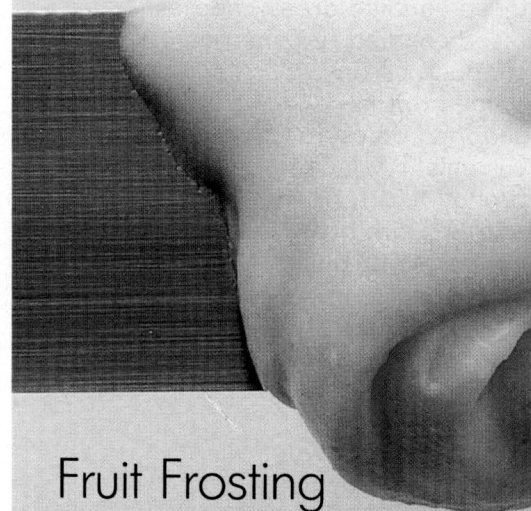

Fruit Frosting

⅓ cup margarine or butter, softened
1½ teaspoons lemon juice
Dash of salt
2 tablespoons instant fruit flavored drink mix
3 cups powdered sugar
¼ cup milk
½ cup chopped nuts (optional)

Fills and frosts two 9-inch layers

1. Beat margarine until light and fluffy. Stir in lemon juice, salt and drink mix. Beat in powdered sugar until smooth.

2. Place milk in 1-cup measure. Microwave at MEDIUM-HIGH (70%) until very warm, 30 to 45 seconds. Add milk to frosting, 1 tablespoon at a time; beat until frosting is desired consistency. Stir in chopped nuts.

Mocha Nut Frosting

- 6 tablespoons margarine or butter, softened
- 1 teaspoon vanilla
- 3½ cups powdered sugar
- ¼ cup cocoa
- ¼ cup milk
- 4 teaspoons instant coffee
- ½ cup chopped nuts

Fills and frosts two 9-inch layers

1. Beat margarine and vanilla until light and fluffy. Beat in powdered sugar and cocoa until smooth.

2. Place milk in 1-cup measure. Microwave at HIGH (100%) until hot, but not boiling, 30 to 45 seconds. Combine instant coffee and 3 tablespoons of the hot milk; stir until coffee dissolves. Add to sugar mixture; beat until frosting is smooth. Stir in chopped nuts. If thinner consistency is desired, stir in remaining milk, a few drops at a time; beat until frosting is desired consistency.

Vanilla Butter Frosting

- ⅓ cup margarine or butter, softened
- 1½ teaspoons vanilla
  Dash of salt
- 3 cups powdered sugar
- ¼ cup milk
- ½ cup chopped nuts (optional)

Fills and frosts two 9-inch layers

1. Beat margarine until light and fluffy. Stir in vanilla and salt. Beat in powdered sugar until smooth.

2. Place milk in 1-cup measure. Microwave at MEDIUM-HIGH (70%) until very warm, 30 to 45 seconds. Add milk to frosting, 1 tablespoon at a time; beat until frosting is desired consistency. Stir in chopped nuts.

Baked Pie Shell ▲

⅓ cup shortening
2 tablespoons margarine or butter, softened
1 cup all-purpose flour
½ teaspoon salt
3 tablespoons cold water
3 or 4 drops yellow food coloring (optional)

Makes one 9-inch pie shell

1. Cut shortening and margarine into flour and salt until particles are size of small peas. Combine water and food coloring; sprinkle over flour mixture; toss with fork until particles are just moist enough to cling together. (It may not be necessary to use all the water.) Shape pastry into ball. Flatten to ½ inch. Roll out on floured pastry cloth to scant ⅛-inch thick circle, 2 inches larger than inverted pie plate, with stocking-covered rolling pin.

2. Fold pastry into quarters. Lift carefully into pie plate. Unfold and fit loosely into plate; press firmly against bottom and side. Do not stretch pastry or it will shrink while microwaving. Let pastry relax about 10 minutes to reduce shrinkage.

3. Trim overhanging edge of pastry to generous ½ inch. Fold under, even with plate, to form standing rim. Flute, keeping rim high to contain bubbling. Prick crust with fork on bottom and side ½ inch apart. Microwave at HIGH (100%) until crust appears dry and opaque through bottom of plate, 5 to 7 minutes. If using oven other than Sharp Carousel, rotate plate half turn every 3 minutes.

Graham Cracker Crust ▲

3 tablespoons margarine or butter
1 cup fine graham cracker crumbs
¼ cup granulated or packed brown sugar

Makes one 9-inch pie crust

1. Place margarine in 9-inch pie plate. Microwave at HIGH (100%) until melted, 30 seconds to 1 minute. Add graham cracker crumbs and sugar; mix thoroughly. Press mixture firmly against bottom and side of pie plate.

2. Microwave at MEDIUM-HIGH (70%) until hot, 2 to 4 minutes. If using oven other than Sharp Carousel, rotate pie plate once or twice during cooking. Cool completely before filling.

Chocolate Cookie Crust ▲

¼ cup margarine or butter
1¼ cups fine chocolate wafer cookie crumbs

Makes one 9-inch pie crust

1. Place margarine in 9-inch pie plate. Microwave at HIGH (100%) until melted, 30 seconds to 1 minute 15 seconds. Add chocolate cookie crumbs; mix thoroughly. Press mixture firmly against bottom and side of pie plate.

2. Microwave at MEDIUM-HIGH (70%) until hot, 2½ to 4½ minutes. If using oven other than Sharp Carousel, rotate pie plate once or twice during cooking. Cool completely before filling.

Deep Dish Apple Pie

- 1 tablespoon sugar
- ½ teaspoon ground cinnamon
- 5 cups sliced peeled apples
- ½ cup sugar
- 2 tablespoons all-purpose flour
- ½ teaspoon ground cinnamon or cloves
- ¾ cup buttermilk biscuit baking mix
- ⅓ cup milk
- 2 tablespoons sugar

Makes 4 to 6 servings

1. Mix 1 tablespoon sugar and ½ teaspoon cinnamon; set aside. Combine apples, ½ cup sugar, the flour and ½ teaspoon cinnamon or cloves in 1-quart casserole. Cover. Microwave at HIGH (100%) until apples are tender and sauce is bubbly, 3 to 4 minutes.

2. Mix buttermilk biscuit baking mix, milk and 2 tablespoons sugar just until moistened. Drop by spoonfuls onto hot apple mixture. Sprinkle with cinnamon-sugar mixture. Microwave at HIGH (100%) until topping is set, 4 to 6 minutes. Serve with whipped cream, if desired.

Pumpkin Cheese Pie ▲

Graham Cracker Crust (page 180)
1 package (8 ounces) cream cheese
1 cup canned pumpkin
¾ cup packed brown sugar
3 eggs
1½ tablespoons all-purpose flour
1 teaspoon ground cinnamon
½ teaspoon ground nutmeg
½ teaspoon vanilla

Makes 9-inch pie

1. Prepare crust. Set aside. Place cream cheese in medium bowl. Microwave at MEDIUM (50%) until softened, 1 to 2 minutes. Add remaining ingredients. Beat at medium speed of electric mixer until smooth and well blended.

2. Microwave at MEDIUM-HIGH (70%) until hot and thickened, 6 to 8 minutes, stirring every 2 minutes. Pour into crust. Reduce power to MEDIUM (50%). Microwave until filling is firm to the touch, 10 to 15 minutes. Center may appear soft-set. Garnish with pecan halves, if desired. Refrigerate until set.

Quick Cherry Pie ▲

Baked Pie Shell (page 180)
1 cup sugar
¼ cup cornstarch
⅛ teaspoon salt
2 cans (16 ounces each) pitted tart red cherries (water pack), drained
½ teaspoon almond extract
⅓ cup sliced almonds

Makes 9-inch pie

1. Bake pie shell. Set aside. Blend sugar, cornstarch and salt in medium bowl. Stir in cherries.

2. Microwave at HIGH (100%) until mixture is translucent, 8 to 11 minutes, stirring once or twice during cooking. Stir in almond extract. Pour into pie shell. Sprinkle with almonds. Chill.

Crème de Menthe Pie ▲

3 cups miniature marshmallows
⅓ cup half-and-half
¼ cup green crème de menthe
3 tablespoons white crème de cacao
　Chocolate Cookie Crust (page 180)
1 cup chilled whipping cream

Makes 9-inch pie

1. Combine marshmallows and half-and-half in medium bowl. Microwave at MEDIUM-HIGH (70%) until marshmallows are melted, 2 to 4 minutes, stirring once or twice during cooking. Blend in crème de menthe and crème de cacao. Refrigerate until cool and thickened but not set. Prepare crust while filling cools.

2. When marshmallow mixture is thickened but not set, beat whipping cream in chilled bowl until stiff. Fold marshmallow mixture into whipped cream. Pour into crust. Refrigerate until set, 2 to 4 hours. Garnish with chocolate curls, if desired.

Creamy Chocolate ▲ Almond Pie

1 package (3⅝ ounces) regular chocolate
　pudding mix
2 cups milk
　Chocolate Cookie Crust (page 180)
½ teaspoon almond extract
¾ cup chilled whipping cream

Makes 9-inch pie

1. Blend pudding mix and milk in 1½-quart casserole. Microwave at HIGH (100%) until thick and bubbly, 4 to 7 minutes, stirring once or twice. Place plastic wrap directly on surface of pudding. Refrigerate until cool but not set, stirring with wire whisk several times. Prepare crust while filling cools.

2. When pudding is cool but not set, stir in almond extract. Beat whipping cream in chilled bowl until stiff. Fold pudding into whipped cream. Spoon into crust. Refrigerate until set, 2 to 4 hours. Garnish with sliced almonds, if desired.

Pudding from a Mix ▲

1 package (3 to 3⅝ ounces) pudding mix

1. Prepare mix according to package directions in 4-cup measure or 1½-quart casserole.

2. Microwave at HIGH (100%) 3 minutes. Stir. Microwave until mixture boils, 1 to 4 minutes, stirring every minute. Pour into serving dishes. Chill. Mixture will thicken while standing.

Blanc Mange

⅓ cup sugar
3 tablespoons cornstarch
¼ teaspoon salt
2¼ cups milk
1 teaspoon vanilla

Makes 4 servings

1. Combine sugar, cornstarch and salt in deep 1-quart casserole. Gradually blend in milk.

2. Microwave at MEDIUM-HIGH (70%) until mixture begins to boil and is slightly thickened, 9 to 11 minutes, stirring every 2 to 3 minutes. Stir in vanilla. Pour into four 6-ounce custard cups. Cover with plastic wrap. Chill until set. Top with fruit, if desired.

Apple Crisp ▶

4 cups sliced peeled apples
2 tablespoons lemon juice
½ cup packed brown sugar
½ cup uncooked quick-cooking or old-fashioned oats
¼ cup all-purpose flour
¼ cup margarine or butter
1 teaspoon ground cinnamon
½ teaspoon salt
⅛ teaspoon ground nutmeg

Makes 4 to 6 servings

1. Place apples in 1-quart casserole. Sprinkle with lemon juice. Microwave at HIGH (100%) until apples are tender-crisp, 2½ to 4 minutes. Set apples aside.

2. Combine remaining ingredients in small bowl. Microwave at HIGH (100%) until hot and bubbly, 1½ to 3½ minutes, stirring after half the cooking time. Spread over apples. Microwave at HIGH (100%) until apples are tender and topping is bubbly, 4 to 6 minutes.

Cherry Cobbler

6 tablespoons margarine or butter
1 cup all-purpose flour
⅔ cup coarsely chopped nuts
⅓ cup packed dark brown sugar
¾ teaspoon ground cinnamon
¼ teaspoon ground allspice
1 can (21 ounces) cherry pie filling
2 teaspoons cornstarch
½ teaspoon lemon juice

Makes 4 to 6 servings

1. Place margarine in small bowl. Microwave at HIGH (100%) until melted, 45 seconds to 1 minute 15 seconds. Stir in flour, nuts, brown sugar, cinnamon and allspice. Set topping aside.

2. Mix cherry pie filling, cornstarch and lemon juice until smooth in 1-quart casserole. Microwave at HIGH (100%) 1 minute. Sprinkle with topping. Reduce power to MEDIUM-HIGH (70%). Microwave until filling is translucent and bubbly, 6 to 8 minutes. Serve warm or cold with ice cream or whipped topping, if desired.

Directions for Baked Custard are in Learn While You Cook, page 31.

◄ Snowflake Macaroon Cupcakes

  3 cups shredded coconut
  ⅓ cup sugar
  1 egg white
  ¼ cup plus 2 tablespoons all-purpose flour
  ½ teaspoon baking powder
  ½ teaspoon almond extract
  2 egg whites
  ⅓ cup sugar

Makes 12 to 18 cupcakes

1. Combine coconut, ⅓ cup sugar and 1 egg white in small bowl. Microwave at HIGH (100%) 2 minutes. Mix flour, baking powder and almond extract into coconut mixture.

2. Beat 2 egg whites until foamy. Beat in ⅓ cup sugar, 1 tablespoon at a time; beat until stiff peaks form. Fold meringue into coconut mixture. Spoon batter into paper-lined muffin cups. Top each cupcake with a candied cherry, if desired.

3. Place 6 cupcakes at a time around outer edge of carousel, leaving center empty. Microwave at MEDIUM-HIGH (70%) until wooden pick inserted in center comes out clean, 2 to 3½ minutes. Repeat with remaining cupcakes. If using oven other than Sharp Carousel, rearrange cupcakes twice.

◄ Peanut Butter Slices

  ½ cup packed brown sugar
  ½ cup peanut butter
  ¼ cup margarine or butter, softened
  1 egg
1¼ cups all-purpose flour
  ¼ teaspoon baking soda
  ¼ teaspoon salt

Makes about 4 dozen

1. Beat brown sugar, peanut butter and margarine in medium bowl until light and fluffy. Beat in egg until blended. Mix in remaining ingredients. Shape into 12-inch roll. Refrigerate 1 to 3 hours.

2. Cut roll into ¼-inch slices. Line carousel or baking sheet with waxed paper. Place 12 slices in circle on carousel. Microwave at MEDIUM-HIGH (70%) until dry, 1 to 3½ minutes. If using oven other than Sharp Carousel, rotate baking sheet once or twice during cooking. Let stand 1 to 3 minutes; remove. Repeat with remaining slices, 12 at a time.

Strawberry Floating Island ▲

¼ cup sugar
2 teaspoons cornstarch
  Dash of salt
1½ cups milk
2 eggs, separated
½ teaspoon vanilla
1 pint strawberries, rinsed and hulled
    or 1 package (16 ounces) whole
    strawberries, thawed and drained
¼ cup sugar
½ teaspoon vanilla

Makes 4 servings

1. Blend ¼ cup sugar, the cornstarch and salt in 1-quart casserole. Stir in milk. Blend in egg yolks. Microwave at MEDIUM-HIGH (70%) until mixture coats a metal spoon, 2½ to 5 minutes, blending with wire whisk once or twice. Chill. Stir in ½ teaspoon vanilla.

2. Just before serving, divide strawberries among 4 small bowls. Beat egg whites until foamy. Beat in ¼ cup sugar, 1 tablespoon at a time; continue beating until stiff peaks form. Beat in ½ teaspoon vanilla. Pour custard sauce over strawberries. Top each with meringue.

3. Microwave at MEDIUM-HIGH (70%) until meringues are set, 45 seconds to 1 minute 15 seconds. If using oven other than Sharp Carousel, rearrange once during cooking.

Cinnamon Baked Apples

4 large baking apples (2½- to 3-inch diameter)
4 tablespoons red cinnamon candies

Makes 4 servings

1. Core apples without cutting through bottom skin and peel about 1-inch strip of skin from stem end of each apple. If necessary, cut thin slice from bottom of each apple so it will stand upright.

2. Arrange apples in shallow baking dish. Place 1 tablespoon of the cinnamon candies in center of each apple. Microwave at HIGH (100%) until apples are tender, 4 to 6 minutes. If using oven other than Sharp Carousel, rearrange apples once.

Applesauce

4 cups sliced peeled tart apples
½ cup water
¼ to ½ cup sugar
¼ teaspoon ground cinnamon

Makes 4 to 6 servings

1. Place all ingredients in 1-quart casserole; cover.

2. Microwave at HIGH (100%) until apples are tender, 7 to 10 minutes. Mash apples to desired consistency. Serve warm or chilled.

Variation: Add 3 tablespoons red cinnamon candies to applesauce. Microwave at HIGH (100%) 30 seconds to 1 minute 30 seconds. Stir until candies are dissolved.

Peaches with ▲ Raspberry Sauce

1 package (10 ounces) frozen sweetened
   raspberries
4 peaches, peeled and cut into halves
2 teaspoons cornstarch
½ teaspoon grated lemon peel

Makes 4 servings

1. Remove raspberries from package and place in
1-quart container. Microwave at MEDIUM (50%)
until raspberries are thawed, 2 to 4 minutes, turning over every minute and gently breaking apart
as soon as possible. Let stand 5 minutes.

2. Place peach halves in rectangular baking dish,
12 × 8 inches or 10-inch square casserole. Cover
with plastic wrap. Microwave at HIGH (100%)
until peaches are heated through, 2 to 6 minutes. If
using oven other than Sharp Carousel, rearrange
peaches once or twice during cooking. Set aside.

3. Drain raspberry juice in small bowl. Blend in
cornstarch and lemon peel. Microwave at
MEDIUM-HIGH (70%) until thick and bubbly, 2 to
4 minutes, stirring once or twice during cooking.
Place 2 peach halves in each of 4 small bowls. Stir
raspberries gently into sauce. Top each bowl of
peaches with one-fourth of raspberry mixture. Top
with whipped cream, if desired.

Variation: Substitute 8 canned peach halves and
omit cooking peaches.

Blueberries and Vanilla Cream

½ cup water
1 envelope unflavored gelatin
¾ cup sugar
1 cup half-and-half
½ teaspoon vanilla
¼ teaspoon salt
¾ cup dairy sour cream
2 cups frozen blueberries
¾ teaspoon lemon juice
⅓ cup sugar
2 teaspoons cornstarch

Makes 4 servings

1. Microwave water at HIGH (100%) until boiling,
45 seconds to 1 minute 15 seconds. Stir in gelatin
until dissolved. Combine gelatin mixture and ¾
cup sugar in medium bowl; stir to dissolve sugar.
Stir in half-and-half, vanilla and salt. Chill until
mixture begins to set. Beat with electric mixer until
smooth. Beat in sour cream. Spoon into 4 lightly
oiled individual dishes. Chill at least 4 hours.

2. Microwave blueberries at MEDIUM-HIGH
(70%) until completely thawed, 4 to 5½ minutes.
Let stand 5 minutes. Drain well, reserving juice.
Mash ⅓ cup of the blueberries in small bowl. Add
reserved juice and lemon juice. Blend in ⅓ cup
sugar and the cornstarch. Microwave at HIGH
(100%) until thick and bubbly, 45 seconds to 1
minute 30 seconds. Let stand until cool. Stir in
remaining blueberries. Unmold vanilla cream onto
dessert plates. Top each with one-fourth of the
blueberry mixture.

Chocolate Almond Fondue ➤

1 package (11½ ounces) milk chocolate chips
2 tablespoons half-and-half
¼ cup almond liqueur
  Pound cake squares
  Ladyfingers, split
  Banana chunks, sprinkled with lemon juice
  Mandarin orange sections, drained
  Pineapple slices, drained and quartered

Makes 6 to 8 servings

1. Combine chocolate chips and half-and-half in small bowl or 1-quart casserole.

2. Microwave at MEDIUM-HIGH (70%) until chocolate is melted, 2 to 4 minutes, blending with wire whisk once or twice during cooking. Stir in liqueur. Serve from bowl, reheating as needed, or in fondue pot over low heat. Dip pound cake squares, ladyfingers, banana chunks, mandarin orange sections and pineapple slices into fondue with fondue forks or skewers.

Variation: Omit liqueur. Increase half-and-half to ⅓ cup. Add ½ teaspoon almond extract.

Variation: Omit liqueur. Increase half-and-half to ⅓ cup.

Butterscotch Fondue

1 package (12 ounces) butterscotch chips
⅓ cup half-and-half
  Ladyfingers, split
  Banana chunks, sprinkled with lemon juice
  Marshmallows

Makes 6 to 8 servings

1. Combine butterscotch chips and half-and-half in small bowl or 1-quart casserole.

2. Microwave at MEDIUM-HIGH (70%) until butterscotch chips are melted, 2 to 6 minutes, stirring once or twice. Serve from bowl, reheating as needed, or in fondue pot over low heat. Dip ladyfingers, banana chunks and marshmallows into fondue with fondue forks or skewers.

CANDIES & TOPPINGS

Microwave candy making requires no special skill, nor constant watching and stirring. Old-fashioned favorites are almost as easy to microwave as the popular short-cut versions. When you're in a hurry, a dessert sauce can be microwaved while the family is eating dinner. Make small batches of jam or jelly at any season of the year, using fresh or frozen fruit or bottle juices. Your kitchen will stay cool and clean-up is easy.

Fudge

3 cups semi-sweet or milk chocolate chips
1 can (14 ounces) sweetened condensed milk
¼ cup margarine or butter
1 cup chopped walnuts

Makes about 2 pounds

1. Place all ingredients except nuts in large bowl.

2. Microwave at MEDIUM (50%) until chocolate chips are melted, 3 to 5 minutes, stirring once or twice during cooking. Stir in nuts. Pour into well-greased square baking dish, 8 × 8 inches. Refrigerate until set.

Variation: Substitute 1 cup peanut butter chips for 1 cup of the chocolate chips.

Microwaving Candies and Toppings

Recipe Conversion

Almost any candy or topping recipe can be adapted to microwaving by using a microwave method and time. No change in ingredients is needed. Traditional caramels require great care because they boil very high when they are stirred and could cause burns.

Jams and jellies should be made in small batches; they need a large utensil to contain boiling. Use the same proportion of fruit, sugar and pectin. Paraffin for sealing jars must be melted conventionally; it will not melt in the microwave oven because it is transparent to microwave energy.

Select a large container for sugary mixtures, which boil high in the microwave oven. The utensil should be 2 to 3 times as large as the volume of candy or jelly mixture.

Stir candies, jellies and sauces a few times during cooking. Frequent stirring is not necessary because mixtures will not scorch.

Select HIGH (100%) for sugary syrups and fruit mixtures. Reduce power for chocolate, which is sensitive to microwave energy.

Test jelly for doneness with a metal spoon. Two large drops on the edge of the spoon should run together to form a single drop.

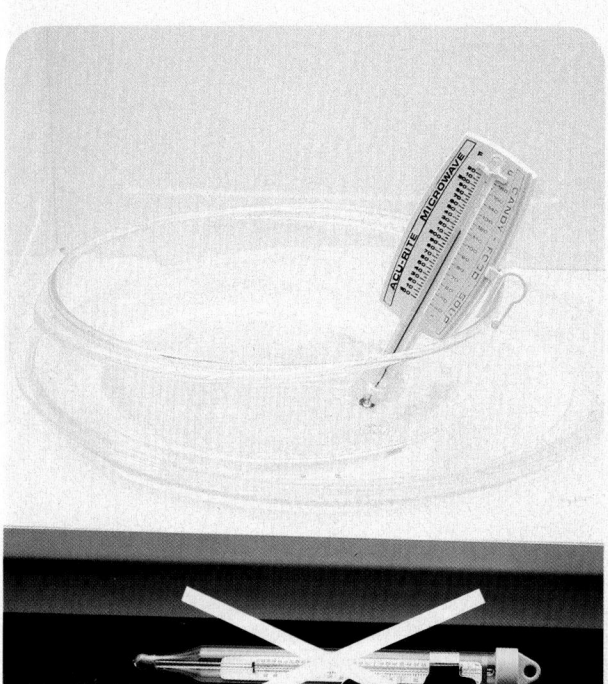

Use a special microwave candy thermometer or the old-fashioned cold water test for candies. Do not use a conventional candy thermometer inside the microwave oven.

Cold water test. Drop a small amount of mixture into a dish of very cold tap water. Shape into a ball. Soft Ball (234° to 240°) will flatten when re-moved from water. Firm Ball (244° to 248°) does not flatten. Hard Ball (250° to 266°) should feel very firm but still pliable.

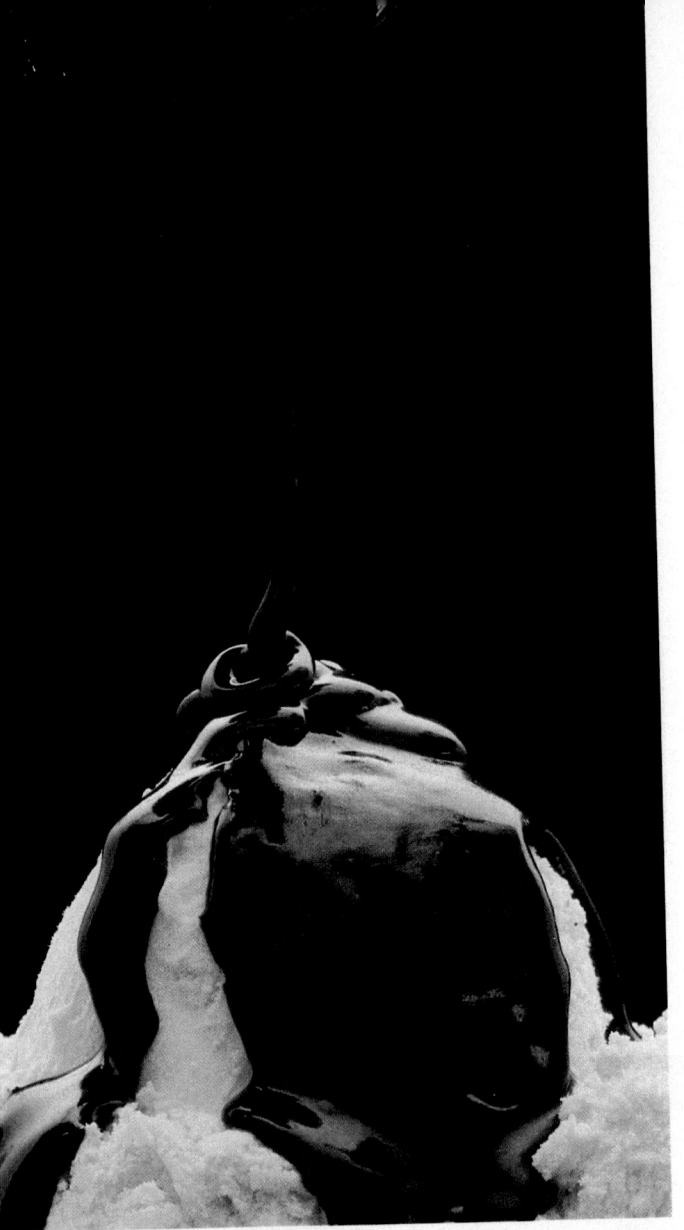

Chocolate Sauce ▲

- 2 ounces unsweetened chocolate
- ¼ cup milk
- ½ cup sugar
  Dash of salt
- ¼ teaspoon vanilla

Makes ¾ cup

1. Combine chocolate and milk in 2-cup measure or small bowl. Microwave at MEDIUM (50%) until melted, 1 to 2 minutes, stirring 2 or 3 times.

2. Blend in sugar and salt. Microwave at MEDIUM-HIGH (70%) until sugar is dissolved, 45 seconds to 1 minute 30 seconds. Stir in vanilla. Serve over cake or ice cream, if desired.

Lemon Sauce ▲

- ½ cup sugar
- 1 tablespoon cornstarch
  Dash of salt
- ½ teaspoon grated lemon peel
- 1 cup water
- 1 tablespoon lemon juice
- 2 tablespoons margarine or butter
- 1 egg yolk, slightly beaten

Makes 1½ cups

1. Combine sugar, cornstarch, salt and lemon peel in deep 1-quart bowl. Blend in water and lemon juice.

2. Microwave at HIGH (100%) until sauce is thickened and clear, 2½ to 4½ minutes, stirring after half the cooking time. Stir in margarine and egg yolk. Microwave at HIGH (100%) until bubbly, 30 seconds to 1 minute.

Hot Vanilla Sauce

½ cup packed brown sugar
1 tablespoon plus 1½ teaspoons
    all-purpose flour
  Dash of ground nutmeg
½ cup milk
¾ cup half-and-half
1½ teaspoons vanilla or rum extract

Makes 1½ cups

1. Combine sugar, flour and nutmeg in medium bowl. Stir in ¼ cup of the milk until smooth. Stir in remaining milk and half-and-half.

2. Microwave at HIGH (100%) until thickened, 5 to 7 minutes, stirring 2 or 3 times. Stir in vanilla. Serve over cake or fruit, if desired.

Cherry Sauce ▲

1 can (17 ounces) pitted dark sweet
    cherries
1 tablespoon cornstarch
1½ teaspoons lemon juice
1 teaspoon grated lemon peel

Makes 1 cup

1. Drain cherry juice into 1-quart bowl; blend in cornstarch until smooth. Microwave at HIGH (100%) until clear and thickened, 2½ to 4 minutes, stirring once during cooking.

2. Stir in cherries, lemon juice and peel. Microwave at HIGH (100%) until sauce bubbles and cherries are hot, 1 to 2 minutes. (For thicker sauce add 1 teaspoon additional cornstarch.)

◄ French Chocolates

- 1 package (12 ounces) semi-sweet chocolate chips
- 1 cup ground walnuts
- ¾ cup sweetened condensed milk
- 1 teaspoon vanilla
- Dash of salt
- Shredded coconut, chopped nuts or powdered sugar

Makes 50 to 60 candies

1. Place chocolate chips in medium bowl. Microwave at MEDIUM-HIGH (70%) until melted, 2 to 4 minutes, stirring twice. Stir in walnuts, condensed milk, vanilla and salt. Cool 5 minutes.

2. Shape into ¾- to 1-inch balls. Dip into coconut, chopped nuts or powdered sugar. Place on greased baking sheet and refrigerate until set.

Rocky Road Candy ►

- 1 package (6 ounces) semi-sweet or milk chocolate chips
- 2 tablespoons half-and-half
- 1 teaspoon vanilla
- 2 cups miniature marshmallows
- 1½ cups chopped nuts
- 1 cup shredded coconut

Makes about 2 dozen candies

1. Combine chocolate chips and half-and-half in medium bowl. Microwave at MEDIUM-HIGH (70%) until chocolate chips are melted, 1 to 3 minutes, stirring once during cooking.

2. Stir in vanilla and remaining ingredients until coated. Press into greased square baking dish, 8 × 8 inches. Chill.

Chocolate Bourbon Balls ►

- ½ cup margarine or butter
- 4 cups powdered sugar
- 1 cup finely chopped nuts
- ¼ cup bourbon
- 1 package (6 ounces) milk chocolate chips
- 3 tablespoons half-and-half

Makes about 3 dozen candies

1. Place margarine in medium bowl. Microwave at HIGH (100%) until melted, 1 to 2 minutes. Mix in sugar, nuts and bourbon. Refrigerate until firm.

2. Shape into 1-inch balls. Refrigerate until firm. Combine chocolate chips and half-and-half in small bowl. Microwave at MEDIUM-HIGH (70%) until chocolate chips are melted, 1 to 2½ minutes, stirring once or twice. Stir until smooth. Drizzle chocolate over candies. (Reheat chocolate as needed.) Chill.

◄ Cherry Squares

½ cup packed brown sugar
½ cup margarine or butter, softened
1 egg
½ teaspoon vanilla
¾ cup all-purpose flour
½ cup whole wheat flour
⅛ teaspoon ground allspice
⅛ teaspoon ground nutmeg
   Dash of salt
½ cup chopped walnuts
1 jar (12 ounces) cherry preserves
½ teaspoon grated lemon peel
3 tablespoons powdered sugar

Makes 16 to 24 candies

1. Beat brown sugar and margarine in medium bowl until fluffy. Beat in egg and vanilla until smooth. Mix in all-purpose flour, wheat flour, allspice, nutmeg and salt. Stir in nuts. Spread in greased square baking dish, 8 × 8 inches. Place baking dish on inverted saucer in oven.

2. Microwave at MEDIUM-HIGH (70%) until top is dry, 5 to 10 minutes. If using oven other than Sharp Carousel, rotate dish 2 or 3 times during cooking. Mix cherry preserves and lemon peel; spread over batter. Let stand until cool. Sprinkle with powdered sugar. Chill before serving.

◄ Divinity

2 cups sugar
⅓ cup water
⅓ cup light corn syrup
¼ teaspoon salt
2 egg whites
1 teaspoon vanilla
½ cup chopped nuts

Makes about 3 dozen candies

1. Combine sugar, water, corn syrup and salt in 2-quart casserole; cover. Microwave at HIGH (100%) 5 minutes. Stir well. Microwave, uncovered, at HIGH (100%) until a hard ball forms when a small amount is dropped in cold water, 4 to 6 minutes. Cool 3 to 4 minutes.

2. Beat egg whites until very stiff. Pour sugar mixture in a steady stream over egg whites, beating constantly until mixture holds its shape and starts to lose its gloss. Stir in vanilla and nuts. Drop by teaspoonfuls onto waxed paper.

Peanut Brittle

- 1 cup sugar
- ½ cup light corn syrup
- Dash of salt
- 1 to 1½ cups shelled raw peanuts
- 1 tablespoon margarine or butter
- 1½ teaspoons baking soda
- 1 teaspoon vanilla

Makes about 1 pound

1. Grease baking sheet heavily. Combine sugar, corn syrup and salt in 3-quart casserole. Stir in peanuts. Microwave at HIGH (100%) until light brown, 8 to 10 minutes, stirring once or twice.

2. Stir in remaining ingredients until light and foamy. Quickly spread on greased baking sheet. Spread as thin as possible for brittle candy. Cool; break into pieces.

◄ Easy Pineapple Preserves

1 can (8 ounces) crushed pineapple
   (juice pack), undrained
1 tablespoon cornstarch
2 tablespoons honey
1 teaspoon grated orange peel

Makes ¾ cup

1. Mix all ingredients in deep 1-quart bowl.

2. Microwave at HIGH (100%) until thickened, 2 to 4 minutes, stirring after half the cooking time. Pour into prepared jars, seal and refrigerate.

◄ Apple Jam

2 medium apples, cored and peeled
1½ cups sugar
1 teaspoon lemon juice

Makes 1 to 1½ cups

1. Combine apples and sugar in medium bowl. Microwave at HIGH (100%) until apples are tender, 3 to 5 minutes. Beat softened apple mixture with electric mixer until well blended.

2. Microwave at HIGH (100%) until mixture is slightly thickened, 3 to 4 minutes, stirring once during cooking time. Stir in lemon juice. Pour into prepared jars, seal and refrigerate.

◄ Raspberry Jam Plus

2 packages (10 ounces each) frozen
   raspberries
2½ cups sugar
1 tablespoon lemon juice
3 tablespoons plus 1½ teaspoons
   liquid pectin

Makes 2½ to 3 cups

1. Place frozen raspberries in 2-quart casserole. Microwave at HIGH (100%) until thawed, 4 to 6 minutes. Stir in sugar and lemon juice. Microwave at HIGH (100%) until mixture boils, 8 to 10 minutes, stirring after half the cooking time. Blend in liquid pectin.

2. Microwave at HIGH (100%) until mixture comes to a rolling boil, 3 to 4 minutes. Microwave at HIGH (100%) to continue boiling, 1 minute. Pour into prepared jars, seal and refrigerate.

INDEX